CONTEMPORARY SOCIAL THEORY

General Editor: ANTHONY GIDDENS

This series aims to create a forum for debate between different theoretical and philosophical traditions in the social sciences. As well as covering broad schools of thought, the series will also concentrate upon the work of particular thinkers whose ideas have had a major impact on social science (these books appear under the sub-series title of 'Theoretical Traditions in the Social Sciences'). The series is not limited to abstract theoretical discussion – it will also include more substantive works on contemporary capitalism, the state, politics and other subject areas.

CONTEMPORARY SOCIAL THEORY

General Editor: ANTHONY GIDDENS

Published titles

Tony Bilton, Kevin Bonnett, Philip Jones, Ken Sheard, Michelle Stanworth and
   Andrew Webster, *Introductory Sociology*
Anthony Giddens, *A Contemporary Critique of Historical Materialism*
Anthony Giddens, *Central Problems in Social Theory*
Steve Taylor, *Durkheim and the Study of Suicide*
John Urry, *The Anatomy of Capitalist Societies*

Forthcoming titles

Martin Albrow, *Weber and the Construction of Social Theory*
Clive Ashworth, Chris Dandeker and Terry Johnson, *Theoretical Sociology*
David Brown and Michael Harrison, *Industrial Sociology*
Simon Clarke, *Marx, Marginalism and Modern Sociology*
Emile Durkheim, *The Rules of Sociological Method* (intro. by Steven Lukes)
Boris Frankel, *The Modern State*
Anthony Giddens, *Between Capitalism and Socialism*
Anthony Giddens, *Sociology: A Brief but Critical Introduction*
David Held, *Bureaucracy, Democracy and Socialism*
Geoffrey Ingham, *Capitalism Divided*
Jorge Larrain, *Marxism and Ideology*
Claus Offe, *Structural Problems of the Capitalist State*
Ali Rattansi, *Marx and the Division of Labour*
Gerry Rose, *Deciphering Sociological Research*
John Scott, *The Development of the British Upper Class*
John B. Thompson and David Held (eds), *Habermas: Critical Debates*

Theoretical Traditions in the Social Sciences

Published title

Barry Barnes, *T. S. Kuhn and Social Science*

Forthcoming titles

Ted Benton, *Althusser and the Althusserians*
David Bloor, *Wittgenstein and Social Science*
Chris Bryant, *Positivism in Social Theory*
John Forrester, *Jacques Lacan*
John Heritage, *Garfinkel and Ethnomethodology*
Athar Hussain, *Foucault*
Bob Jessop, *Nicos Poulantzas*
Julian Roberts, *Walter Benjamin*
James Schmidt, *Maurice Merleau-Ponty and Social Theory*
Dennis Smith, *Barrington Moore and Historical Sociology*
Robin Williams, *Erving Goffman*

Durkheim and the Study of Suicide

Steve Taylor

First published 1982 by
THE MACMILLAN PRESS LTD
London and Basingstoke
Companies and representatives throughout the world

ISBN 0 333 28645 6   (hard cover)
ISBN 0 333 28646 4   (paper cover)

Typeset in 10/12pt Times by
ILLUSTRATED ARTS

Printed in Hong Kong

To Clive Ashworth, Olive Banks and Eric Dunning

Contents

Preface

I should like to express my gratitude to all the officials who agreed to talk to me about their work; London Transport for their co-operation in part of this research; the Lanchester Polytechnic, Coventry, for financial assistance with part of the study; a number of people, including Peter Baehr, Alf Barrett, Stan Cohen, Nick Tilley and Jock Young, who have been kind enough to comment on parts of the text; Anne Southall, who assisted with some of the field-work; and Anthony Giddens, who was a most helpful and encouraging editor. My greatest debt is to Clive Ashworth of Leicester University – without his painstaking help and keen critical intelligence this work would not have been written. The errors and shortcomings that remain are, of course, Durkheim's.

Steve Taylor

Acknowledgement

The author and publishers are grateful to Olwyn Hughes on behalf of Ted Hughes, and Harper & Row, Publishers, Inc., for permission to quote an extract from 'Lady Lazarus' in *Ariel* by Sylvia Plath. Copyright © 1965 by Ted Hughes.

Introduction

My interest in suicide, which stemmed from a long-held fascination with 'daredevil' and risk-taking behaviour, was stimulated by the work of the late Erwin Stengel, who was the first to show that most serious suicidal acts, including many that actually end in death, are in fact risk-taking exercises and, in this respect, may be usefully likened to medieval ordeals. From this point of view the problem for suicide research is not so much why people put a determined end to their lives as why many more *gamble* with death and allow fate to decide whether or not they go on living.

The traditional sociological approach to suicide involving the explanation of comparative suicide rates, which I discuss in Part I of the book, seemed to me to have two important deficiencies. First, a relatively uncritical reliance on official suicide rates, and second, a lack of interest in studying what may be termed the micro-social contexts of suicidal acts which led students to misunderstand the nature of suicide, especially its risk-taking dimension. The research undertaken for this book is devoted to the examination of these two problems.

Part II examines the production of official suicide statistics where I attempt to develop the excellent critiques advanced by Douglas and Atkinson into a *demonstration* of the dangers of the use of such data for research purposes.

Part III discusses more 'individually orientated' approaches to suicide, documents and attempts to explain the risk-taking nature of certain suicidal acts, and concludes with the development of an alternative social-psychological approach to suicide.

At each stage of the work I have tried to relate specific debates and issues in suicide research to the more general debates within the social sciences. In this context Durkheim's work remains a massive influence, for, despite a tendency in recent work to caricature Durkheim as responsible for anything that seems 'bad' in modern social science, for example 'conservatism', 'functionalism', 'positivism' or 'anti-psychological social determinism', he remains the most difficult of all the leading figures in the social sciences to 'pigeonhole'. In fact, I shall try to show how modern students of suicide have not so much 'progressed beyond' Durkheim, as they often like to believe, but rather, by returning to one or other of the horns of the philosophical dilemmas that Durkheim tried to synthesise, they have returned research conceptually to the state it was in prior to *Suicide*. Indeed, seen from a Durkheimian perspective, the respective parties of many of the most intense debates in the social sciences, for example between 'social' or 'individual' explanations or positivist *vs* interpretative methods, are united by far more than separates them, in particular a shared positivist view of natural science and a common commitment to an empiricist epistemology.

In Chapter 1, I differentiate Durkheim's approach to suicide from those adopted by later students and, in the final chapter, despite significant reservations about Durkheim's theory of suicide, I draw upon many of his most important insights to develop an alternative, structural, theory of suicide.

While suicide appears to be a topic of great interest to both 'lay' and 'professional' people, at present there are relatively few sociologists working in this field. Therefore, I have tried to write a text which will be of interest to those whose main concern is either with suicide research or sociological research.

Part I

Explaining the Suicide Rate

1

Durkheim's *Suicide*

The spirit of scientific endeavour and the growth of scientific knowledge in the seventeenth and eighteenth centuries increasingly drew
the observer towards the conclusion that, as Morris puts it, 'the
things and events he experienced were determined and controlled
by forces within the world rather than outside it'.[1] The spectacular
advances of the natural sciences led many to the belief that diligent
application of the same principles and procedures to the study of
human behaviour would, ultimately, produce an understanding of
the social world equivalent to the scientist's grasp of the natural
world. Thus debating the meaning and morality of social phenomena increasingly gave way to a *factual* interest in them and traditional concern with the 'evilness' (or otherwise) of suicide – should
people do it?[2] – was transcended by the question of *why* people do
it. In this quest students were encouraged not to search themselves
for essences and ultimate truths, but rather, to 'distance' themselves
from their material; social phenomena were, after all, only 'facts',
and as such could be analysed objectively.[3] In this undertaking the
observer must clear his mind of preconception, and base analysis on
careful observation and description. Morselli, in his classic study,
explained that suicide is 'connected to the natural development of
society', and that this only became apparent through the adoption
of a scientific approach:

> This new aspect of suicide could not become clear when
> metaphysical systems prevailed; it was necessary to collect all the
> facts, to unite them together, to consider their analogy and differ-
> ences, to do, in short, precisely the reverse of what philosophy had
> done up to that time. That is not to start from a preconceived

system, but to base arguments on facts supplied by observation and, when possible, by experiment.[4]

Concern with the 'facts about suicide' took two apparently distinct avenues. First, there were studies of individual cases of suicide, many of which linked suicide to forms of 'inherited madness'.[5] Second, there were comparative studies of official suicide rates which tended to explain variations in terms of various 'environmental' factors. While there were, and indeed continue to be, some bitter disputes between those who study individual cases of suicide and students of suicide rates;[6] both approaches, by attempting to uncover the 'determining causes' behind a seemingly 'individual' act, sought to unseat the Romantic view of humans as the willers, or authors, of their own fate. The new 'social scientists' argued that just as humans had achieved greater freedom (i.e. to exercise their will) first by recognising, then understanding and ultimately controlling some of the Earth's natural forces, so too could they attain further dimensions of freedom by understanding those social and/or psychological forces that (at present) 'really' control them even though they may *believe* that their actions are the product of their own 'free will'.[7] Therefore, if humans are to become social scientists, one of their first steps must be to rid themselves of the conceit that they are the independent willers of their own actions. Regarding the study of suicide Morselli explained that:

> The old philosophy of individualism had given to suicide the character of liberty and spontaneity, but now it became necessary to study it no longer as the expression of individual and independent faculties, but certainly as a social phenomenon allied with all the other racial forces.[8]

Many of these early students were convinced science could explain even moral behaviour and, in this context, official rates of immoral phenomena – apparently precise, quantifiable social facts that could be related statistically to other social phenomena – provided an excellent source of data for a nascent science of society, for they could be used to *demonstrate* the importance of 'external factors' in the causation of 'individual' actions.

By the middle of the nineteenth century most European countries were publishing suicide rates.[9] Suicide was classified along with murder, prostitution, alcoholism and other crimes under the general category of moral statistics. As these phenomena were necessarily seen as moral problems (rather being morally problematic) the moral statisticians used their data as a quantitative index of the moral health of a society. With the accumulation of statistics it became apparent not only that there were significant variations in the suicide rates of districts and countries, but also that these variations remained remarkably consistent over time. If suicide were the result of impulse and individual free will, the early statisticians reasoned, then the statistical rates would be random and not consistent.[10]

Buckle, for example, proposing his scientific theory of history, claimed that:

> All the evidence we possess respecting it points to one great conclusion, and can leave no doubt [in] our minds that suicide is merely the product of the general condition of society, and that the individual felon only carries into effect what is a necessary consequence of preceding circumstances. In a given state of society, a certain number of persons must put an end to their own lives. This is the general law; and the special question as to who shall commit the crime depends, of course, upon special laws; which, however, in their total action, must obey the large social law to which they are all subordinate . . . the existence of the regularity is familiar to whoever is conversant with moral statistics.[11]

Competing explanations of the causes of variations in rates of moral phenomena included race, culture, industrialisation, the decline of religion, economic and geographical conditions, but students were united in the general belief that moral problems could be explained scientifically and the specific assumption that official rates of moral phenomena, such as suicide rates, 'proved' the non-existence of free will and therefore the possibility of a positivist science of society.

Morselli, discussing the impact of the work of the early social statisticians, wrote with approval that:

> [statistical laws] . . . helped to change radically the metaphysical idea of the human will . . . and served as a formidable weapon to

deny the reality of independent human actions, and to declare that *the same laws exist in the moral as in the physical world* [my emphasis].[12]

A distinct scientific perspective on suicide was thus forged – a perspective which, largely because of Durkheim's qualified adoption of it, has influenced most sociological research into suicide. The legacy bequeathed by the moral statisticians was a conception of suicide as an immoral (deviant) 'thing', whose proven statistical distribution must necessarily be the result of (material) forces which were 'outside' individual wills.

The optimism with which these early social statisticians saw enumeration as providing a key which would unlock the problem of the relation between the individual and society is seen, for example, in Morselli's claim regarding suicide statistics:

From the investigation of comparative statistics, it appears that the true nature of suicide may now be reckoned amongst the most certain and valuable discoveries of experimental psychology. By applying to this social phenomenon the eminently positive method of numerical progression and of proportional averages, we have discovered its organic character, so to speak, have understood clearly its inward workings, and have explained scientifically its historical evolution.[13]

Though today, few would claim such undiluted optimism for official statistics (and indeed, in other parts of his work, Morselli himself expressed far more caution), the major sociological works on suicide are dependent on official suicide rates and the uncritical use of suicide statistics by sociologists and others is one of the major problems explored in some depth later. However, concern here is with attempts to explain suicide rates, and by far the most ambitious is Durkheim's *Suicide* which, despite criticism, 'modification' and 'improvement', remains the most important sociological work on suicide.[14]

The Polemics of *Suicide*

While the moral statisticians' explanations of suicide and other social phenomena in terms of 'extra-individual' causes had a profound influence on Durkheim's treatment of the problem,[15] *Suicide* transcended previous works in at least four important respects. First, while many previous writers had suggested that the steadily increasing suicide rates of western societies were linked to declining moral controls, Durkheim was the first (and many would argue the only) student to develop the notion into a logically consistent and complete theory of suicide. Second, Durkheim's analysis was wholly sociological and he explicitly rejected 'non-sociological' explanations, such as climate or race, as causes of suicide. Third, while Durkheim wanted sociology to be scientific, he did not agree that there was a unified scientific method as such which could simply and uncritically be imported into the study of social behaviour. Social facts, he insisted, could only be explained with reference to special (i.e. Durkheimian) rules and methods.[16] Finally, following from the previous point, *Suicide*, which like Durkheim's other works expressed an opposition to nominalistic reductionism, represented an important, though by no means complete, break with the positivist approaches of competing works.[17]

This last point requires some clarification, for even such well known Durkheimian students as Alpert and Nisbet have 'credited' Durkheim with being one of the founding fathers of the positivist, hypothetico-deductive school of sociology.[18] It is a popular view that Durkheim's work, particularly *Suicide*, was the main link between modern, scientific sociology and Comte's original formulation. One of the problems in discussing positivism, as Giddens has observed, is that nowadays the word is used very indiscriminately, often as a term of abuse.[19] This raises a number of problems, for example, distinguishing between those who call themselves positivists and those, such as Popper, who reject the term when it is applied to them.[20] However, for purposes of the present discussion, I shall refer to positivism as a total philosophical position embodying an ontology grounded in nominalism and phenomenalism; an epistemology holding that the only certain knowledge we can attain comes from observation, or experience, and a variety of methodologies, inductive, hypothetico-deductive, methodological-individualistic for example, based on a belief in the unified logic of scientific practice. Durkheim, in one way or another, was clearly opposed to each of these positions; nevertheless, in the study of suicide, the myth of a strong, positivist, sociological tradition from Durkheim to recent studies of suicide rates persists, and thus a sociological student of suicide stated that the major division in the sociology of suicide is 'Durkheim and the positivists *vs* Douglas and the phenomenologists'.[21] This misrepresentation of Durkheim stems, in part, from a fairly widespread misunderstanding of his intentions in *Suicide*. The popular view is that Durkheim's aim was to demonstrate to the world in general, and to a sceptical French academia in particular, the necessity for an independent academic discipline concerned with the study of society. In fact, sociology was undergoing a revival in France prior to the publication of *Suicide*, and Durkheim's main concern was with demonstrating the truth of *his* sociology, particularly to those who had rather different views on the subject. The work is thus not so much aggressively sociological, as distinctly *Durkheimian* sociological. It is then *doubly* polemical: aimed at demonstrating the importance of sociology (to the world) and the truth of Durkheimian sociology (to those who had alternative conceptions of the discipline).[22]

In order to achieve these twin ambitions Durkheim, like the other prophets of the 'new' sciences of humanity, had to define his project in terms of the scientific spirit of earlier and contemporary works. Sociology, he argued, apparently echoing the pronouncements of many others, must not content itself with philosophical speculation, it must concern itself with facts:

> Instead of contenting himself with metaphysical reflection on social themes, the sociologist must take as the object of his research groups of facts clearly circumscribed, capable of ready definition, with definite limits, and adhere strictly to them.[23]

It is not difficult to see how this and other statements, particularly early in the work, could have persuaded critics that Durkheim was arguing the case for a positivist sociology, comparable to that employed in modern 'scientific' sociology. However, while in these more recent works 'facts' are nominal and phenomenal, for Durkheim a 'social fact' was holistic; it was trans-subjective, constraining and, above all, it was real.[24] The relationships between suicide rates and rates of external association are factual, Durkheim argued, but these relationships were not explanations in themselves: rather, they were the *products* of social facts, suicidogenic currents, which were real although they could not be experienced by sensory per-

ception. Thus, according to Durkheim, facts such as rates of external association were only means of reaching the real causes of
suicide, which he attributed to an imbalance of currents of egoism,
altruism, anomie and fatalism.

However, the empiricist-orientated sociologists who 'rediscovered' *Suicide*, while admiring Durkheim's attempt to relate
(observable) suicide rates to (observable) rates of external association, were less than happy with his attempts to explain both of them
in terms of non-observable, (and thus unknowable) 'suicidogenic
currents'. Therefore, in so far as *Suicide* influenced subsequent
sociological research it is fair to say that, given its original intentions, it has had a rather one-sided influence; that is, sociologists
have tended to confine themselves to the relationships between
suicide and 'social factors', or 'social structures', and have been
inclined to ignore, or 'explain away', Durkheim's notion of 'currents', or 'forces', acting upon individuals. Bierstedt describes the
reaction of contemporary sociology to this aspect of Durkheim's
work as follows:

> These views, however [i.e. of 'collective sentiments'], proved to
> be serious obstacles in the general acceptance of and reaction to
> Durkheim's general sociological theory. American sociologists
> were especially resistant to them on the ground that Durkheim
> seemed quite clearly in these words to be hypostatizing abstrac-
> tions, to be making 'things', as it were, out of words, to be violat-
> ing the law of parsimony – sacred to the scientific method – in
> creating entities beyond necessity, and to be declaring that
> society is somehow more 'real' than the individuals who compose
> it. Long suspicious of German metaphysics and nurtured instead
> on an empirical and nominalistic tradition, the Americans
> viewed this approach with disfavour and demanded to know in
> what the 'reality' of society consists if not in individuals. They
> were similarly suspicious, and for the same reasons, of any
> independent entity called a 'collective consciousness', an entity
> with its own reality and, as Durkheim insisted, external to
> individuals.[25]

I shall return to this issue when discussing more fully Durkheim's
influence on subsequent sociological works on suicide, but it is first
necessary to examine in more detail Durkheim's specific intentions

in *Suicide* and his unique explanation of variations in suicide rates.

In *The Rules of Sociological Method*,[26] published two years before *Suicide*, Durkheim had argued that sociology is an autonomous discipline with its own theories and concepts which are not reducible to those of the neighbouring sciences. Social phenomena cannot be understood simply in terms of the motives and wishes of individuals. People are born into societies which are already organised and which thus influence them independently of their own volition. Societies, therefore, have 'a reality of a different sort from each individual considered singly'. In short, society is external to the individual, social facts are therefore autonomous and cannot be explained by reference to individual facts.

> Sociological method as we practice it rests wholly on the basic principle that social facts must be studied as things, that is, realities external to the individual. There is no principle for which we have received more criticism; but none is more fundamental. Indubitably for sociology to be possible, it must have above all an object all its own. It must take cognizance of a reality which is not the domain of other sciences.[27]

If this fundamental principle is not accepted, Durkheim argued, then 'the only possible subject of observation is the mental states of the individual, since nothing else exists' and social institutions, being only the superficial expression of individual needs, would call for no special attention. Those who sought to base the discipline on the psychological constitution of the individual were in fact 'robbing sociology of the only object proper to it'.[28]

Suicide was to be the vindication of this fundamental principle: a *demonstration* of the extent to which individual behaviour was determined by a collective reality 'as definite and substantial as those of the psychologist or the biologist'.[29] Suicide seemed a particularly suitable subject for such a demonstration for a number of reasons. First, the popularly held view of suicide was that it was a supremely individual act and if it could be shown that such acts were in fact governed by the society in which the individual participated, then Durkheim would have proved the truth of his general thesis by the very case seemingly most unfavourable to it.

Second, Durkheim had the work of the moral statisticians to draw upon and, in particular, their attempts to explain variations in suicide rates in terms of 'extra-individual' causes. The (known) regularity of suicide rates must have seemed to Durkheim very suitable material for 'proving' his thesis that society is external to the individual. As Nisbet puts it, 'the idea, the plot, and the conclusion of *Suicide* were well in Durkheim's mind before he examined the parish registers'.[30]

Third, suicide, and particularly the rising suicide rates of western societies, represented a concrete and specific social problem, especially in France where the rates were relatively high.[31] Many writers saw rising suicide rates as further evidence of the increasing social malaise sweeping European societies as a result of the declining influence of traditional institutions of social control.[32] The theme of social dissolution was a pervasive one in nineteenth-century French thought, and Durkheim was intent upon demonstrating how *his* sociology could explain the connections between social control and suicide and point to some remedies. 'The progress of a science', he wrote, 'is proven by the progress towards the solution of the problems it treats'.[33] Suicide was also clearly relevant to the fundamental problem of Durkheimian sociology, uncovering the bonds that integrate men into society and regulate their baser instincts, for it represented the most extreme manifestation of the dissolution of those bonds.

The Explanation of Suicide

Durkheim began by distinguishing between the explanation of the suicide rates and the explanation of individual acts of suicide.[34] Drawing attention to the consistency of the comparative variations of European suicide rates, Durkheim reasoned that the suicide rate is therefore 'a factual order, unified and definite, as shown by both its permanence and its variability'. The study of individual cases of suicide will not explain this regular statistical distribution.

Many previous studies had, of course, tried to explain the regularity of suicide rates in terms of 'extra-individual' causes, but these explanations were 'non-sociological' and, therefore, the first task was a refutation of these explanations. Using concomitant variations Durkheim attempted to show that there was no positive correlation between suicide rates and the frequency of psychopathic states. While they may be relevant to certain individual cases of suicide, the *social* phenomenon (the suicide rate) cannot be explained in terms of psychopathic states. With similar logic, Durkheim rejected race and heredity (normal psychological states) and cosmic factors as explanations of the suicide rate. Finally, he argued that if the suicide rate is determined by imitation, then a map of the geographical distribution of suicide would show cases radiating from a centre, where the rate is particularly high, to other regions. However, this is not the case: next to a region where the rate is particularly high can be found one where it is particularly low.[35]

Durkheim then went on to develop his own explanation. The suicide rate, he argued, is a social phenomenon and, therefore, can only be explained sociologically. The causes of variations in suicide rates are to be sought 'in the states of the various social environments' in which they occur. Durkheim was then, as Lukes puts it, attempting to discover 'what explanatory relations are there between forms of social life and individual acts of abandoning it?'[36]

Durkheim justified his approach as follows: by elimination, suicide must depend on social causes, but there is little point in attempting to classify individual cases of suicide into types. The nature of the act and the inadequacy of the data do not permit such an approach, as De Boismont's efforts revealed.[37] An alternative method, however, was to 'reverse the order of study' and determine types of suicide, not from their preliminary ascribed characteristics, but from 'the causes which produce them'. Durkheim then went on to argue that this approach, descending from causes to effects, is in fact the only method for studying the social suicide rate and explaining its formation and variation:

> No description, however good, of particular cases will ever tell us which ones have a sociological character. If one wants to know the several tributaries of suicide as a collective phenomenon one must regard it in its collective form, that is, through statistical data from the start. The social rate must be taken directly as the object of analysis: progress must be made from the whole to the parts . . . We must then immediately discover its causes and later consider their repercussions among individuals.[38]

However, these causes are not to be located in the 'causes' ascribed by officials, nor in the reasons that the individuals themselves give for their actions. These are no more than 'apparent causes', because they are merely 'individual repercussions of the general state', and even then they express it unfaithfully, 'since they are identical while it is not'. Individuals and their motives must therefore be 'disregarded' and the causes sought within society, in order to determine the forces which produce in communities a collective inclination to suicide.[39]

Supposedly from his analysis of statistical data, Durkheim developed four types of interrelated social causes which were derived from his conception of social and moral order. Durkheim's main interest was the relationship between the individual and society; and in particular, the tensions arising from the ways in which 'social man' imposes himself upon 'physical man'.[40] Society, he argued, constrains individuals in two ways: first, by attaching them to socially given purposes and ideals (integration) and second, by moderating their (potentially infinite) desires and aspirations (regulation).

Egoism and altruism are derived from the notion of integration. In the case of egoistic suicide the bond attaching man to life relaxes because that attaching him to society is itself slack. The individual becomes remote from social life and suffers from an excess of individualism.[41]

Egoistic suicide was derived from correlations between suicide rates and more or less integrating social contexts: Durkheim used religious differences, familial comparisons, and political upheavals to illustrate this type of suicide. Catholic countries had consistently lower suicide rates than predominantly Protestant ones, and even with nationality controlled, in Bavaria, Prussia and Switzerland, Catholic districts had lower suicide rates (varying from 20 per cent to 300 per cent).[42] These differences, Durkheim argued, cannot be explained in terms of a disparity in the attitudes of the two religions to suicide, since both unreservedly condemn it. The main difference between them is that Catholicism involves an established set of beliefs and ritual practices around which the life of believers is closely bound. In contrast, Protestantism is more individualised and permits a far greater degree of free enquiry, consequently the Protestant is more frequently 'alone before God'. In times of crisis the Protestant is more likely to be thrown upon his own resources and is thus less 'protected' from suicide than the Catholic. The comparatively higher suicide rates associated with Protestantism are a result of that Church being less integrated than the Catholic church. Suicide rates also tend to be higher in more educated societies and in particular, amongst highly educated and professional groups; this is due to 'the weakening of traditional beliefs and to the state of moral individualism resulting from this'.[43]

Similarly, the statistics illustrate that married people have proportionally lower suicide rates than the unmarried of the same age. However, according to the figures, after a time married women without children cease to be more protected from suicide and are in fact one and a half times as likely to commit it as the unmarried. Hence the protection from suicide comes not from the (regulating?) influence of marriage itself, but from the integration provided by family life and children. Married people with children have a higher 'coefficient of preservation', but childless marriages do not provide a strong enough integrating milieu to offer the same protection from suicide.[44] On average, suicide is inversely related to family density.[45]

Finally, suicide rates, particularly amongst urban populations, decrease in times of war or political upheaval. This is because social disturbances 'concentrating activity towards a single end, at least temporarily, cause a stronger integration of society'.[46]

Suicide then varies inversely with the degree of integration of religious society, domestic society, and political society. Individuals are more likely to commit suicide when they are egoists, when they think primarily of their own interests and desires and are not sufficiently integrated into the social groups around them. Therefore: 'suicide varies inversely with the degree of social integration of the social groups of which the individual forms part'.[47]

Altruistic suicide, the opposite of egoistic suicide, results from the over-integration of the individual into society. In altruistic suicide the individual's ego is not sufficiently developed to resist the demands of society and he kills himself in order to *conform* to social imperatives. Women who respond to the ritualistic obligation to kill themselves on the death of their husbands, and military leaders after defeat in battle, are two examples of such suicides. Altruistic suicide is a characteristic of primitive and traditional societies, but can still be found in modern societies in a tightly knit social group such as the army.[48]

Anomie and fatalism, on the other hand, are derived from the second dimension of social morality – the regulation, by society, of individual desires and aspirations. Anomic suicide occurs as a result of a person's activity 'lacking in regulation' and this may be indicated by the positive, statistical correlations between suicide rates and economic crises. Suicide rates rise in times of economic depression and, more surprisingly, in times of greater prosperity.[49] Economic change, therefore, influences the suicide rate not because of poverty as such – indeed 'poverty may even be considered a protection' – but because periods of economic fluctuation have the effect of placing large numbers of individuals in circumstances where the norms that had previously regulated their conduct are no longer appropriate to their changed conditions of life. They are thus left in a state of moral deregulation, or anomie, and are consequently less protected from suicide. Durkheim used a similar argument to explain the positive correlations between suicide and divorce.

Durkheim distinguished between acute and chronic anomie. The former refers to sudden crises, such as an economic crisis, which might cause the suicide rate to vary from time to time but would not be 'a regular constant factor'.[50] He was, however, more concerned about the latter (though he found it more difficult to identify empirically) which he saw as the condition of modern social existence most reponsible for the gradual (pathological) rise in suicide rates. In modern societies, social existence is no longer ruled by custom and tradition and individuals are increasingly placed into situations of competition with one another. As they come to demand more from life, not specifically more of something but simply more than they have at *any* given time, so they are more inclined to suffer from a disproportion between their aspirations and their satisfactions, and the resultant dissatisfaction is conducive to the growth of the suicidogenic impulse.

Anomic and egoistic suicide clearly have similarities in so far as both result from 'society's insufficient presence in individuals'.[51] But there is a difference in the nature of the deficiency. In egoistic suicide, the individual is deficient in 'collective activity and is no longer able to find a basis for existence in life'. In anomic suicide, society's influence in restraining individual passions becomes diminished and the individual is lost 'in an infinity of desires'.[52]

Some critics have suggested that Durkheim failed to make a clear and precise distinction between egoistic and anomic suicide.[53] In fact, Pope has argued that Durkheim's main purpose in introducing a second key variable, anomie, was to enable him to explain correlations not accounted for by egoism, thus giving the theory the appearance of being both complete and irrefutable.[54] Certainly, on several occasions, Durkheim was inclined to merge the concepts; referring, for example, to the 'identical cause' that produced egoism and anomie.[55] Similarly, he stated that egoism and anomie 'are usually merely two different aspects of one social state' without explaining under what conditions they were, and were not, aspects of the same state.[56] However, to suggest, as Johnson has, that all Durkheim's correlations can be explained in terms of egoism and that his theory may be more usefully restated as 'the more integrated (i.e. regulated) a society, group, or social condition is, the lower its suicide rate', is not only to rob the theory of much of its explanatory power, but also to take from the work its *critical* element.[57] An analysis which *restricts* itself to the integration (or lack of integration) of the individual into the prevailing norms of society thereby avoids discussion of the *content* of those norms (and the nature of the society). Clearly, this was not Durkheim's intention in *Suicide*. He was interested in the quality of social norms and, particularly in his discussion of chronic anomie, he was concerned with the way in which the norms of modern society, stressing as they did self-interest, competition and socially approved dissatisfaction, were themselves conducive to the aggravation of suicidogenic impulses. Thus, in a Durkheimian formulation, it is possible for individuals to be both moderately, or adequately integrated and yet still vulnerable to suicide if those norms into which they are integrated are too weak to regulate their baser instincts. Durkheim saw the rising suicide rates of European societies as a manifestation of social pathology, and considered that the rise was largely due to the relationship between modern social conditions and anomic states.

Fatalistic suicide, the polar opposite of anomic suicide, resulted from excessive regulation and oppressive discipline as, for example, in the suicides of slaves. Durkheim considered that this type of suicide was 'of very little contemporary importance' although, in some cases, the suicides of young husbands and childless women may be the result of oppressive regulation.[58]

Having identified the social types of suicide, Durkheim then attempted to show that they corresponded to psychological states.[59] Egoistic suicide was characterised by states of apathy and indifference; altruistic suicide by energy, passion and determination; and anomic suicide by irritation and disgust. There were also mixed types of suicide: egoism–anomie (agitation and apathy), anomic–

altruistic (exasperated effervesence) and ego–altruistic (melancholy and fortitude). Although Durkheim did not satisfactorily (except by implication) link his morphological to his etiological classification, this part of the work does demonstrate that he was not trying to create some radical disjunction between supposedly 'external' and 'internal' explanations of human behaviour as some commentators have claimed. In fact Durkheim, by admission, started 'from the exterior' out of necessity:

> We do not expect to be reproached further, after this explanation, for wishing to substitute the exterior for the interior in sociology. We start from the exterior because it alone is immediately given, but only to reach the interior.[60]

Although Durkheim was not the dogmatic advocate of crude 'sociologistic' explanation, nearly all his critics (and many of his admirers) have depicted him as an 'implacable foe' of psychological explanations. Thus Hendin, for example, interprets Durkheim's call to treat social facts as 'things' as 'making the psychology of suicide seem irrelevant';[61] while Havighurst, in a monumental misunderstanding of *Suicide* wrote that 'Durkheim neglected the self. One can read all of Durkheim on suicide and it appears as though all of suicide depends on status and society.[62] Gibbs, one of the leading sociological students of suicide explained that:

> As a radical advocate of purely sociological explanations of social phenomena, Durkheim had an axe to grind. Above all, he was an implacable foe of psychological explanations; and throughout his career Durkheim attempted to demonstrate the pervasiveness of social factors in human behaviour.[63]

Similarly Pope, who devoted a whole book to Durkheim's *Suicide*, claimed that in *Suicide* Durkheim was attempting to demonstrate the superiority of sociological explanations over psychological ones.[64]

In fact, Durkheim was not opposed to psychology as such; indeed, he was a keen student of the psychology of his day and, as Douglas has observed, even contributed to some of its debates.[65] Rather, Durkheim was opposed to *individualistic* explanations; that is, reducing explanation to states of individual consciousness.[66] This is not a criticism of 'studying the individual', but in fact a criticism of not *studying* the individual and instead, merely accepting individual consciousness at, as it were, face value. Durkheim makes this quite clear in his criticism of Tarde's claim that 'in sociology we have through a rare privilege, intimate knowledge both of that element which is our individual consciousness and of the compound which is the sum of consciousness in individuals':

> This first assertion is a bold denial of all contemporary psychology. Today it is generally recognised that psychical life, far from being directly cognisable, has on the contrary profound depths inaccessible to ordinary perception, to which we attain only gradually by devious and complicated paths like those employed by the sciences of the external world. The nature of consciousness is therefore far from lacking in mystery for the future.[67]

Of course, Durkheim was interested in the boundaries between sociology and psychology,[68] but it was a later generation of students who created the disjunction between supposedly 'internal' and 'external' factors in the explanation of suicide. Durkheim was concerned with the way in which society superimposes itself on individuals, but his sociology was not an attempt to show that social facts impinge on individuals from without and, as it were, 'propel' them like billiard balls in given directions; but rather that society, the collective experience of humanity, 'lives in' the subjective experiences of individuals. When Durkheim wrote about society being external, he was not advocating some crude social determinism where forces *physically outside* individuals 'push' them in given directions, but rather that society is external to each individual considered singly.[69] Thus a collective current, such as a wave of patriotic feeling, is 'almost wholly exterior' to individuals, since each contains only a spark of it.

The Form of the Explanation

Durkheim attempted to explain suicide rates in terms of other (factual) social phenomena – currents of egoism, altruism, anomie (and fatalism). It is the balance of these forces which determines the suicide rate of a group at a given time. These social causes are 'real living active forces' and the relative strength of their presence gives each society its own 'suicidogenic current':

> As these currents are collective, they have, by virtue of their origin, an authority which they impose upon the individual and they drive him more vigorously on the way to which he is already inclined by the state of moral distress directly aroused in him by the disintegration of society. Thus, at the very moment that, with excessive zeal, he frees himself from the social environment, he still submits to its influence.[70]

Psychiatrists, if they refer to *Suicide* at all, tend to dismiss it as an example of nineteenth-century collectivist metaphysics and appear to share Stengel's view that the work is 'only of historical interest today'.[71] Sociologists, while generally applauding the way in which *Suicide* demarcated an area of analysis specifically for sociology, have tended to ignore Durkheim's form of explanation and concerned themselves instead with those factors which *physically* constrain individuals. Thus Cresswell, for example, has argued that:

> Durkheim embodied [his] ideas in a unitary concept, the collective consciousness, which could now be supplanted without losing the value of his insight by the term, 'limiting factors'. Limiting factors, as structural limitations placed upon the individual – simply by virtue of the way society is constituted – have in their sum effect unintended but measurable consequences. Hence the possibility that the suicide rate for a particular group will reflect, to a measurable degree, changes in the composition of the group, for example in proportions of sexes, races and religions and different marital states.
>
> Because of the complexities involved in the use of Durkheim's ideas and arguments . . . later writers had considerable justification, in my view, in ignoring his philosophical realism and concentrating on the insights which he gave.[72]

Similarly, Pope claimed that 'Durkheim's conception of social reality as an emergent, irreducible system of forces may be rejected without diminishing appreciation of *Suicide*'.[73]

In short, for many sociologists, especially those who have actually studied suicide, the realist aspects of Durkheim's theory constitute an unnecessary hindrance to proper 'sociological' and 'scientific' understanding. Instead, they concentrate on those nominalist aspects of the work,[74] and indeed, some commentators have argued that for Durkheim the notion of 'suicidogenic currents' was little more than a metaphor. Lukes, for example, suggested that the language of 'forces' and 'currents' was 'distinctly inappropriate analogical language' and was 'at odds with the central social-psychological theory advanced in *Suicide*'.[75] However, given Durkheim's intentions, as opposed to those who followed him, the language was quite appropriate. Certainly the language of currents conveyed through a group mind was not metaphorical, for Durkheim was consistently so explicit about the nature of his explanation. He insisted that his concepts were not fictions, but realities.

> It is not a mere metaphor to say of each human society that it has a greater or lesser aptitude for suicide; *the expression is based on the nature of things*. Each social group *really* has a collective inclination for the act, quite its own, and the *source* of all individual inclination, rather than their result [my emphasis].[76]

According to Durkheim, currents of egoism, altruism and anomie are necessarily present in all societies and incline men in different, often contradictory, directions. This is because the individual has a certain personality (egoism), that he is responsive to the demands of the community (altruism), and that he is sensitive to progress and change (anomie). When these forces balance one another the individual is in a state of equilibrium and (more) protected from suicide. However, if one of them exceeds in strength to the detriment of others then, as it becomes 'individualised', it becomes 'suicidogenic'.[77] Individuals are thus (normally) restrained from suicide by two dimensions of polar opposite forces in a state of dynamic equilibrium and it is a change in strength of one or more of these forces, causing disequilibrium, that is *primary* in the causation of suicide, i.e. moving a suicide rate either way. To give an example from Durkheim's study, suicide rates were generally increasing in European societies; however, the crisis and political troubles affecting France in 1848 spread through Europe and were accompanied by a drop in the suicide rates. Durkheim's theory would argue that this was due to stronger currents of altruism which, at least for a time, offset the general tendency towards increasing egoism and the suicide rate fell.

Conclusions

Durkheim argued that although suicide appears to be purely an individual phenomenon, its causes are essentially social. The clinician, studying individual cases of suicide isolated from each other, finds suicide to be related to psychopathic states and believes these to be the causes. But this does not explain why a consistent number of people kill themselves over a given time. To find the causes of this social phenomenon, one must look beyond individual cases of suicide in order to find what gives them unity. This reveals that each population has a collective inclination for suicide and the causes of this must be sought in the characteristics of the social group, not individuals taken separately. Durkheim's work on suicide appeared to vindicate the fundamental idea of his sociology, that societies are heterogeneous to individuals and give rise to phenomena which can only be explained when taken as a whole. Aron has thus summarised Durkheim's achievement: 'There are, therefore, specific social phenomena which govern individual phenomena. The most impressive, most eloquent example is that of the social forces which drive individuals to their deaths, each one believing that he is obeying only himself.'[78]

2

The Sociologistic
Perspective on Suicide

Social-Factor Studies

It is a popular view that *Suicide* has had a profound and celebrated influence not only on the sociology of suicide, but also on the general development of the discipline. Merton, for example, referred to it as perhaps the greatest piece of sociological research ever done,[1] while Selvin has claimed that 'the empirical analysis in *Suicide* is as vital today as it was in 1897 – perhaps more so'.[2] However, although *Suicide* helped to shape a distinct sociological perspective, such homages to Durkheim should not obscure the significant reservations that later generations of students had about the work.

In the previous chapter it was observed that sociologists, while latching eagerly on to Durkheim's demonstration of the relationship between a seemingly 'individual act' and various 'structural variables', were rather less enthusiastic about his explanation of both in terms of 'suicidogenic currents'. What impressed most later students (particularly those who actually engaged in research) was not so much Durkheim's theoretical analysis of suicide rates, but rather the fact that so many of *Suicide's* empirical associations were subsequently confirmed. It is often argued that (much of) Durkheim's theory must be 'right' because the facts confirm that suicide is indeed related to religious differences, economic change, etc.[3] Maris, for example, having tested the relationship between the suicide rate of Cook County, Illinois and 'core sociological variables', concluded that:

> So much for the empirical analysis. The question now is 'what can we make of it?' We ought to be in a better position to criticise and

suggest reformulations of Durkheim's theory of suicide and to be loyal to the radical spirit in which this book was conceived. Paradoxically, however, the major explanatory postulate of our work *supports* Durkheim . . . Championing the heuristic value of irreverence in science does not require heretical results. It could be that Durkheim was in some measure right about the causes of suicide.[4]

For Durkheim, of course, these statistical associations were only manifestations of (and hence ways of reaching) the real causes of suicide (egoism, etc.) which were to be located in the differing moral authority of various groups. If, for the purposes of this discussion, we refer to Durkheim's approach as 'sociological', then many of the works that have followed him are, in this restricted use of the term, 'non-sociological' in the sense that 'society' has been decomposed into 'structures', or 'factors', which it is felt, given a sophisticated enough methodology, can be isolated and their (causal?) influence on suicide tested. For many, the significant contribution of *Suicide* is the way in which Durkheim's pioneering research helped to illustrate some of the most important 'limiting factors' associated with suicide.

Given this qualified interpretation of suicide, it is hardly surprising to find that much subsequent research into suicide rates, including many studies claiming to 'follow' Durkheim, has been restricted to mere 'fact finding'; that is to 'uncovering', or 'testing', the relationship between suicide and particular (material) factors. Geisel, for example, attempted to test 'Durkheim's' social-integration theory by examining the influence on the suicide rates of age, rural–urban residence, marital status, sex, race and occupation.[5] Each positive correlation was taken as evidence supporting Durkheim's theory. Similarly, Labovitz and Brinkerhoff, examining the relationship between industrialisation and suicide rates found that technological efficiency, urbanisation and occupational structure were related positively to the national suicide rates.[6]

In order to distinguish mere 'fact-finding' studies from those which are searching for some underlying order to the relationship between suicide and other social phenomena, I shall refer here to the former as social-factor studies of suicide rates. Adopting this approach Sainsbury, for example, examined the suicide rates of each London borough and found high suicide rates positively correlated with some factors (such as social mobility and social isolation) but not with others (such as unemployment or overcrowding).[7] Summarising such research findings, Stengel concluded that:

> Suicide rates have been found to be positively correlated with the following factors: male sex, increasing age, widowhood, single and divorced state, childlessness, high density of population, residence in big towns, high standard of living, economic crisis, alcohol and addictive drugs consumption, broken home in childhood, mental disorder and physical illness.[8]

I shall examine some of the implications of this approach when discussing suicide research in general in Chapter 6; however, two points may be made here specifically in relation to social-factor studies of suicide rates. First, while some of these works, for example those by Dublin[9] and Sainsbury,[10] are undertaken with care and precision; many more make no attempt to control for confounding variables and the results are thus invalid, even in terms of the narrow empiricism in which they are conceived. A curious, yet common, error is the belief that tests of significance designed for *random* populations may be usefully applied to *empirical* populations: many of those who relate suicide to a single empirical variable, say religion, have implicitly assumed that all those in religious group X have nothing else in common other than their religion. Therefore, we should hardly be surprised to find that efforts to 'explain differing rates of suicide on the basis of religious affiliation have been largely unsuccessful'.[11]

Second, whereas Durkheim's theory represented a logical attempt to account systematically for a potentially infinite number of particular associations, social-factor studies, in contrast, assume that, first, we must know the (finite number of?) 'facts about suicide', particularly the relationship between suicide and 'core variables' such as sex, race, occupation, etc., *before* constructing general theories (i.e. how can one construct a theory before knowing the facts that the theory is to explain?)[12] However, such research, rather than 'building up' into increasingly 'general' explanation has rather tended to go the opposite way and, as might be imagined, 'broken down' into more and more particular explanations. Looking, for example, at the relationship between suicide rates and occupation, suicide rates have been found to be highest in 'high' and 'low' status occupations.[13] However, some occupational groups have high rates (for example, dentists) while others have low rates (for example, engineers). Furthermore, occupational rates vary from place to place. Thus firemen in the United States have a relatively low rate in general, but a particularly high rate in Los Angeles; while lawyers have a high rate in Oregon, yet a relatively low rate in the United States as a whole. If, in attempting to explain such variations, the focus is restricted to the categories 'occupation' and 'suicide', then explanation becomes increasingly 'population specific'. With no clear theoretical framework, explanation does not order data, rather data orders explanation, with each 'new' discovery demanding its 'own' explanation.

Social-factor studies of suicide rates are only one aspect of a far wider concern which appears to be to try to correlate suicide rates with every conceivable factor; suicide rates have even been tested to see if time, day and month of birth are significant (thus bringing social science uncomfortably close to astrology).[14] Much of this research appears to be undertaken with the conviction that knowledge of a phenomenon is roughly proportional to the quantity of facts that are 'known' about it. With such an epistemology 'fact gathering' becomes a legitimate end in itself. Suicide, it is assumed, will ultimately be explained when 'enough' facts about it are 'known', and each further 'bit of information' is seen as another piece of the jigsaw. Many studies of suicide rates are, therefore, undertaken with no explicit theoretical framework, although underlying all of them is the implicit theory that the empirical world can be directly observed and that explanations will 'emerge' when 'enough' observations have been made.[15] Although many such studies may bear a superficial resemblance to Durkheim's work in so far as they study statistics and sometimes claim to be 'developing' his ideas, in no useful sense can they be described as following in a Durkheimian tradition.

The Sociologistic Perspective

Even amongst the more theoretical, thorough and systematic attempts to explain suicide rates there has been relatively little progress since *Suicide*.[16] Some commentators have claimed that the magnitude of Durkheim's achievement has inhibited later students.[17] Certainly no one since Durkheim has attempted to construct such a complete and embracing theory of suicide rates. Later studies have tended to limit their attentions either to refining and developing aspects of Durkheim's theory, or constructing alternative theories which attempt to explain *specific* associations, such as the suicide rates of particular status groups especially, in recent works, 'marginal' status groups such as blacks[18] or women,[19] cultural and subcultural groups.[20] The post-Durkheimian literature on suicide rates is characterised by much duplication of error, repetition of 'findings', uncritical acceptance of data, and relatively little innovation and originality. Concern here, however, is not so much with reviewing the merits and shortcomings of many particular studies,[21] but rather with defining some of the more important general characteristics of the sociology of suicide and discussing the implications for further research. Thus in attempting to discuss development since Durkheim, I shall focus specifically only on those few works which have generally been viewed as worthy successors to *Suicide*, in so far as they are considered to go in some important respect 'beyond' Durkheim. These works develop theories of suicide which, like Durkheim, try to reveal an underlying order which produces the consistency and stability of various suicide rates. However, unlike Durkheim, they seek the sources of this order at a nominal and phenomenal level and attempt to explain suicide in terms of a mechanistic physical constraint, as opposed to a moral and ideal constraint. To put it simply, while Durkheim was insistent that society was something more than the sum of its parts, later students by and large abandoned this notion and concentrated instead on the relationships between the various and apparent parts of society. Thus I have termed these later studies 'sociologistic' in order to distinguish them from Durkheim's 'sociological' approach.

Halbwachs, in a thorough and systematic reappraisal of *Suicide*, which included an attempt to examine the reliability of the data, generally confirmed Durkheim's correlations, but claimed that most (for example, the relatively high rates associated with Protestantism) could be explained more plausibly in terms of the differing way of life of urban and rural cultures.[22] The relatively higher rates consistently found in urban areas were caused by a higher degree of social isolation which, according to Halbwachs, was *both* a structural cause of and an individual motivation for suicide. Similarly, many subsequent students have taken the position that social integration, or isolation, is *the* key variable in variations in suicide rates.[23] The proposition that the suicide rate varies inversely with the degree of social integration of the social groups of which the individual forms part, remains both a consistent research finding and the closest sociology has come to generating a law-like proposition. Most later students have seen it as the main, and in some cases the only, contribution of Durkheim's theory.[24]

Gibbs and Martin, however, claim that even this aspect of Durkheim's theory could never be subjected to a formal test as he provided no clear *empirical* definition of social integration.[25] They propose instead the concept of status integration. People occupy a number of statuses and when they are incompatible (i.e. their tenancy does not overlap), the individual is subject to a greater degree of role conflict and the resultant strain of conflicting expectations impairs the stability and durability of social relations. Therefore, the suicide rate of a population varies inversely with the degree of status integration of that population. Evaluating their own theory, Gibbs and Martin claim to have produced a formal, testable theory with a high degree of predictive power.[26] However, as Chambliss observes, although the work has the appearance of a general theory, it is in fact merely the test of a single proposition and the preliminary postulates are unnecessary and misleading.[27] There are also problems in the operationalisation and testing of this proposition. Status integration is supposed to measure the stability and durability of social relationships in a given population over time, but what Gibbs and Martin actually provide is a static index of role occupancies, which is hardly a basis for 'measuring' (even indirectly) social relations over time. Furthermore, as Gibbs and Martin offer no evidence that the individuals who actually kill themselves suffer disproportionately from a lack of status integration, the proposition has hardly been 'tested'; at best, a positive relationship between suicide and status integration can only be inferred. Even then there are problems, because role conflict, the idea which links status integration to suicide, is defined solely in terms of statistical status incompatibility and does not take into account the fact that different statuses might have different meanings to members of society. In other words they are attempting to 'measure' with an absolute yardstick when, in terms of the logic of their own theory, it is not necessarily legitimate to do so. As Hagedorn and Labovitz note, although there are few male lion tamers and few male ballet dancers, there is likely to be more role conflict amongst the latter group.[28] However, Gibbs and Martin do point to what is in their terms an important deficiency in Durkheim's work and they do, in a quite ingenious manner, attempt to provide a concrete and testable theory of suicide rates.

Sociologists have also been interested in the relationship between status change and suicide; in particular, the positive correlations between status loss and suicide and high status and suicide.[29] In what is probably the most original post-Durkheimian study of suicide rates, Henry and Short argue that the common element which links high status and social isolation, the two factors most consistently and positively associated with suicide, is external restraint.[30] First, continued involvement in any social relationship involves some element of (horizontal) restraint as the individual has to take into account the behaviour of others if the relationship is to continue; second, those playing the subordinate role in the relationship are subject to a higher degree of (vertical) external restraint than those playing the superordinate role. When an individual experiences frustration (which is more likely, for example, in an economic depression), the more he is externally restrained the more likely it is that he will direct his aggression at others (commit homicide) and the less he is externally restrained the more likely it is that he will direct his aggression at himself (commit suicide).

It is often argued that Henry and Short's work goes beyond Durkheim's because it provides a testable theory which attempts to link sociological *and* psychological variables in explaining the causes of suicide, whereas Durkheim considered only the former. The psychological part of Henry and Short's thesis, however, is little more than the adoption of a crude frustration–aggression theory.[31] In fact the original part of Henry and Short's work is the attempt to show, with the concept of external restraint, which status groups are likely to 'prefer' suicide or homicide.[32] However, as Henry and Short conceive of restraint only in *physical* terms, i.e. literally *outside* the individual, they fail to consider the more or less restraining quality of norms and values; nor can they relate the experience of a lack of restraint to suicide and homicide. Their approach, rather than incorporating psychological explanation, in fact effectively *precludes* examination of the social-psychological variables that might mediate between more or less restraining norms and individual acts of destruction. Further, it is also doubtful if the method used by Henry and Short actually demonstrates the validity of their thesis. To support their theory, Henry and Short offered *absolute* rates of suicide and homicide for specific years. This data does show that suicide rates are higher in high-status categories and homicide rates higher in low-status categories. But the observation that high-status categories have higher suicide rates does not 'prove' that these groups have a greater preference for suicide than members of low-status categories. This may only demonstrate that they are more frustrated and hence more aggressive in general. Nor is it enough to show that *within* the higher-status categories the suicide rates are higher than the homicide rate. This does reveal that higher-status citizens prefer suicide to homicide, but it does not show that their preference is any greater than the lower-status category where the suicide rate may also be higher than the homicide rate. Gold criticises Henry and Short for precisely this error, and proposes instead a suicide–murder ratio, where the total amount of suicide and homicide of a category is taken into account and an index of preference for suicide is obtained by dividing the homicide rate by the sum of suicide rate and comparable homicide rate.

Gold goes on to argue that Henry and Short's correlations may be more plausibly explained in terms of the varying child-rearing practices associated with high and low-status groups. Working-class children who tend to be punished physically are more likely to express themselves with physical aggression, while middle-class children who are more often punished psychologically tend to turn their aggression inward.[33]

Maris adopts a concept of external constraint broadly similar to Henry and Short's notion of external restraint.[34] According to Maris, Durkheim's work has two major weaknesses. First, his tendency to generalise made him overlook important details and second, he understated the role of 'individual factors' in the causation of suicide.[35] Not only are these criticisms scarcely relevant to *Suicide*, but it is hard to see how 'Maris's study offers any remedy to these 'errors'. His own work is full of unsupported generalisations as, for example, when he argues, without providing any evidence, that fatalistic suicide predominates in the Negro and suburban areas; while the nearest he gets to considering 'individual factors' is one comment about 'internal restraint' also having to be considered.[36]

Maris claims that the correlations found in his study can be accounted for by the concept of external constraint, a concept which combines integration and regulation. However, in view of Gibbs and Martin's criticism of Durkheim's notion of integration, it is interesting to note that the concept of external constraint is impossible to operationalise. For example, Maris suggests that we might measure integration by counting an individual's 'interpersonal-dependency relationships', although he provides no definition of an interpersonal-dependency relationship. It would be hard enough to measure one's own interpersonal-dependency relationships. For example, does one count all friendships, or include only some whilst excluding others? If so, what criteria should be used? Frequency of contact? Should relatives that one keeps in touch with but does not see be included? And what about relatives one is obliged to see but, given some choice in the matter, would happily never see again? The problems would be endless, and Maris's bland assumption that such a measure of integration could be established from coroners' records is difficult to justify.

Maris's study is interesting, however, because it contains both an explicit commitment to a 'Durkheimian' approach and yet an implicit abandonment of interest in the areas of social life that most passionately interested Durkheim. Concern with the relationship between individual acts and collective morality has been substituted by the search for the material factors which physically constrain individuals, and the struggle between individual desire and collective obligation has been displaced by a partitioning of 'internal' and 'external' causes.

However, despite the general rejection of Durkheim's social realism by most later students, almost all subsequent sociological research into suicide has been shaped by *Suicide*. In particular, sociologists have accepted the important distinction that Durkheim made between explanations of acts of suicide and explanations of suicide rates, and it was generally accepted that 'the foremost task of sociological studies of suicide is to explain differences in rates'.[37] They have also followed Durkheim in searching for the social causes of suicide in correlations between suicide rates and various other rates of external association and, like Durkheim, they have assumed that the examination of individual motives for suicide and the study of the micro-social contexts of suicidal acts are largely irrelevant to the sociological explanation of suicide.[38] Furthermore, most subsequent explanations of suicide rates by sociologists in terms of integration, status and restraint are derived from Durk-heim's massive insights. Methodologically then, due to the influence of *Suicide*, a distinct sociological, or as I have termed it here sociologistic, perspective on suicide has evolved, and it is to some general observations on this perspective that I now turn.

Some Observations on the Sociologistic Perspective

The 'Non-Suicide' Rate

This objection, which is essentially numerical rather than theoretical, was first raised by Delmas in response to Durkheim's *Suicide*.[39] With a logic that would now be described as 'lateral thinking' it was argued that, as suicides are (fortunately) such a tiny proportion of any population, they cannot reasonably be used to *demonstrate* that some social contexts are more 'protecting' than others. For example, the Republic of Ireland has a suicide rate (1.8 per 100,000 per year) which is *six* times lower than that of England and Wales (10.8 per 100,000 per year).[40] In Durkheimian terms we could attempt to explain these differences, for example, in terms of the more integrated, and hence 'protecting', social life of the Republic of Ireland. If, however, these figures are inverted and we compare the numbers of those 'protected' from suicide each year, then the differences, 99,998.2 as opposed to 99,989.2, are nominal in spite of the supposedly more 'preserving' influence of Catholic, rural society.[41]

This observation clearly has the greatest implications for those studies which attempt to explain cross-cultural comparative variations in suicide rates. Hendin, for example, attempted to explain the seemingly very significant differences in the suicide rates of Sweden and Norway in terms of the different child-rearing techniques of those cultures.[42] A critic would be entitled to express surprise, however, that despite the different child-rearing practices and profound cultural variations noted by Hendin, more or less identical numbers of people decide, year in and year out, *not* to commit suicide.

The Ecological Fallacy

Sociologists have long had their attention drawn to the fallacy of assuming that the associations derived from comparisons of groups are valid estimates of the associations that would be obtained from individual data.[43] Nevertheless, in relating suicide rates to other rates of external association, most sociological studies of suicide from Durkheim onwards have been prone to this error.

Durkheim, for example, observed that there was a positive correlation between suicide rates and the proportion of people in each French department with independent means. Such an ecological association *in itself*, however, tells us nothing about the relationship between independent means and suicide, for it is consistent with either of the following hypotheses: none of the people who committed suicide had independent means or, all of the people who committed suicide had independent means. Ecological associations are quite permissible when the unit of analysis is the group rather than the individuals in it, but this is not the case with studies of suicide rates where Durkheim and others have been theorising about the relationship between the properties of a social group and an individual act.[44]

Of course, if the student carries his replications down to individual data, as Durkheim sometimes did, then there is no ecological fallacy. It is not then a necessary consequence of the sociologistic approach to suicide, but the general reluctance of sociologists to move beyond broad comparisons of group rates and consider individual data has meant that the ecological fallacy is still prevalent, with more or less damaging consequences in most works on suicide by sociologists, including the better ones by Gibbs and Martin, Henry and Short, Gold and Maris, discussed in the previous section.[45] Henry and Short, for example, show that suicide and homicide rates are affected by changes in the business cycle. They argue that this is the result of aggression caused by the frustration of having goals blocked, but provide no evidence to show that individuals who committed suicide or homicide suffered this frustration. They do not, therefore, support their most fundamental hypothesis empirically. In general, the notion that there has been some profound methodological advance in the study of suicide since Durkheim cannot be sustained.

Veil of 'Statistical Proof'

Douglas has written that: 'Throughout the western world today there exists a general belief that one knows something only when it has been counted . . . Though this epistemological assumption was first applied to the natural sciences, it has come to dominate western man's thought concerning human affairs as well.'[46] Many of the earliest social scientists were inclined to see the objectivity and rationality of the physical sciences in idealised terms, and were enthusiastic about the possibilities of applying scientific methods to social phenomena. It was felt that in this way the study of society could *transcend* philosophical debate and theories of society could thus be 'proved' (or 'disproved'). Moral statistics were used in a polemical debate to prove the possibilities of an objective science of man and society. As Douglas observed:

> In an age torn by many basic conflicts . . . any honest social thinker had to be deeply troubled by the elusiveness of certainty in his quest for understanding man and his actions, and by the difficulty of convincing other social thinkers and the public that any given position was correct. Both problems could best be solved by using the ideas and methods of mathematics and the natural sciences: what could be more certain than ideas and findings based on the ultimate criteria of scientific methods and knowledge? And what could be more convincing to one's friends and enemies? Who could deny the truth of a finding or an explanation so obviously based on forms of science?[47]

Douglas argues that this is why Durkheim chose a 'scientific', statistical approach for a work aimed at proving the truth of his social philosophy.[48] The consistency of the relations between suicide and other social phenomena, Durkheim claimed, proved the existence of real and constraining causes which he called collective representations.

It is here that we encounter one of the core dilemmas of Durkheimian sociology. Durkheim was quite clear that collective human existence is something other than people think it is; if this is not the case, then it calls for no *special* attention, certainly not an independent academic discipline concerned with the study of society. But Durkheim was also insistent that this discipline must transcend philosophical debate and reasoned argument; it must be factual and produce propositions capable of scientific proof.[49] However, if social reality is necessarily beyond our experience as participating members of society, how then do we know it exists in order to have scientific statements made about it?

In attempting to resolve this problem Durkheim tries to get the best of two contradictory worlds. Without relinquishing his realism, he nevertheless maintains that we may know social reality exists by experiencing its effects as, for example, in the stable relations between suicide and rates of external association. This demonstrates, Durkheim claimed, that individual actions are determined by a social reality which has its origins in *collective* human life.[50]

Whereas many critics and 'followers' of Durkheim have merely misunderstood the nature of the Durkheimian enterprise, his more sophisticated empiricist critics have observed that Durkheim's thesis has not been proved in the manner he claimed. The facts about suicide cannot validate Durkheim's case, it is argued, for these had already been established in earlier (non-sociological) works. Proof had to come from Durkheim's analysis of those facts; but this proof is not forthcoming because Durkheim did not define his causal concepts in a manner precise enough to allow for empirical refutation.[51] Durkheim was thus able to interpret the facts in such a way as to support his preconceived theory. Even facts which potentially threaten it, such as a low suicide rate in predominantly Protestant England, or a low rate amongst relatively well-educated Jews, can quite conveniently be brought within its ambit.

The justification for the low suicide rate amongst Jews is a good example of Durkheimian logic and thus illustrates the nature of his explanation and the contradiction contained within it. The Jew, even though he is usually well educated, is 'disinclined' towards suicide because of the different meaning that education has for Jews. They seek knowledge for protection in a hostile word; it is therefore superimposed on collective beliefs and does not undermine them.[52] This explanation is, of course, quite *consistent* with Durkheim's general theory of suicide, which does not assume a consistent order at a phenomenal level but argues that suicide is the product of social meanings which are caused by combinations of egoism, anomie, etc. However, such an explanation is *inconsistent* with Durkheim's *claim* that his theory is both derived from and proved by the data and empiricist critics are, therefore, quite entitled to question Durkheim's claim of 'proof'. You are talking, our (scientific) language critics seem to be saying to Durkheim's ghost, but your theory is not 'really' scientific because it refuses to commit itself to the phenomenal world for 'validation' (or 'refutation'). However, two points can be made in this context. First, while it is true that no specific empirical finding, for example a Catholic population with a high suicide rate, can disprove the theory this does not mean, as some have claimed, that the theory is so flexible as to be irrefutable. In the final analysis it is not the statistics but Durkheim's logic, reason and argument on which the theory rests. Durkheim develops a model of suicidal meanings from a series of logical propositions derived from a distinct conception of humanity.[53] The theory can indeed be embarrassed by its illogical relationship to the empirical world and could be refuted, or displaced, not by some empirical finding as such, but by the development of a more rational, logical model. In the later Chapters of this work I shall attempt such an exercise by revealing logical inconsistencies between suicidal phenomena and Durkheim's model.

The second point to be made here is that even if one accepts the empiricist critique of the 'non-testability' of Durkheim's theory, then precisely the same charges must be raised against the later sociological studies which, at best contain similarly ill-defined concepts,[54] and at worst are mere *ad hoc* interpretations of empirical particulars. Kruijt, for example, examined the suicide rates of western societies since the Second World War and identified some significant trends, such as the rise in the number of suicides of males between twenty-five and fifty-five years of age since the early 1960s.[55] He argued that this increase was caused by increasing affluence which produced more 'anomie' amongst this group. Similarly, as we have seen, increasing suicide rates of women have been attributed to the increasing emancipation of participation in the labour force, the increasing suicide rates of blacks to their growing alienation and so on. Such *ad hoc* 'interpretative empiricism' is only explanation in the crudest sense. In the first place, as many explanations as the observer wishes to think of can usually be found to 'fit' the trends;[56] second, explanation defined in terms of descriptive particulars can never transcend them, they are 'temporary, snapshot, ten-for-a-penny descriptions'.[57] However, even these crude, intuitive generalisations, when veiled in statistical 'proof', often give the impression of being testable, refutable theories. Many of these later students, like Durkheim, have also been inclined to assume that the facts speak for themselves, and that once the statistical facts have been uncovered the explanations must be 'true'.

These observations do not, of course, lead to a refutation of sociologistic theories of suicide, but they do suggest that they have not been demonstrated as 'scientifically' and as unequivocally as their authors have sometimes claimed. In general, studies of suicide rates have been characterised by a rather circular argument. It has been assumed that variations in suicide rates between groups must be due to some sort of fundamental differences between those groups, i.e. the general theory is right by assumption. Theories are then advanced and apparently tested and confirmed by the data.

'Externalistic' Explanations

In the nineteenth century it became increasingly popular, particularly amongst medical and psychological students of human behaviour, to try to explain crime, prostitution and the like as manifestations of mental illness. Esquirol, for example, wrote that suicide (rather than being 'wicked') 'shows all the characteristics of mental disorders of which it is in fact only a symptom'.[58] The scientist's problem was to find the causes of the illnesses which, amongst other things, made suicide more likely. In contrast, there were those, like the moral statisticians, who drew attention to the relationship between immoral acts and environmental factors.

A distinction of sorts was thus forged between approaches which sought explanations of deviance in terms of individual (or 'internal') causes and those which sought them in environmental (or 'external') causes. In the study of suicide, the debate between respective advocates of supposedly 'internal' and 'external' explanations became most intense in France, largely due to the influence of Durkheim's *Suicide*.[59] In response to Durkheim's sociological explanation of suicide, the heirs of the medical point of view claimed that social factors were irrelevant in the causation of suicide. De Fleury, for example, argued that suicide is always a consequence of mental disorder, the primary causes of which are bio-psychological rather than social. Therefore, as suicidal tendencies are biologically 'built into' individuals, sociology is irrelevant to the explanation of suicide. Similarly, Courbon (in response to Halbwachs's thesis) argued that suicide derived from anxiety and depression and these are, through their biological nature, as independent of social factors as colour of eyes or reaction time.[60] However, although suicide has been found to be more common in particular diagnostic conditions,[61] it is now generally held that suicide is not necessarily an indication of mental illness and that social factors must *also* play an important part.[62] In more recent research a popular position is that suicide is the result of both external factors (i.e. literally outside individuals, urbanisation for example) and internal factors (personality for example) and a proper, or ultimate, explanation of suicide should take cognizance of both.[63] The problem with Durkheim's analysis, it is argued, is that he took account of only external factors. Thus Stengel observed, with explicit reference to Durkheim's theory, that it is now 'recognised' that the individual and the group cannot be understood apart from each other,[64] while Maris and other sociologists have warned against following Durkheim and neglecting 'individual factors'.[65] Similarly Van Del argued that:

Durkheim pointed to social factors as the major influences in the development of suicide tendencies. But social factors are not the only variables to be considered in the dynamics of suicide, for a suicidal individual may isolate himself from society and live in a lonely, suicidal world still beset by suicidal forces but independent of social influences.[66]

Here Van Del, like so many of Durkheim's critics, assumes that *Suicide* is concerned with the external, material world, at the expense of the internal causes which emanate from the individual himself. However, Durkheim cannot be held responsible for such a dichotomy, for he would not have acknowledged the distinction around which it revolves. He made his position on this issue quite clear in another work:

Since we have made constraint the outward sign by which social facts can be most easily recognised and distinguished from the facts of individual psychology, it has been assumed that according to our opinion, *physical* constraint is the essential thing for social life. As a matter of fact, we have never considered it more than the material and apparent expression of an *interior* and profound fact which is wholly ideal; this is moral authority. The problem of sociology consists in seeking, among the different forms of external constraint the different forms of moral authoriity corresponding to them and in discovering the causes which have determined these latter [my emphasis].[67]

It was in fact Durkheim's *successors*, by confining their attentions to *physical* constraint, who helped to create the supposed radical disjunction between internal and external explanations of suicide. Gibbs and Martin, for example, quite explicitly adopt this position,[68] While in the studies by Henry and Short and Maris, restraint and constraint were defined purely in physical terms. Charges of social determinism and wishing to substitute the exterior for the interior in sociology, often raised unjustly against Durkheim, may quite legitimately be levelled against these later works. Just as there are crude Marxists, so too are there 'crude Durkheimians'.

Restriction to Completed Suicide

Although Durkheim used biographical data to try to classify the 'individual types' of suicide,[69] most sociologists have confined themselves exclusively to the statistics and have made little, or no, attempt to clarify and extend their general knowledge of the phenomenon they are seeking to explain.[70] I shall discuss the implications of this position in Chapter 7, but a couple of preliminary points can be made here. First, as sociologists have told us little or nothing about that majority of suicidal actions that do not end in death (other than assuming that some of them must be 'failed' suicides), their explanations are at best partial and limited and, until the position is altered, there can be no sociological explanation of suicide.

Second, and more important, sociologistic studies of suicide are misleading in so far as they assume that a clear-cut distinction can be made between 'genuine' suicidal acts (which are aimed at death) and various other 'false' suicidal acts (which are aimed at survival). However, students who have studied the micro-social contexts of suicidal acts have observed how frequently, in most 'serious' suicidal acts, only hairbreadth differences separate death from survival.[71] In most suicidal acts (including many that result in death) the outcome is left to chance. Often an individual will initiate an act of (potential) self destruction, while at the same time allowing for the *possibility* of intervention from others. From the definitions of suicide given by most sociologists, such actions would not *really* be suicidal, and if sociologists wish to use a conception of suicide which excludes risk-taking, then they should *not* use official suicide rates where many gambles with death are recorded as 'suicides'.[72] On the other hand, if sociologists do employ a broader conception of the suicidal act, one that involves the notion of a gamble with death, then this would mean the student having to use data from a wider range of sources.[73] The general point to be made here is that sociologists, largely as a result of their refusal to study what Douglas calls 'real world suicidal actions', have been using a concept of suicide which does little justice to the complexities of the phenomenon.

Conclusions

The previous section outlined some recurring weaknesses in the sociologistic perspective on suicide; but while these problems are *characteristics* of sociologists' approach to suicide, they are not necessary *consequences* of it. For example, it was noted that most sociologistic works on suicide lapse into the ecological fallacy, but there is no reason why studies should necessarily commit this error. In short, the observations made above may refute particular studies, but not the general perspective.

However, while there are problems to be explored and perhaps solved within the limits imposed by the sociologistic perspective (for example, Gibbs and Martin's attempt to provide a more testable theory of integration, or Gold's discussion of the social-psychological variables that might mediate between social conditions and rates of suicide) the position taken here is that the most fruitful avenues for further enquiry lie in two areas typically ignored by sociologists of suicide. Both stem from sociologists' reliance on official suicide rates.

First, when reviewing the relevant literature, one finds how generally indifferent most students have been to the quality of the data upon which their theories are based and through which they are tested. This appears still to be the case, in spite of an important shift in emphasis in the study of deviance away from exclusive concern with the forms of deviant behaviour to include 'the processes by which persons come to be defined as deviant by others'.[74] The research of the societal-reaction theorists, despite its obvious shortcomings and limitations,[75] has demonstrated that social rules are not implemented in a more or less mechanical fashion and the assignment of individuals to deviant statuses is the product of processes of judgement, argument and negotiation. One of the most important implications of this is that the student is increasingly forced to treat as problematic what he once took for granted; for example, the validity, reliability and comparability of official rates of deviant behaviour.[76] However, this appears to have had relatively little impact on the study of suicide rates where, apparently, students feel entitled to continue using the official statistics in a relatively uncritical manner until they have been 'proved' to be unreliable.[77]

Second, although in most areas of deviance students have shown greater willingness to try to 'appreciate', or 'understand', the phenomenon they are studying, sociologists of suicide have done virtually nothing in this direction. They have not, for example, attempted to examine the micro-social contexts of suicidal actions, nor have they shown any apparent interest in the wealth of non-sociological literature on suicide.

The remainder of this work is devoted to the exploration of these two problems. Part II examines the problems relating to the quality of official suicide statistics, while Part III attempts to develop an alternative, social-psychological approach to suicide, one that derives types of suicide not from the statistics, but from the micro-social contexts of suicidal actions.

Part II

The Social Construction of Official Suicide Rates

3

Some Critiques of Official Suicide Rates

The suicide rates have always played a most important part in suicide research. They have been looked upon as the perfect instrument for measuring and comparing the size of the suicide problem in populations . . . Two years ago, in a symposium at Washington, a distinguished sociologist dismissed doubts about their reliability and comparability as part of the folklore of psychiatry.[1]

Four Perspectives on Official Suicide Rates

Questions about the viability of official suicide rates as a primary source of data for suicide research have usually concerned themselves with whether or not such statistics are *valid* in principle and *reliable* in practice; these are essentially problems related to *defining* what suicide is and problems of *recognising* whether or not suicide has taken place.

Of course, few would deny that 'errors' in the reporting of suicides do occur and, therefore, there must be some discrepancy between the officially recorded and the 'real' volume of suicide. It is generally accepted that the official suicide rates tend to underestimate the real distribution of suicide because it seems inevitable that due to deliberate concealment, lack of evidence, etc., some suicides will be 'hidden'.[2] Estimates regarding the extent of possible error vary;[3] but while this is clearly important, it is not simply a question of proportions, for it is also important to try to discover the nature of these 'errors in reporting'. For if the problem is to be defined in these terms, it is crucial to discover whether these errors are *random* (and therefore tend to cancel each other out) or *systematic* (thus reducing their research value to an unacceptable degree).

Most students of suicide rates have either assumed, or occasionally attempted to argue, that suicide rates are at least working approximations of truth. It has been argued, for example, that at least in industrialised countries, systematic techniques of investigation, careful search procedures, better informed officials and the very regularity of the rates themselves (irrespective of the coming and going of particular officials) serve as evidence of a reasonable level of reliability.[4] On the other hand there are those who argue, usually on the basis of a few cases known to them personally, that suicide rates are a far too unreliable, or even invalid, source of data for research.

It would be a mistake, however, to imply that researchers are either totally 'for' or 'against' the use of official suicide rates; rather they vary in the level of confidence, or more aptly in the lack of confidence, they have in the statistics. Four positions can be identified. In the first place there are students (like Durkheim) who are content to undertake longitudinal, cross-cultural comparisons of suicide rates. I shall refer to this as a position of *general acceptance* of suicide rates: a position usually identified with (though by no means confined to) sociological approaches to suicide.

General acceptance of suicide rates involves making at least three fundamental assumptions: (1) that the researcher's definition of suicide corresponds to that employed by the officials who compile the data (assumption of *validity*); (2) that this definition is applied efficiently and consistently (assumption of *reliability*); and (3) that the definition employed and the search procedures used are the same in all the populations under consideration (assumption of *comparability*). Students using suicide rates in a Durkheimian manner are thus assuming that the statistics are valid in principle, reliable in practice and are cross-culturally comparable. There are other students, however, who are more concerned about the problem of reliability, or 'accuracy', of suicide rates. That is, they do not dispute that suicide is in principle subject to statistical analysis, but they have doubts as to whether or not, in practice, official suicide rates always provide a viable index of the 'real' or 'true' rate. A distinction can be made between two general sets of arguments.

The first, which I shall refer to as a position of *limited acceptance*, is probably held by the majority of researchers who argue that although suicide rates are useful as a rough, or approximate, index of suicidal behaviour, they are too unreliable for the kind of cross-cultural comparative analyses undertaken by some sociologists. While these students may well accept that it is possible to arrive at a fairly precise definition of suicide which reflects that employed by officials (assumption of validity), they would not accept that suicide is necessarily efficiently recognised by officials (doubts about relia-bility), and they would certainly not accept that definitions and search procedures do not vary cross-culturally (rejections of cross-cultural comparability).[5] Thus researchers adopting a *limited accep-tance* view, if they used suicide rates at all, would probably use them to engage in the type of 'social-factor' analysis described in Chapter 2. It would, for example, be quite legitimate to study the suicide rate of a city over, say, a ten-year period to search for relevant causal fac-tors. For example, Stengel and Cook studied the suicide rate of a town during a period of migration of many of its younger inhabit-ants,[6] while Hassall and Trethowan monitored the suicide rate of Birmingham in the years following the change from domestic coal gas to natural gas.[7] Studied in this way the suicide rate is not so much an object of enquiry in its own right, or a 'social fact' requiring socio-logical explanation, but rather a 'guide' to forming hypotheses, another source of data contributing to some eventual explanation.

Whereas the suicide rate of a city, or a country, over a relatively short period of time is seen as potentially useful data,[8] those holding a limited-acceptance position would draw the line at the kind of longitudinal, cross-cultural comparisons undertaken by Durkheim and others. A headline from the medical journal *Pulse* reflects the medical concern with the problem of accuracy: **'Figures Hide True Rate of Suicides'**: 'The true incidence of suicide is hard to ascertain. Varying methods of certifying deaths, different registration and coding procedure and other factors affect the extent and complete-ness of coverage, making international comparisons impractic-able.'[9]

Increasing concern with the accuracy of suicide statistics, particu-larly amongst medical researchers, was voiced at the Fourth Inter-national Conference for Suicide Prevention. Stengel and Farberow drew attention to the varying methods of certifying deaths as suicides, between countries and even within some countries; for example, in some countries the judiciary was involved while in others it was not. However, they did not dismiss the use of official statistics provided they were used in a 'responsible' (i.e. *limited*) manner.[10]

In general, those who adopt a position of *limited acceptance* are quite optimistic that, given more systematic application of classificatory procedures, suicide rates will become an increasingly reliable source of data,[11] and indeed many psychiatrists are sympathetic to the more recent works of sociologists which, like their own studies, have searched for relevant 'factors'.[12] There are other students, however, who doubt if (at present at least) there is anything to be gained from *any* sort of analysis of official suicide rates and are thus suspicious of any conclusions reached from a study of them. This position I shall refer to as a *sceptical* view of suicide rates. Those who adopt this stance even doubt the primary assumption made by all users of suicide rates (assumption of *validity*) that, at least within the same culture over a relatively short period of time, it is probable that researchers are employing a conception of suicide that corresponds to that used by the officials who compile the data.

Although recently there has been increased sociological concern regarding the validity of suicide rates, the *sceptical* position was originally associated mainly with those psychiatrists and physicians who, from the study of individual cases of suicide, argued that the *discrepancy* between the *criteria of proof* required for a coroner's verdict of suicide, and that required for a post-mortem diagnosis of 'the cause of death', is so great as to invalidate the statistics for purposes of scientific (i.e. medical) study. That is, these students are suggesting (usually on the basis of specific cases known to them) that suicide verdicts are *frequently* inconclusive (i.e. 'open', or 'misadventure') *even when the 'medical evidence' for suicide is conclusive*. In short, it is argued that suicide is a 'medical' (or psychiatric) problem, and there is, therefore, little point in singling out for special attention a group of cases whose 'homogeneity' has been established on non-medical grounds. Those adopting a *sceptical* position argue that the proportion of cases where a suicide verdict is not brought in, although a medical practitioner would be satisfied that an individual killed himself, is high enough, at present at least, for all official suicide rates to be treated with the utmost scepticism.[13]

However, even those holding a *sceptical* view of official suicide rates are not necessarily opposed to statistical methods as such, or the analytical tools available for analysing such data. Their critique is not against subjecting human behaviour to analysis by means of pre-defined scientific categories, their complaint is simply against official suicide statistics.[14] Researchers could, for example, analyse statistics on attempted suicide (or whatever) for significant variables providing they had been compiled in a systematic and reliable fashion (e.g. by themselves, or other psychiatrists, etc.).[15]

Those holding a *sceptical* view of official statistics on suicide are not simply concerned with the extent of the 'errors'. Often asserted, though never really clearly articulated and certainly not demonstrated, is the suggestion that deaths which come to be officially recorded as suicides (even in 'advanced' countries with relatively efficient bureaucratic apparatus) are not merely a 'useful sample' of 'real' suicides, but in fact a *highly selective* and therefore unrepresentative sample and, second, that comparative variations are more likely to be reflections of different collection procedures. Swedish psychiatrist Ruth Ettlinger, for example, expresses both these doubts in her discussion of the certification of death in Sweden:

> It is well-known to all of us that the official WHO statistics are marked by considerable sources of error . . . We know, for instance, that the WHO statistics have not yet arrived at a common definition of what is considered suicide in the various countries and that no agreement exists as to the registration of suicide and accidents in cases of doubt. We also know that the statistics are based on a primary material which is often impaired by religious, social and even medical prejudices and that these prejudices differ from one another in the various cultural, social and geographical regions . . . We know, for instance, that many observers are inclined to explain the apparent differences in the WHO suicide statistics for the Scandinavian countries as a result of the different ways of registration applied in each of the countries concerned. Thus, it is assumed that the suicide frequency in Norway which, according to WHO is only about half of that in Sweden and Denmark is due to the difference in ways of registration.[16]

She goes on to suggest, however, that even in the Swedish suicide statistics (which are probably better than most) there are probably considerable sources of error, particularly with respect to death by drug poisoning and thus, by implications, at present official statistics are an unreliable source of data.

Some sociologists, for example Wilkins[17] and Atkinson (in his earlier work),[18] have shown some concern with the problem of the accuracy of suicide rates. Atkinson argued that suicide must be seen as a process consisting of the period leading up to the act, the time between the suicidal act and death or some other outcome, and the time between death and registration as a suicide. Those who use official statistics have ignored the fact that social integration also plays an important part in the second and third stages of this process. Here again is the implication that suicide rates should be treated with the utmost scepticism.

The fourth and, for purposes of this discussion, final position with regard to official suicide rates I shall refer to as one of *rejection*. Rejection of official rates of deviant behaviour is a position recently associated with the social phenomenologists and ethnomethodologists. However, these students are not strictly concerned with problems of accuracy; rather it is their intention to demonstrate the impossibility (or at least improbability) of constructing *any* valid rate of deviant behaviour. I shall deal with some specific critiques later in this chapter and confine myself here to a few general comments about the position of *rejection* of official statistics.

The ethnomethodologists have developed their critique of official statistics as part of a wider attack on what they variously describe as 'orthodox', 'conventional' or 'traditional' sociology.[19] The development and expansion of ethnomethodology in contemporary sociology owes much to Garfinkel's interpretation of Schutz's phenomenology.[20] Schutz approved of Weber's attempts to base sociology upon the subjective meanings that individuals assign to their actions, but argued that Weber had not gone 'far enough' in this direction:

[Weber] breaks off his analysis of the social world when he arrives at what he assumes to be the basic and irreducible elements of social phenomena. But he is wrong in this assumption. His concept of the meaningful act of the individual – the key idea of interpretive sociology – by no means defines a primitive, as he thinks it does. It is, on the contrary, a mere label for a highly complex and ramified area that calls for much further study.[21]

The 'further study' should involve the attempt to analyse, rather than take for granted, the ways in which individuals 'accomplish' social interaction. Reciprocity of perspectives cannot be assumed, it has to be explained. However, modern sociology, the ethnomethodologists argue, has retreated from the problems bequeathed by Weber and Durkheim and simply assumed that social action (unless it is deviant) is some form of normative orientation to 'social structure' or 'external constraint'. That is, sociologists have assumed that individuals internalise social norms and these provide the rules that guide role playing in society. Thus society is seen to 'impose' itself upon individuals from without (as can be seen, for example, by the regularity of the suicide rates).

The main criticism made by the ethnomethodologists is that social rules are not immutable and unambiguous: individuals do not internalise rules as if they had been 'branded', rather 'society' is the 'active' and creative 'accomplishment' of its members in their interactions with one another and the sociologist's primary task (a phenomenology of intersubjectivity) is to try to explain the images, beliefs, assumptions, etc., that people draw upon to order their interactions.

Sociology (and related disciplines), by failing to distinguish between 'surface' and basic interpretative, or 'normative', rules,[22] have operationalised crude notions of role playing, where terms like 'deviant' and 'conformist', etc., are not seen as problematic *in themselves*. This may be illustrated by taking the example of Cicourel's work on juvenile justice.[23] 'Law-abiding', 'criminal', etc., are examples of surface rules; rules 'that enable the actor to link his view of the world to others in concerted social action'. However, Cicourel attempts to demonstrate that when we examine the processes by which individuals actually come to be assigned to categories such as 'delinquent' we find not that rules are 'obvious' and applied 'automatically' and consistently, but rather that the decision-making processes can only be understood in terms of the stock of knowledge and everyday procedures of the various officials; police, probation officers, social workers, etc. (i.e. interpretative rules). Thus given 'rates' of deviance are simply the result of the 'tacit unanalysed properties' which produce given decisions.[24]

As rates of deviance are produced by the everyday workings of the organisations of social control, it is not therefore a problem of accuracy (i.e. underestimating, or in some other way 'misrepresenting', the 'real' rate), for this presupposes an absolutist definition of a phenomenon such as suicide, which is simply waiting to be 'recognised' or not. Indeed, from this perspective suicide rates may well be 'accurate', in the sense of reliably reflecting the workings and procedures of given organisations, but they are quite clearly unsuitable for the kind of statistical and explanatory research typically undertaken by sociologists and others.

In this approach then, the sociologist's task is not to explain why particular populations produce given suicide rates, but rather why particular *organisations* produce given suicide rates.[25]

I have outlined four positions with regard to official suicide rates. They can be *accepted*, accepted with *limitations*, rejected given the present methods of compilation and finally, the very notion of a 'real' suicide rate should be abandoned. These positions may be summarised in table form (see Table 3.1).

TABLE 3.1

	Assumptions of		
	Validity	Reliability	Comparability
General acceptance	Accept	Accept	Accept
Limited acceptance	Accept	Doubtful	Very doubtful
Scepticism	Doubtful	Reject	Reject
Rejection	Reject	Reject	Reject

These positions are, of course, ideal-typical, but they are intended to clarify the various uses that have been made of the official statistics and also the different positions adopted by particular theorists. For example, in his more recent work Atkinson has moved from a *sceptical* to a *rejectionist* position[26] and, while a *rejectionist* position is normally attributed to Douglas, he offered an alternative set of arguments on suicide rates that bring him closest to a *sceptical* position.

I shall first examine some of the implications of the rejectionist position and here, and in the following section on problems of accuracy, I shall focus predominantly on the work of Douglas, who developed a most original and powerful critique of official suicide rates.

Douglas's Critique

Douglas begins by reminding us that suicide rates, like suicidal acts themselves, are the result of involved and complex social processes, although the meanings of the statistics appear obvious:

> *The difficulty, however, is that one is still relying upon human judgement for the data, not simply upon sensory experience, which one also used to observe the mercury expansion and contraction against a calibrated scale, but actually upon the complex faculties of human judgements in interaction with each other.*[27]

Given these problems, Douglas argues, researchers must first look at relations between the 'measuring instrument' and the phenomenon. However, in attempting this exercise himself, Douglas becomes drawn in two different directions, and ends up advancing not one, but two contradictory and irreconcilable sets of arguments.

In some statements Douglas denies the reality of suicide as a unitary phenomenon and argues that researchers have been mistaken in assuming that 'suicidal' actions have a 'necessary and sufficient, unidimensional meaning throughout the western world'. Examination of the problematic nature of the meanings of 'suicidal' acts will reveal that the very idea of a 'real suicide rate' is a misconception.[28] This stance – clearly a *rejectionist* position – I shall from here on refer to as Douglas's *hard* thesis. However, at other times in his discussion, Douglas adopts a *softer* thesis – far closer to a *sceptical* position – and argues that suicide rates may well be systematically biased. 'It will be my purpose . . . to show that official statistics on suicide are probably biased in a number of ways, often in the same direction, such that the various sociological theories of suicide will be unreliably supported by these official statistics.'[29]

The contradiction between these two positions should be quite apparent, although Douglas himself makes no reference to it. If there cannot be such a thing as a 'real' suicide rate as Douglas has suggested, why then (in the *softer* version) bother to discuss sources of systematic biases? Biases from what? In Douglas's terms the only answer is from some 'true', or 'real', suicide rate. And once the notion, or even the possibility, of a true suicide rate is acknowledged then, in principle at least, there is a possibility that some set of statistics *could* reflect it.

Most discussion of Douglas's work has centred on his *hard* (*rejectionist*) thesis and the important doubts he raised about sources of systematic bias have been generally ignored. However, as the two positions advanced by Douglas are contradictory, I shall treat them as *distinct* arguments and discuss each separately.

I have already suggested that writers such as Sudnow, Cicourel, Douglas and others who ostensibly adopt a *rejectionist* position, were not concerned with the reliability of official statistics, rather they were using their research to illustrate a *particular* manifestation of a *general* weakness in 'conventional' sociology, i.e. its indulgence in unwarranted abstractions.[30] In this context they attempt to show that official statistics of deviant behaviour *cannot* correspond to some set of 'real world' events. Official statistics are dependent on the reports of many observers who examine particular situations, or 'real world' events, and then, on the basis of their investigations, make a decision in assigning an event to an appropriate category. Researchers cannot assume, Douglas argues, that their formal definitions of suicide necessarily correspond to those employed by the various officials who decide whether death is 'suicide', 'misadventure', or whatever. It is necessary, therefore, to examine (1) the objective criteria used to decide how to categorise a death and (2) the search procedure used to determine whether or not these criteria are met.[31]

In this context Cicourel, who unlike Douglas undertook detailed empirical work into this problem, has argued that the decisions of law-enforcement personnel (or anyone else for that matter, including researchers) can only begin to be understood in terms of their 'background expectations'; that is, 'seen but unnoticed features of common discourse whereby actual utterances are recognised as events of common, reasonable, plain talk'.[32] Background expectations make the world of objects recognisable and intelligible to (a) the observer himself and (b) to others through his reports which, in the case of official law-enforcement personnel, become the 'facts', which when aggregated produce official rates of crime. An ethnomethodological approach to delinquency, therefore, would direct the researcher's attention to the theories of delinquency employed by laymen, particularly the police, probation and court officials when deciding the existence (or non-existence) of juvenile delinquency:

What is needed are studies showing how folk theories articulate with actual practice, adequate descriptions of the environment of objects attended by members and the organising features of their practical activities. How natives describe events and objects provides a basis for contrasting abstract notions such as 'contract', 'debt', 'crimes' and 'rape' with folk or members' categories.[33]

It follows, therefore, that sets of statistics on deviance – which are derived from the reports of numerous observers each with their own background expectancies and folk theories – cannot necessarily be assumed to be indices of the 'same' phenomena. According to Cicourel, they cannot be interpreted without reference to the background expectations of the observers upon whose reports they are based.

Hindess, in his critique of the ethnomethodological critique of official statistics, notes that the ethnomethodologists confuse and obscure the (logical-positivist) distinction between 'theoretical' and 'observational' categories:

It seems that we are concerned with two different orders of things. On the one hand there are real world things or events – real or proper things. On the other hand there are things that are not things at all – things improper. The latter are a result of an imposition of an order or classification on things proper by some observer. Thus, what is called the real suicide rate is the product of further transformations and codifications of numerous things improper by some bureaucratic apparatus. The real suicide rate is a function of the organisation producing suicide statistics.[34]

The *rejectionist* position argues that there can be no clear-cut or unambiguous interpretation of official categories (such as 'suicide') in terms of some set of 'real world' events. First, it cannot be assumed that official categories have the same meaning for different observers and it is therefore unlikely that observers follow the same rules in assigning particular cases to given categories. Second, assignment to categories is usually the *result* of negotiation and argument, and therefore judgements are likely to involve certain arbitrary elements. But, in spite of these 'difficulties', why can assignment to categories not be carried out consistently? The ethnomethodologists' argument (as we have seen) is that while classification (into deviant categories) is 'guided' by 'surface' or 'normative' rules, it can never be *determined* by these rules, because they do not have a clear and unambiguous meaning to members of a society who employ different sets of '*interpretative*' rules in actually assigning 'events' or 'objects' into given categories. Thus there is only an 'apparent', or tenuous, connection between sets of official statistics and the 'real world' events to which they are intended to refer.

The implication of these arguments for research into deviance, Douglas and Cicourel both suggest, is that researchers should abandon analysis of official rates of deviance (and by implication other forms of supposedly 'hard' and easily quantifiable data, such as questionnaire responses, etc.) in favour of more detailed and 'exact' observations and descriptions of social life. Douglas, for example, takes sociologists to task for their 'failure to see the need for careful observations and descriptions of suicidal phenomena' before attempting to explain them;[35] while Cicourel, on the basis of broadly similar assumptions, has attempted to demonstrate that the 'data' (collected by observers on the basis of a variety of background expectancies) cannot simply be assumed to correspond to the structure of a given environment of objects. However, to *demonstrate* this necessarily presupposes that some (more or less) accurate description *can* be made of the environment of objects.

We thus reach a position where 'careful description' is assumed to be possible, but is not provided by official statistics. However, this argument cannot be used to deny the *possibility* of a real rate of deviance. If it is possible (in principle at least) to have accurate descriptions of 'real world' events, then it is also possible to aggregate these descriptions and, for want of a better word, call them statistics.

The arguments advanced by the *rejectionists*, however, to deny the possibility of 'real' rates of deviance also preclude the possibility of *any* accurate description. For example, Cicourel argues that the world becomes intelligible to members through their background expectancies, and the researcher's job is to illustrate these background expectancies and explain their effect. Therefore we have two sets of reports: the initial observer's report, and the researcher's report based upon the observer's report. However, as Hindess has observed:

Before [the researcher's] reports can be used to estimate the effect of background expectancies . . . we need to know how [the researcher's] descriptions relate to the environment of objects in question. To do this we call in a third observer to examine [the researcher's] observation of the initial observer. This leads to the absurdity of an infinite regression, at no stage of which is the environment of objects available other than in the form of an observer's report (rendered intelligible by the action of his background expectancies).[36]

Douglas's arguments, taken to their logical conclusions, reveal a similar apparent 'inaccessibility to the world'. Douglas argues that we must see suicide verdicts as the end result of an argument. If we do this we shall realise that the meaning of the term 'suicide' is highly variable and this in turn will lead us to abandon the notion of a 'real' suicide rate. But since *any* such categorisation is the result of a judgement, how then do we undertake research? In fact, in his analysis of the social meanings of suicide, Douglas uses data collected by a variety of other researchers based upon what they or other observers considered in their (negotiated?) judgements to be 'suicide' and 'attempted suicide'.[37] While this would seem to most to be quite an acceptable use of data, in terms of the logic of Douglas's *hard* thesis, it entails precisely the same 'fundamental misconceptions' for which 'conventional sociologists' were criticised. If it is *necessarily* illegitimate for sociologists to use data based on officials' judgements (often made after consultation with experts) of what they considered to be 'suicide', why is it then legitimate for Douglas to use data based on a variety of other researchers' judgements of what they considered to be suicide? Douglas's *hard* thesis, it seems, precludes the possibility of studying suicide at all. If the *only* thing that a variety of phenomena have in common is that they have been given the label 'suicide', then they do not constitute a field of study. They are quite literally different things and, although described by the same word, there is no reason why they should be grouped together and an attempt made to 'classify' their various 'social meanings'.

The ethnomethodologists' ('hard') critique of official statistics may be summarised as follows. There exists an 'environment of objects' and 'real world' events which are made available to us by observers' reports, and these reports themselves (including researchers' reports) can only be organised through background expectancies, tacit assumptions, interpretative rules, etc. Therefore, this realm of objects can never really be 'known'; it is available to us only in a variety of distorted forms. However, if 'undistorted reality' can never 'really' be known, it follows that the effect of these distorting mechanisms (background expectancies, etc.) can also never be known, documented, or their effect demonstrated. Thus it becomes irrelevant for Douglas to hypothesise about sources of systematic bias in suicide rates, or Cicourel to try to reveal this effect of background expectancies.

Whereas positivists are sceptical of any data that cannot be observed, ethnomethodologists are sceptical even of data based on simple observational categories. As we have seen, they argue that such classification is not 'given', but is based on background expectations, etc. However, they do not share the *rationalist* concern with the fundamental categories through which human experience is ordered, but have instead an *empiricist* concern with demonstrating that the researcher's observations are more 'real', or 'true', (i.e. better observations) than those of law enforcement personnel, coroners or whatever. However, in attempting this exercise, they are forced to fall back upon observation and experience in order to demonstrate the greater 'truthfulness' of their accounts. These accounts therefore are open to the same 'fundamental' objections that were levelled by the ethnomethodologists against 'conventional' social scientists. The ethnomethodologists have reduced 'knowledge' to a position of complete 'social relativism', which 'disposes' not only of official statistics, but also the possibility of any rational knowledge of the world – including the 'alleged' 'demonstrations' of the invalidity of official statistics. Hindess dismissed their critique in the following brutal way:

> What, then, are we to make of [the ethnomethodologists'] accounts of the workings of statistics-producing organisations? These accounts are produced within an irrationalist problematic in which there is no place for rational proof and demonstration. It follows that the supposed demonstrations offered by these authors are theoretically worthless. A manuscript produced by a monkey at a typewriter would be no less valuable.[38]

However, as I have implied above, it is important to distinguish between the ethnomethodologists' *hard* thesis (usually advanced in their 'programmatic statements') and their *soft* thesis (more characteristic of their empirical research). Both Cicourel and Douglas in their *actual* analysis of statistics-producing organisations are suggesting *something rather different from the position outlined above*, i.e. that official statistics are not a useful source of data because they do not represent the 'real' distribution of some social phenomenon. However, critics such as Hindess have addressed themselves only (or mainly) to the 'hard' thesis.

This situation is made clear in Cicourel's reply to Hindess's critique. Cicourel devotes several pages of the 1976 edition of *Juvenile Justice* to an attempt to repudiate Hindess's argument. All he does in fact is to make the contradictions in his own position more obvious. Cicourel argues that if Hindess had taken the trouble to examine his empirical work properly he would have found his charges 'weak and misleading':

> Hindess fails to compare the programmatic statements in *'Method and Measurement in Sociology'* with the actual research of the present book . . . Contrary to claims made by Hindess *my research on juvenile justice can be used to improve crime statistics and to estimate and control possible sources of error* . . . My concern is with the limitations of descriptive statistical accounts and the observers' reports are designed *to call attention to routine and normal sources of error or misclassification that are inherent in data reduction procedures* [my emphasis].[39]

This is quite correct; however, Hindess's concern was not with Cicourel's empirical work as such, but with the arguments used by the ethnomethodologists to dispose of the possibility of accurate statistics. Cicourel does not attempt to deal with this argument, except by stating that his work was really concerned with different problems, including possibly making the statistics more accurate. Thus tacit assumptions, etc., are actually being studied to *improve* observational categories.

The rejectionist *argument*, taken to its logical conclusions then leads to a position where either (a) no explanation of the world is possible, or (b) the fundamental 'errors' of conventional sociology are simply duplicated under different guises. Let me, by way of summary, clarify this point. If there is nothing to social reality other than the 'interpretative procedures' and 'constituted' meanings' of actors then 'it' cannot be studied, the only thing that can be examined is those 'interpretative procedures', etc., which must be expressed in the same language as they express themselves, i.e. observer and actor categories must coincide with each other. However, if this is the case then there is no point at all in study, because study merely repeats *what is* and in no way *explains* it. Conversely, if there is an 'it' to study, an 'it' not necessarily the same as common-sense meanings, this will involve an imposition of 'abstractions' upon the subject, a fact which makes ethnomethodology in essence no different from the positivistic tradition that it purportedly criticises.

Sources of Systematic Bias

Those adopting a *sceptical* view of suicide rates are arguing that (it is likely that) the official statistics are systematically biased to an extent that makes them unacceptable for research. Curiously enough Durkheim came close to developing this line of argument, quite explicitly when some set of statistics threatened to contradict his theory,[40] and implicitly, when he considered officials' interpretations of the motives for suicide.

> What are called statistics of the motives of suicides are actually statistics of the opinions concerning such motives of officials . . . The value of improvised judgements, attempting to assign a definite origin for each special case from a few hastily collected bits of information is, therefore, obviously slight. As soon as some of the facts commonly supposed to lead to despair are found in the victim's past, further search is considered useless, and his drunkenness or domestic unhappiness or business troubles are blamed, depending on whether he is supposed recently to have lost money, had some troubles or indulged in a taste for liquor. Such uncertain data cannot be considered a basis of explanation for suicide.[41]

Durkheim did not pursue the implications of this observation for he was concerned to point out that suicide cannot be explained in terms of the *particular* motives that individuals or officials give for the act. However, it would have taken only one step further to argue (in terms of Durkhiem's *own* logic) that we need not necessarily accept the *decisions* of the officials (and therefore the statistics) for the 'motives', or 'explanations', ascribed by the officials are not simply 'tagged on' as separate, or supplementary data, as Durkheim *chose* to imply, but are obviously an important *part of the decision-making process*. That is, for a death to be recorded as a 'suicide' there must also be *facts* (such as drunkenness, domestic troubles, etc.) which provide, at least in the officials' view, an explanation for the suicide. Thus while Durkheim rejected 'such uncertain data' as not relevant to a scientific explanation of suicide, he nevertheless used (in a completely uncritical way) official statistics which were based on this uncertain data. Therefore, even though we may agree with Durkheim that officials' 'motives' are not the 'real' causes of suicide, the fact that *they* hold these beliefs means that the presence or absence of 'evidence' will lead the officials towards or away from a verdict of suicide. It is evidence of such 'motives' that renders the death meaningful in terms of the prevailing conceptions of social reality. As Berger and Luckmann have observed:

> Death posits the most terrifying threat to the taken-for-granted realities of everyday life. The integration of death within the paramount reality of social existence is, therefore, of the greatest importance . . . All legitimations of death must carry out the same essential task – they must enable the individual to go on living in society . . . [and] not paralyse the continued performance of the routines of everyday life.[42]

Part of 'repairing' the fabric of everyday life involves *explaining* the death, rendering it accountable and deaths which appear not to be due to natural causes, particularly deaths which 'could be suicides', present particular problems in 'repair' work. Suicide is something which, by definition, an individual brings upon himself. Thus for a death to *be* a 'suicide', not only has a physiological explanation to be provided, but also a *psychological* explanation. In western society is it generally believed that people kill themselves because of profound unhappiness with their life situations and this, in turn, is the result of social and/or psychological problems.[43] A 'normal', happy, adjusted person killing himself makes 'no sense'. Therefore, if a death *really* is a 'suicide', then there must be evidence of 'abnormality', unhappiness, disturbance, etc. The 'facts' of the biography must match the 'facts' of death. In discussing our attempts to render actors as 'consistent objects' Lofland has observed that: 'There must be a *special* history that specially explains current and imputed identity . . . the *present evil* of current character must be related to *past evil* that can be discovered in the biography.'[44]

It would seem that the 'past evils' that officials believe provide a 'motive' for suicide would have an important influence on the decision-making process and it seems most unlikely that a mind such as Durkheim's, having come so far, would not have grasped this. It seems more reasonable to suppose that, given the polemical intentions of *Suicide*, he chose not to pursue the implications of his own embryonic statistical 'critique'.

Douglas had no such reservations and developed his soft critique around the importance that officials attach to finding 'socially adequate motives' for suicide and argued that evidence of certain external states (such as social isolation or status loss) which serve as indicators of suicidal motives (such as depression or crisis) would systematically bias the official statistics. With reference to the Henry and Short thesis for example, Douglas argues that, in times of economic crisis, we should expect the suicide rate to rise in direct proportion to status, because officials will be presented with a greater number of situations that *mean* suicide.[45]

Similarly, with respect to the most consistent sociological finding, the negative relationship between social integration and suicide, Douglas argues that social integration may influence the rates of both attempted and successful concealment of suicide because first, assuming suicide is judged negatively, the more integrated an individual is the more he and his significant others will try to avoid having his death categorised as suicide and second, the less likely it is that officials would *consider* his death suicidal.[46]

Douglas suggests that if positive correlations were found between rates of successful concealment of suicide and social integration, this would produce a 'fundamental bias in the testing of almost all sociological theories tested with official statistics, a bias that would result in the acceptance of these theories regardless of the state of real world events'.[47] For example, varying rates of concealment could account for the fact that suicide rates are higher in urban than in rural areas, that they are especially high in areas of high social mobility, etc.

The problem however, which Douglas does not even consider, is how we might operationalise this hypothesis and actually 'reveal' these concealments. If trained coroners (or medical examiners), policemen, pathologists and other experts have been 'misled', or 'conned', into thinking that a 'suicide' was really an 'accident', then the researcher is going to require access to a very privileged source of information (a spiritualist perhaps?) to *demonstrate* that the deceased 'really' killed himself; although he may infer it. Also, we may ask how the researcher is to devise a measure of integration. Durkheim used an observable (suicide) to measure a non-observable (egoism), but an observer wishing to follow Douglas's lead who then went on to construct some alternative concrete measure of integration would lay himself open to the same sort of charges that were levelled at Durkheim and others. Alternatively, one could simply use 'common sense' regarding whether or not a population was integrated. Douglas implies this when he writes: 'In general it seems clear that the average degree of social integration of individuals is higher in rural areas than in urban areas'.[48] However, Douglas was very critical of sociologists for using their 'common-sense' knowledge of suicide to help 'explain' their data; indeed it was one of his *major* criticisms of the sociological approach.

As Douglas did not test his own hypotheses of attempted and successful concealment, his alternative 'explanation' of the stability of the suicide rates remains at the level of *argument*. The problem is that until we have some 'evidence', all sorts of equally plausible arguments are possible.[49] For example, with respect to successful concealment, Douglas argues that if the deceased was known to the officials then it is less likely that his death will be recorded as suicide. This may be so, but equally, if it was 'really' suicide, the officials, because of their intimate knowledge of the deceased, may also be in a better position to 'know' that he was depressed, continually talking of suicide, etc.[50]

Douglas's main contribution to the suicide rate problem was the production of several powerful and persuasive arguments suggesting systematic biases.[51] However, his hypotheses, in their present form are impossible to test effectively. To try to *demonstrate* systematic biases in the official statistics one would have to study first, the beliefs, theories and assumptions held about suicide by the officials responsible for categorising such deaths and second, one would have to devise a methodology for demonstrating that these beliefs have an independent (and therefore biasing) effect on the statistics. The following chapters in this Part of the work attempt this exercise, but first, I shall briefly consider some responses to Douglas's critique.

Responses to Douglas

Despite the general critical acclaim that *The Social Meanings of Suicide* quite rightly received, it has had very little influence on the ways in which sociologists actually study suicide. In the first place, many subsequent studies of suicide rates make no reference to Douglas[52] and second, those who do mention him tend to side-step, rather than confront his arguments. Maris, for example, suggests that 'In part Douglas's criticism is just a plea for different sources of data. Of course, most of us realise the limitations of using official statistics.'[53]

There are two observations to be made here. First, although Maris apparently 'realises' the limitations of official statistics, this has no effect on his own researches. Second, it is clear that Douglas's 'plea' was not simply for *additional*, but for *alternative* sources of data.[54] Finally, there are those like Sainsbury and Barraclough and Cresswell who curiously attempt to argue that the very stability of the rates provides evidence of their reliability.[55] Cresswell, for example, argues that:

> The existence of stable rates of suicide can be taken as evidence for the operation of structural or cultural factors which help in generating the suicide rate, which, it is argued, will remain unchanged **so long as these remain unchanged. Since Douglas's denial of the** influences of social factors does not provide a basis for predicting the generation of stable rates but, if anything, the reverse, their existence becomes for him a problem.[56]

However, the whole point about Douglas's ('soft') critique is that it offers and *alternative* explanation (or more exactly, a basis for an alternative) of the phenomenon that intrigued Durkheim and so many others: the consistency of suicide rates over time and place. There is little point, therefore, in claiming that such consistency is 'evidence' for the inadequacy of Douglas's position. Questions regarding the viability of official suicide rates are *only* going to be answered by systematic and controlled study of the ways in which the data is produced. Although Douglas himself did no empirical research on this problem at least one student, Atkinson, has attempted to build on some of his insights.[57] Atkinson examined the procedures employed by coroners and other officials to assign sudden and unexplained deaths to various categories, suicide, misadventure, etc. He argues that coroners (like the rest of us) have ideas and beliefs about circumstances, situations and individuals typically associated with suicide. Their investigations reflect these beliefs and in categorising a death – which in most cases involves deciding whether or not it is suicide or accident – they are lead towards, or away from, a suicide verdict by the presence, or absence, of 'suicidal cues' relating to evidence of suicide notes or threats, mode of death, location and circumstances of death and the biography of the deceased. For example, certain modes of dying such as hanging and drowning, or certain biographical details, such as a broken home in childhood or a history of mental troubles, are seen as suggestive of suicide. It is then through evidence of 'suicidal cues' that officials are able to impute suicidal intent.

Like Douglas, Atkinson suggests that those who use official statistics to explain suicide may only be formalising the criteria used by officials to infer suicide and these, in turn, are only reflections of the general meanings that society associates with suicidal actions. From this basis, unlike Douglas, he argues that the data from coroners' courts is not to be rejected but is, on the contrary, of 'central significance' to the study of the social meanings of suicide.

> Not only do coroners, to an admittedly unknown extent, share the prevalent definitions of suicide in society at any one time, but they are also in a position to reaffirm these definitions publicly and even perhaps introduce new ones. By defining certain deaths as suicides, they are in effect saying to others in society: 'These kinds of deaths are suicides, these are the kinds of situations in which people commit suicide and these are the types of people who commit suicide.'[58]

Atkinson argues that coroners, researchers and those in the media draw from and, at the same time, help to define the definitions of suicidal situations prevalent in a society at a given time and this means that it is more likely that individuals in such situations will contemplate a suicidal solution to their problems.[59]

Conclusions

Four perspectives on official suicide statistics were identified and discussed. It was argued that they should neither be *accepted* nor *rejected*, but the question of their viability for research purposes could only be examined by further empirical study. Douglas's hypotheses and Atkinson's research are the most important contributions in this direction and the research reported in the following chapters is an attempt to develop some of their ideas. It has also been suggested here that further research must not only examine the procedures, beliefs and assumptions employed by officials, but it must also document the influence of these beliefs. In this context it will be argued that attempts to establish the meaning of sets of official statistics (or any other social phenomena) are essentially theoretical exercises which must transcend the mere comparison of observational categories.

4

Proving Suicide

Official Procedures

In the previous chapter it was argued that the questions students have raised about the viability of official suicide statistics for research purposes could only be answered by more systematic study. Official statistics are products of the system of theoretical categories in terms of which they are compiled and the bureaucratic and organisational procedures by which they are collected. Their evaluation for research, therefore, involves consideration of two interrelated sets of questions. First, analysis of the adequacy of the theoretical and conceptual categories of production and second, examination of the extent to which the data produced by the officials reflects these conceptual categories. I shall consider the first of these questions later in the work, where I shall try to show how many acts of self destruction that result in death fit comfortably into neither the category of 'suicide' nor 'accident'. In this part of the work I shall be more concerned with the latter problem and its implications for research based on official suicide rates. In this context I shall use the term 'bias' to refer to systematic deviations from the *theoretical* suicide rate.

The ethnomethodologists have quite rightly shifted the focus of research into official statistics towards the routine, taken-for-granted procedures employed by the officials who compile the data. In relation to suicide rates the most important contributions have come from Douglas and Atkinson and, as will be quite clear, the present research owes much to their work. However, as we have seen, the ethnomethodological critique of positivism degenerates into either a similarly 'positivistic' concern with 'more accurate' statistics or a position of complete agnosticism, where the student acknowledges (or implies) that questions regarding the viability of the statistics can never really be 'answered'. Cicourel's response to Hindess, in which he stresses that his real concern was with 'more accurate' statistics, is an example of the former position. However, from this point of view, the ethnomethodological position is essentially no different from the positivist one it criticises, for in both of them there is the assumption of some 'true' rate of suicide which is, in some mysterious way, independent of human thought about suicide. Alternatively, Atkinson, who does not lapse back into positivism, argues that there are two rival interpretations of suicide rates. One can claim that the factors commonly associated with suicide 'really are' in some way causally related to suicide or one can argue that they are merely 'seen to be' causes of suicide by the officials who compile the data. Which interpretation is correct, however, according to Atkinson remains 'unclear'.[1] The aim of the research documented here and in the following chapter was to pursue this question further and to try to *demonstrate* the viability (or otherwise) of official suicide statistics. Data for this part of the work was collected from two main sources: first, from a participant-observation study of a coroner's office in the Midlands over a six-month period and second, from interviews with five (other) coroners and their officers. The first section briefly outlines some of the official functions of the coroner, the second makes some observations on the nature of the work, while the final section examines some of the ways in which officials try to establish suicidal intent.

In England and Wales a death certificate may only be issued by a registered medical practitioner or a coroner. If a doctor is satisfied that the causes of death are natural he will sign a certificate which is then taken to the local Registrar of births, deaths and marriages, who will sign a certificate permitting disposal of the body. To issue a death certificate a doctor will either have examined the body soon after death, or have treated the deceased within fourteen days of death ('14-day rule'). Cases where a doctor feels unable to specify the causes of death (which includes all unnatural deaths) are referred to a coroner. In England and Wales this comprises about 20 per cent of all deaths. Coroners are appointed by the local authority, most of them (215 in 1975) are part-time and qualified in either medicine or law. There are fourteen full-time coroners in England and Wales (most of whom are qualified in law and medicine) and these full-time officials are responsible for dealing with about a third of all cases. Coroners have several officials and experts to assist them, the most important of whom are coroners' officers, full-time policemen attached permanently to the coroner's court, and specialist pathologists. The former provide for the coroner evidence from the scene of death, statements from witnesses, relatives, etc., while the latter furnish him with detailed evidence regarding the exact cause of death.

The original coroners were local dignitaries, knights, squires or the lord of the manor who were informed of deaths in order to attend to the affairs of the estate and decide whether or not legal proceedings were necessary. Even today, in most cases coroners are informed as a matter of common law obligation, although statute requires that coroners are always informed in cases of the death of foster children, certified mental patients, prisoners and all cases where the relatives wish to remove the body from England or Wales.[2]

Most cases that are referred to a coroner come from medical practitioners, but occasionally a registrar will refer a case when he is not satisfied with the doctor's statement of cause of death and sometimes, cases are reported directly by the police. As might be expected, a higher proportion of deaths are referred to coroners in urban areas, particularly in areas of high social mobility and the so-called twilight zones, where a local or 'family' doctor is less likely to know the deceased or his history.[3]

If a coroner is satisfied, after an examination, that death is due to natural causes the registrar is informed accordingly (only coroners, registrars and the Home Secretary can issue certificates for the disposal of a body). These are known as 'Pink Form A' cases. If, however, a death appears to be unnatural or the cause of death cannot be discovered, then the coroner will normally order a post mortem. By far the greatest proportion of deaths dealt with by the coroner are found to be due to natural causes. Once a coroner is satisfied that the causes of death are natural then he completes side B of the pink form and the registrar is informed accordingly.[4] Inquests, therefore, are held only in a minority, usually about twenty per cent, of cases either when the cause of death is unknown, or death appears to be due to unnatural causes (Figure 4.1 overleaf).

The inquest is thus a relatively small part of the officials' work, though it is the most public part. Most cases do not reach the inquest

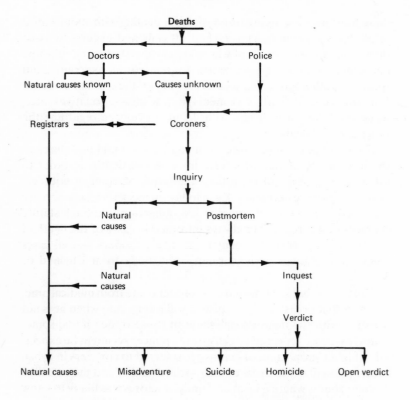

FIGURE 4.1   *Registration of deaths in England and Wales*

stage and in those that do, most of the work, taking statements, etc., is done before the case comes to court. The scope of the inquest is laid down in Coroners' Rules No. 26.

> The proceedings and evidence at an inquest should be directed solely at ascertaining the following matters:
> (a)   who the deceased was
> (b)   how, when and where the deceased came by his death
> (c)   the persons, if any, to be charged with murder, man-slaughter and infanticide or of being accessories after the fact, should the jury come to the verdict that the deceased came to his death by murder, manslaughter or infanticide
> (d)   particulars required for the time being by the Registration Acts to be registered concerning death.

In practice fifteen possible verdicts are open to the coroner, but the majority, usually over eighty per cent, are either recorded as 'misadventure' or 'suicide'. The category 'open verdict' is usually employed when there is some doubt as to whether or not death was due to suicide or misadventure. Very rarely is a coroner involved in criminal or civil issues. For example, in cases of murder, all a coroner's jury has to establish is that cause of death was homicide, the case then goes for trial and the coroner is no longer involved. In the words of one coroner whom I interviewed: 'You must understand that an inquest is a *purely factual enquiry* aimed only at establishing how an individual came by his death, it is not concerned with criminal, civil or political issues.'

Normally every effort is made to hold an inquest within a week to ten days of the discovery of the body, though sometimes there is considerable delay, usually due to difficulties establishing the identity of the deceased or the availability of witnesses. Witnesses are examined by the coroner and then, if desired, 'by any other properly interested persons'. There are normally four main classes of witnesses: (a) relatives, friends, associates, etc.; normally identity witnesses are called from this class (b) lay witnesses, for example observers and bystanders (c) expert witnesses, for example medical witnesses and (d) police witnesses. The procedure of inquests is relatively flexible, but normally the order of witnesses is as follows:

(1) Identity witnesses
(2) Relevant exhibits, e.g. plans, photographs, weapons, etc.
(3) Last seen alive by
(4) First to see the deceased after death
(5) Independent observers
(6) Expert witnesses
(7) Pathologist
(8) Police
(9) Anyone whose conduct might be called into question

Coroners have considerable discretion regarding the conduct of the inquest, the atmosphere is deliberately informal and coroners make every effort to try to avoid further distressing the bereaved. For example, witnesses who are likely to become extremely distressed by giving evidence in court, such as the deceased's wife or children, are only called if it is felt that their evidence is indispensable. Coroners also try to avoid, if possible, raising matters which might (unnecessarily) reflect discreditably upon the deceased or his relatives, for example evidence relating to homosexuality, financial problems, etc. Witnesses are examined in a relatively informal manner; the coroner has their statements in front of him and they are normally only asked to confirm, or sometimes elaborate upon, their earlier statements. It is unusual for an inquest to last more than about half an hour.

The inquest is clearly of central importance in attempting to understand the processes involved in deaths becoming recorded as suicides; however, many of the most important decisions and enquiries are made prior to a case coming to court, and it is therefore first necessary to examine the processes involved in collecting the evidence upon which decisions are based.

Coroners as Historians

This research, as the previous section has illustrated, is not concerned with all types of enquiries made by coroners, but with the minority of cases which reach the inquest stage. Most of these deaths are either known to be, or are suspected of being, due to unnatural causes and the vast majority of these are eventually recorded as misadventure or suicide. For a death to be recorded as suicide it must be *proved* that the deceased died as a direct result of his own actions, and that he *intended* to die from them. Thus although the 'hard' drug user, or the drunken driver, may die as a result of their actions, in suicide it has to be proved that death was the *purpose*, and not merely a probable *consequence* of an individual's action.

Whereas pathologists can normally be certain of the causes of death, intent has to be inferred *retrospectively*. This part of the research is concerned with some of the procedures, processes and problems involved in inferring suicidal intent, and the possible implications for research based upon official suicide rates.

Clearly, a suicide cannot plead 'guilty', confess, or be 'tricked' into an admission of guilt, the evidence upon which decisions are based is then, in legal terms, largely circumstantial. Of course, if the deceased leaves a note, this could (if found to be genuine) be seen as equivalent to a guilty plea. However, in the first place, notes are recovered in only about twenty-five per cent of cases recorded as suicide; and second, as Shneidman and Farberow have shown,[5] such notes taken on their own are not always unequivocal expressions of suicidal intent. For example, notes such as 'I can't go on', and 'Please do not disturb, someone is sleeping', only *become suicidal* when taken in conjunction with other evidence which is seen as indicative of suicide, such as a recently fired gun, an empty bottle of barbiturates and so on. If the writer of the first note had left his wife, and the writer of the second note really was having 'a good sleep', then the notes would be seen as having a very different meaning.

It might be thought that the task of establishing suicidal intent solely, or largely, on the basis of circumstantial evidence is extremely problematic. However, none of the officials I interviewed saw their work this way. When I suggested that in many cases it may be difficult to decide whether or not a death was suicide or accident, I was informed, and this was quite a consistent response, that there were established procedures of investigation which were carried out in *all* cases of sudden and apparently unnatural deaths. A coroner's officer explained to me that:

> Every sudden death is treated, from the outset, as a murder, because, you know, this is how you've got to start. It's no good going to it and making your mind up before the actual causes of death are given and this that and the other . . . you might miss something. But if you treat it as a possible murder then you're not going to miss anything because as I say we're all detectives in here, we're all experienced detectives otherwise we wouldn't have come in here in the first place . . . The police force have got a system of going through a murder enquiry, a set procedure that's known to all detectives, and we use that as we work our way through, and by the time we get to the end of it there shouldn't be any slip-ups . . . It's just impossible really for anything to slip by. That's our check, and on top of that its verified by a post mortem, so we're going to get a true answer in the end.[6]

A system of checks and double checks ensured that important evidence would not be 'missed', and whether or not a death is suicide is determined by the evidence. This is illustrated by an extract from a conversation that I had with another coroner's officer.

ST   I suppose in many cases it must be difficult to decide whether a person killed himself or not?

CO   Well . . . I think you must understand that a suicide is when you've got the deliberate intention of a person to take his own life. When a death is reported to us, if it appears to be other than natural causes, basically you can say the coroner will hold an inquest . . . It's my job to present before the coroner the evidence by calling various witnesses and producing, perhaps, certain exhibits. After the coroner has heard the evidence, um, it will either fall into one of three categories. It will either appear from the evidence that the person deliberately decided to take his own life, he would therefore record a verdict of suicide. If it appears after hearing the evidence that it is an accident . . . the evidence indicated that a person died because of an accident and didn't have any intention of taking his own life, the verdict would be accidental death. But if the evidence isn't clear, either that it is an accident or that he had a clear intention of taking his own life, then he will return an open verdict.

In that extract the coroner's officer is very insistent that decisions are only taken on the basis of evidence. Suicide verdicts are then only brought in when there is *no possible doubt* that the deceased killed himself. If there is any doubt, then an open verdict is returned. This point was made to me rather more forcibly by a coroner whom I interviewed. In an earlier formulation of the research problem, I wrote to several coroners stating that I was interested in the classification of deaths which were 'on the border-line' between suicide and accident. In those original letters I foolishly used the term 'ambiguous deaths', a statement of the problem which brought the following reply from a coroner:

As far as I am concerned there is no such thing as an 'ambiguous' suicide. Suicide is a deliberate act of self killing and each case is very carefully investigated and ultimately decided on the evidence, including medical evidence, presented upon oath in Court. Should there be any doubt about the matter either an 'open verdict' would be recorded or, if the evidence were to support it, a verdict of 'accidental death'.

According to the officials concerned, the classification of death as suicide, or whatever, is dictated by the evidence; and providing the evidence is available and is properly collected then how an individual came by his death is usually apparent. Of course, there were particular cases which were confusing, awkward or unusual, but in general the procedure was not problematic. Investigation was simply a question of applying the correct procedures. Further evidence of this was supplied by the fact that once the officials realised that I was not particularly interested in lists of 'hard' data from their files, they often appeared rather puzzled as to what it was that I *was* interested in.

Unfortunately, coroners themselves have written very little about their work. One exception is Theodore Curphey, the Los Angeles coroner, who suggested that coroners are not always qualified to deal competently with cases where there is a possibility, but not a certainty, of suicidal certification.[7] In order to try to achieve 'more accurate certification', Curphey handed over a number of equivocal, or problematic, cases to a team of experts from the Los Angeles Suicide Prevention Centre. Even here, only a minority, ten per cent of cases were examined by the SPC team, the implication being that the majority of cases apparently fell unequivocally into one or other category. From both the comments of the officials I interviewed and the writings of Curphey and the SPC team, it appears that the problems they see themselves dealing with are problems of *uncovering the 'true facts' surrounding an individual's death*. Curphey called in the SPC psychiatrists because, as well as facts relating to the causes of death and facts from the scene of death, there was another order of facts, psychological facts, which were more likely to be uncovered by psychological experts. Thus regarding suicide rates Curphey wrote that: 'we feel that accurate reports based on *all* the facts are ultimately in the best interests of the community'.[8]

However, facts themselves, no matter how diligently collected, do not 'give' verdicts; for in order to write the reports from which the enquiry is conducted facts have to be *selected* and *interpreted*. They only become significant, relevant, important, etc., within contexts of meaning and understanding. Although it may be stated that it is apparent, from the evidence, that a death was suicide, that 'apparentness' is itself a product of particular assumptions and interpretative procedures. It is the observer's beliefs, understandings, etc., which give the facts *meaning*.

It is useful here to compare the task of the coroner (and his officials) with that of the historian. Both are concerned with past events and both share the common problem that the objects of their enquiries are irretrievably out of their reach. Coroners appear to believe, as traditional historians believed, that the past consists of a complete set of facts waiting 'discovery' and 'documentation'. The observer's task is, therefore, one of retrieving the past in order to establish in Ranke's famous phrase 'how it was when it really happened'. Implicit in such a view is the assumption that there is an authentic (or genuine) past to be 'recovered' and the observer's main problem is not to be 'misled' into accepting a 'wrong' (or false) past.[9]

Any report of the past, however, is to a greater or lesser degree limited and oblique, for it can never contain the full complexity of a living event. A historical account therefore, whether of the French Revolution or Joe Soap's sudden and unnatural death, is a selective reconstruction: an *interpretation* of past events shaped first by the (acknowledged) availability of evidence and second, by the (less commonly acknowledged) values, beliefs, theories, common-sense understandings, etc., of the observer. While reports certainly contain verifiable facts, such as the storming of the Bastille, the empty gun lying by the body, etc., such facts are only meaningful, i.e. only make sense when organised within contexts of meaning. It is erroneous to assume that if one is diligent enough in searching out 'all the facts', the meaning will evolve by itself. Any systematic search for facts necessarily presupposes some form of theory which structures for the observer first, the selection of facts and second, the interpretation of facts.

The aim of this part of the research, outlined in general at the beginning of this chapter, may now be formulated more explicitly: it is first, to try to reveal some of the taken-for-granted assumptions and 'folk theories' employed by officials in the investigation of unnatural deaths and second, to try to demonstrate the influence of these beliefs on the classification of these deaths.

Establishing Suicidal Intent

This part of the work involves data from the participant-observation study, attendance at inquests and the formal interviews. Originally, I had intended to use only interview data, but it became apparent that it would also be useful to see, as far as possible, how the work was done as well as hearing how it was done. In this respect I was fortunate in that one of the coroners I interviewed showed an interest in the work and offered additional assistance, such as access to records, and it was from this coroner that permission for the participant-observation study was obtained.

The participant-observation study consisted in practice of attempting to 'follow through' a number of cases over a six-month period from the initial report of the death through the various stages of investigation to the inquest and the verdict. This involved telephoning, usually on the Monday morning to ask the officers if they 'had anything interesting for me' (i.e. obviously unnatural deaths), it would then involve reading reports of the death, which included various pieces of evidence and photographs, etc., then there would be the statements of the witnesses, the reports of the pathologists and other experts and finally, attendance at the inquest. However, it is important to stress, and I hope that it will become apparent as the discussion progresses, that as well as reading the reports it was also important to simply 'be around' and listen to the discussion of particular cases, ask questions and so on. This point may be illustrated with a brief example. The chief coroner's officer, a detective sergeant of considerable experience, was reading through a statement from a witness, the father of an Asian girl who had died from an overdose of barbiturates. 'Take a look at that Jack', he said to one of the other detectives. The other detective read it and put it down. 'It stinks', he replied. The sergeant nodded in agreement, 'I wonder what he's hiding', he said. I had also read the statement (and it had seemed quite straightforward to me), and after a pause I asked what was wrong with it. The sergeant seemed to have forgotten I was there, he turned and smiled, 'After thirty years in this game you get to know when some bugger's told you a pack of lies', he said. In the light of this, and many other, similar observations, it was interesting to note how often officials in the *formal* interviews *denied* that inspiration, intuition, guesswork, etc., played any significant part in their enquiries. (In fact, in the case referred to above the policeman's hunch was quite right, and it subsequently emerged that the relatives were trying to conceal quite an elaborate suicide pact.)[10]

In requesting information for interviews and other data I simply informed the coroners that I was interested in how deaths came to be recorded as suicides, misadventures or open verdicts; I added that the officials concerned would have a great deal of knowledge, insights, etc., that could possibly be usefully passed on to suicide researchers. At no time did I ever suggest that I would be engaging in any critical discussion of their work, and this is indeed the case. In the first place I am clearly not competent to judge effectively whether or not coroners, policemen, pathologists, etc., are carrying out their work efficiently; in the second place such a question is irrelevant to the thesis offered here. It seemed to me that the officials were indeed carrying out their work efficiently and also with a great deal of tact and sympathy, but the point being made here is not that officials are making 'mistakes', or are 'cheating', and thereby invalidating the data, but rather that the researchers who use suicide statistics have tended to misunderstand what in fact they consist of. A point that I hope will become more apparent by the end of the chapter.

Broadly, investigation into sudden and apparently unnatural deaths consists of searching for evidence from two main sources. First, there is evidence relating to the *'immediate circumstances of death'*. This may be further divided into three areas. First, there is the evidence from the pathologist's autopsy on the causes of death. Second, there is evidence from the scene of death; this consists of 'relics' taken from the scene, 'archeological data' to pursue the 'historical' analogy, such as notes, clothes, bottles, glasses, ropes, etc., photographs of the deceased and additional descriptive evidence; for example, in a case of drowning the officers will want to know if there was evidence of slip marks, if it was wet or dry, hot or cold, how deep the water was and so on. Finally, there will be reports, if any, from eye witnesses. This 'evidence from the body' and 'evidence from the scene of death' will be used to try to piece together the last moments of the deceased.

The second main source of evidence relates to the *biography of the deceased*, 'historical data'. This is not, of course, an attempt to reconstruct a 'complete' biography of the deceased (even if such a thing was possible), it is rather a search for features of the *deceased's past life which may be relevant to (i.e. make more intelligible) the circumstances of his death*. For example, if the driver of a car is killed when his car runs off the road and no other vehicle is involved, then the officials may want to know, for example, if he has any previous convictions for motoring offences, any physical disabilities that may impair his driving and so on. However, *there is only a detailed search into the deceased's biography if, from the circumstances of death, suicide or foul play is suggested.*

Thus the simple answer to the question of how a death becomes recorded as a suicide is that first, it must *look like* a suicide and second, there must be *reasons* for the suicide. From careful investigation of the circumstances of death officials will develop an opinion that suicide is probable, possible, or can be excluded. As Atkinson has shown, certain pieces of evidence, suicidal cues, from the circumstances of death such as the cause of death, position of the body, extent of physical damage, notes, weapons and other 'relics' taken from the scene of death tend to point officials in the direction of investigating the death as a probable, or possible, suicide.[11] However, for reasons that will become obvious as this discussion progresses, I would wish to distinguish between two types of cues, those related to the immediate circumstances of death and those relating to the biography of the deceased. Evidence from the scene of death which is viewed as being suggestive of suicide may, for purposes of the present discussion, be referred to as 'primary suicidal cues'.

The manner of death is usually the most significant of these primary cues. Certain types of death are rarely investigated as 'possible suicides', road traffic deaths are one example. The office where I undertook this research dealt with two cases where individuals (neither with an excess of alcohol in their blood) had been killed when their cars had gone off the road. Although there were no other cars involved and there was no evidence of mechanical failure, neither case was considered as a possible suicide. Similarly, a case where an elderly, but apparently 'firm', man had suddenly walked into the path of an oncoming car, while according to both the driver and an independent witness looking towards the car, was not considered as a possible suicide.[12] There is research suggesting that 'vehicular suicides' are more frequent than normally supposed,[13] and it is possible that people who decide to kill themselves in this way normally 'mistakenly' have their deaths recorded as 'accidents'. However, this source or 'error', even if proved, would not necessarily systematically bias the statistics for it may be assumed to be random.

Other ways of dying, such as hanging, barbiturate poisoning, shooting, drowning and, in communities with a large Asian component (such as the one I was studying) burning, are, once foul play has been excluded, suggestive of suicide. Hanging, particularly once homicide has been excluded, is probably the most unequivocal primary suicidal cue. However, even in cases of hanging, suicide is still not necessarily always recorded, for there is still scope for possible doubt. Some people can in fact hang themselves accidentally while engaging in semi-masochistic sexual activity;[14] others may hang themselves while attempting to frighten others. There are various reasons why people *conceivably* hang themselves by accident and even with such a seemingly unequivocal mode of death as hanging, death need not be recorded as suicide if there are not 'reasons' in the biography to support such a verdict. This is often the case in deaths of those who are felt to be too young to have formed suicidal intent. Atkinson quotes the case of a boy found hanging where death was not recorded as suicide because he had been planning a climbing holiday and it was decided that he could have hanged himself accidentally while practising with the rope.[15] If a 'reason' cannot be found for 'suicide' then a 'reason' has to be found for the 'accident'; the death has to 'make sense' as the following case illustrates:

> *Boy's death link with record.* A suggestion that the Led Zeppelin pop group's record 'Gallows Pole' might have induced David P., aged 16, of Eastern Way, Letchworth, Hertfordshire, to hang himself accidentally in a cupboard at Ickleford school, near Hitchin on August 27th where he worked as a part-time cleaner was advanced at an inquest at Hitchin yesterday. A verdict of death by misadventure was recorded after the coroner, Mr. Francis Shillitoe, said that *there was no evidence that the boy intended to harm himself.*
>
> Detective Inspector Jeffrey Askew said that the record 'was about a man going to the gallows and being hanged for a crime which he allegedly did not commit'. He suggested that the boy put a rope round his neck in the cupboard and then slipped [my emphasis].[16]

Other types of death typically associated with suicide are more equivocal. Other things being equal there is, for example, rather more doubt as to whether death due to barbiturate poisoning is suicide or accident. Clearly the level of the dose, which is revealed by the autopsy results, is an important indicator of intent, and coroners tend to work with an notion of the three to four times the prescribed dose as indicative of suicidal intent.[17] There are, however, various other factors which tend to cloud and confuse the issue. The age, intelligence and general mental ability of the deceased is important when officials are trying to ascertain whether or not the deceased was aware of the consequences of his action. An elderly, senile or unintelligent person is more likely to take an overdose by 'mistake'. As one coroner's officer explained, 'Some of these old dears, they're on that many tablets . . . well, they may get confused and take too many. It doesn't take a lot to finish some of them off'.[18] Others, normally younger people, may die accidentally as a result of taking too many tablets 'for kicks'. Again, whether or not the tablets were taken with alcohol is important. Some barbiturates, Mogodon, the 'suicide-proof' sleeping tablet, for example, is dangerous when taken with alcohol. There is thus the possibility that such deaths may be accidental.

Some students have recently suggested, though it has not yet been proved, that some individuals may die of barbiturate poisoning in a state of 'automatism';[19] that is, taking a prescribed dose of barbiturates with no suicidal intent, and then entering a semi-conscious state of mind where they 'automatically' ingest a lethal quantity of tablets while unaware of what they are doing.

It is relatively common for some people to take what they believe to be a relatively harmless overdose of tablets for 'show', or as a 'cry for help', and then possibly die by 'accident' as it were. Clearly such acts, even though they are self inflicted and result in death, are not necessarily suicide in the legal sense and, as I shall illustrate later, are not always recorded as suicides for the coroner may decide that the evidence was such that the individual did not 'really' want to die.[20] In short, coroners have, through their expert knowledge, a number of possible explanations as to why an excessive amount of barbiturates could have ended up 'accidentally' in someone's stomach. Thus in cases of barbiturate poisoning, and even more so with relatively more equivocal modes of dying typically associated with suicide such as drowning, falls from a high place or in front of a train, or gassing, a coroner will require a great deal of *additional evidence* (i.e. from the biography) in order to determine whether or not a death was suicide or accident.

Mode of death is the most important 'primary suicidal clue': there are, however, other important 'primary clues'. If a coroner feels that the deceased had a good idea or knew what he was doing, for example a pharmacist taking an overdose of tablets, then there is greater indication of suicidal intent. There are also particular cues relevant to particular deaths. Atkinson quotes a coroner who said that in cases of drowning it was more likely to be a suicide if the clothes were neatly folded;[21] in cases of gassing suicides tend to make themselves comfortable with a pillow and perhaps a favourite book; in cases of wrist cutting there will normally be small 'hesitation cuts'; and in cases of shooting, pathologists are asked to specify whether of not the entry of the bullet is conducive to a self-inflicted wound. From the investigation of the circumstances of death, suicide will either be excluded, or the death will be seen as, to a greater or lesser degree, suggestive of suicide. The main point to be made in this context is that, even if the officials may feel they have a pretty good idea whether or not someone killed himself, *evidence from the circumstances of death is rarely, if ever, sufficient to establish a verdict of suicide in law*. Therefore, whether or not a death becomes legally recorded as suicide is also dependent upon 'evidence of intent' that can be discovered in the biography of the deceased ('historical data'). Just as officials do not search the scene of death, or pathologists the body, in a random way, but rather work to established procedures, so too the deceased's background is examined in a systematic way. Police officers are taught what to look for, what is important and why it is important. In the cases of deaths where suicide is suspected, officials are interested in particular aspects of the deceased's past. There are features of an individual's background which are seen as indications of suicidal intent – a history of mental instability would be an obvious example – these will be referred to as 'secondary suicidal cues'.

The experts of the Suicide Prevention Centre who assisted the Los Angeles coroner, Curphey, in his investigations coined the term 'psychological autopsy' to describe their investigations which consisted of a thorough search into the psychological and biographical history of the deceased in order to try to confirm, or rule out, suicidal intent.[22] However, as Atkinson has observed, these experts were only doing, possibly in a more informed and expert way, work that officials engaged in classifying sudden deaths which 'could be suicides' routinely undertake, i.e. examining the deceased's past for evidence of suicidal intent.

This may be seen from the following comments from coroners' officers. In order to try to establish how coroners' officers' enquiries proceeded, I asked them to comment upon particularly equivocal cases:

ST   Supposing a body is taken out of the canal, identity is established, and, after examination, murder is ruled out; how does investigation then proceed?

CO   Well, you'd have to look at the evidence as I said before. If you found a pile of clothes on the canal bank, looked into the history and found that the person was, perhaps, suffering from depression and had attempted in the past to commit suicide, or threatened suicide . . . In other words, is there any clear indication there, not only from what evidence you can find, but *from the general circumstances*, of deliberate intent, then you would bring in a verdict of suicide . . . You might also call in the GP to see what he had to say. The evidence of a GP is often invaluable because he is an unbiased third party. Sometimes relatives are not always . . . very clear. But the GP . . . perhaps, um, has had private consultations with that patient, he may have been treating him for depression, or an anxiety state other than the norm. He may be a chronic depressive. Um . . . there's many different types of *mental diseases which are known to be more prevalent to suicides*. Um, therefore, you have the medical evidence . . . You'd look into the person's background, his school background, his home environment. You'd perhaps contact a vicar, or a teacher, and make general enquiries to *find out how that boy fitted in, and what his mental state* was. And if you found that person *had got everything to live for* . . . and perhaps you found a slip mark on the canal bank . . . In other words if there was *no indication of suicide*, you'd bring in a verdict of accidental death. Now, if there was a *mixture of both* then there would be an open verdict. So what I'm saying is that the law as it stands, where you've got 'suicide', 'open', and 'accidental', then it will fit either into 'suicide' or 'accident', and the 'in-betweens' go into the 'open'. [my emphasis]

In answering a similar question, another coroner's officer described something of the nature of these enquiries, and went on to talk about a case of attempted concealment. Again, the importance attached to evidence that can be discovered in the person's 'background' is apparent:

ST   Can you tell me a little bit more about how enquiries proceed when there is not much to go on from the immediate
circumstances of death. Say a drowning when there is no
note on the body, no evidence of violence, or drugs in the
stomach . . . How does investigation then proceed?

CO   Well . . . the pathologist goes over the body very thoroughly
prior to the actual autopsy. He's looking for bruises, marks,
scratches, he checks fingernails and things like this, to see if
there is any possibility that this person has been attacked or
something like this. That's from his point of view. From our
point of view, we see the relatives and we want background
history right the way through on this person, er, you know
have they had any mental trouble, have they been in mental
homes, er, have they been depressed, have they got any
money worries, and things like this. That's from the immediate relatives. If we can find somebody close to them that
we can talk to, then, of course we can go on to other subjects. You know, in the case of a younger woman, has she
got a boy friend that her husband doesn't know about and
this sort of thing. This is done very discretely, you'll appreciate, but its all thoroughly checked into, and by the time
we've finished taking statements, and our statements are
more like a little enquiry, out of that we should get some
facts. Er . . . we had an Indian lady a few weeks ago, er, was
found in the canal, drowned, and we went right the way
back, the usual thing, to the relatives. And the husband was
saying he couldn't understand why and this that and the
other, she'd had no depression, no money problems, none
of this, none of that, none of the other . . . But when we
made further enquiries from other relatives and close
friends, we found that *there had been a lot of domestic
trouble, she was depressed, because she had been forced
into, er, the marriage hadn't gone very well, and she was very
depressed, and, in fact, she'd said to a friend that she was
going to end it all . . . and did.* But this is digging right the
way back. [my emphasis]

The enquiry referred to above had, despite evasions, uncovered
the 'true facts' and the suspicion of suicide was *confirmed* because
investigation *had revealed problems, in this case depression due to a*

very unhappy marriage, consistent with someone ending their own life.

Similarly, Curphey refers to a case where he was handed a petition signed by several hundred people protesting about a verdict of suicide brought in on a woman neighbour. She was, it was claimed, a good citizen, and a dutiful wife and mother, and the label of suicide was a slur on both her and the community. Curphey handed the case over to the SPC team for further investigation:

> Their [the SPC team's] efforts brought forth a number of interesting facts, chiefly that, although everything in the petition was true, it was also true that the deceased had been a member of Alcoholics Anonymous (because of what had been a chronic drinking problem) and that she had received psychiatric help for anxiety and depression. Also, in the few weeks before her death, she had taken leave of absence from her job and had been to several physicians, from whom she had received a variety of prescribed medication. It was also discovered that two days before her death she had been to see a psychiatrist, who had written a report that he deemed the victim to be acutely depressed and in need of hospitalization.[23]

Curphey quotes this case to demonstrate that the investigation *proved* that the *correct* decision had been made, i.e. because the biography revealed mental problems, alcoholism, depression, absence from work, etc., all 'evidence' of suicidal intent, *facts consistent with someone killing themselves*.

I asked several officials what happened in cases where they suspected suicide, but could not, no matter how deep they searched, find a motive. The general answer was that, in most cases an 'open verdict' would probably be returned. However, in some cases, the absence of suicidal 'motives' may lead to further investigation as possible murder. As one coroner's officer explained, an overdose, for example, 'is something you've got to be careful with, because when there's *no reason* for them taking it themselves . . . this is very suspicious. Did they know they were taking the overdose, or was it given to them?'

Indeed, there was a case on these lines while I was undertaking the participant-observation research. A man was found dead in his car in his garage having died from inhaling poisonous fumes from the engine – not an uncommon way of committing suicide. Investigation however, revealed none of the sort of problems typically associated with suicide; he was apparently happily married, with two small children, there was no history of mental problems, his business was doing well and so on. It was assumed therefore that, as he had returned home late, he had fallen asleep before turning off the engine and a verdict of 'misadventure' was returned. The problem with such an interpretation was to explain how the garage door came to be closed. What was interesting about this case is that a death which looked like probable suicide from the circumstances of death, became seen as a probable accident, because not only was there no evidence of intent in the deceased's biography, but everything seemed to point *against* suicide. In the light of this, the circumstances of death became *re-interpreted*; how did the *accident* occur? It was suggested that the metal 'swing door', which is opened and closed by lifting could have been blown shut, killing the deceased who had obviously decided to spend the night in his car and kept the engine running to keep the heater on. The main point is that, because of lack of evidence of motive, investigation was deflected away from consideration of the death as suicide.

Evidence from the biography of the deceased is, then, particularly important in determining whether or not death was suicidal. The most important areas of investigation are as follows:

(1) *State of mind prior to death*. Officials attempt, not only to reconstruct the deceased's movements prior to death, but also his state of mind. Individuals who were close to him normally give evidence on this, and officials are interested to know if the deceased was depressed, worried about particular problems and so on. Evidence regarding the deceased's state of mind may also be constructed from the actions, and possibly writings (e.g. notes) of the deceased himself.

(2) *Psychological and medical history*. Evidence of mental, and to a lesser degree, physical, illness are particularly significant suicidal cues. If it can be proved that the deceased was suffering from a type of mental illness 'known' to be associated with suicide such as chronic, or manic depression then officials are far more confident in inferring suicidal intent. Similarly, severe physical illness, particularly terminal illness, is 'known' to drive some people to suicide and is therefore an important suicidal cue.

(3) *Evidence of problems*. In the western world it is generally

believed that suicide is often an escape from problems that an individual (perhaps because he is 'ill') feels are insurmountable. It is thus assumed that where one finds suicide one will also find problems that, for the deceased at least, were reasons for his action. Therefore, officials, in their search into the biography of the deceased, look for evidence of the sort of problems commonly associated with suicide. Some of the most common of these are marital tensions, financial worries, worries over health, impending court case and possible disgrace. Of course, evidence of these problems, in itself, is not necessarily an indication of suicidal intent; there must also be evidence that the deceased was worried, depressed, etc., about them.

(4) *General life history of the deceased.* This level of investigation concerns things such as the childhood experiences of the deceased, his work record, marriage and/or other relationships, and whether or not there was evidence of other forms of 'deviance' such as crime, homosexuality, etc. Such investigation stems from the belief that there are some people who for various reasons (childhood experiences or whatever) are particularly unstable, and hence more *suicide prone* than most. This instability, it is believed, will probably have manifested itself in other ways, such as breakdowns and psychiatric help, inability to form relationships, isolation, deviance and so on. The deceased's life style is also seen as important because, and this was a common belief amongst the officials I interviewed, the strains associated with 'high pressure' life styles were seen as sometimes being conducive to suicidal actions.

It is argued here that the 'areas' of a deceased's life history which are investigated and the interpretation of the 'facts' that are discovered, are products of the officials' (expert and common-sense) knowledge of suicide. The officials themselves, however, as illustrated in the second section of this chapter, see their task as the application of routine procedures of investigation to 'uncover facts' which then 'prove' that death was due to this or that cause. In contrast, the present discussion suggests that the facts become intelligible in the way they do as a result of the observer's knowledge of the phenomenon; that is, the observer's knowledge of what suicide *is* and what it *looks like* means that sets of facts either do look like it, do not look like it, or are 'ambiguous'.

Those aspects of the deceased's biography which are investigated, such as his mental history, are seen as important because of the observer's knowledge of suicide in general and his beliefs about the 'types' of people most likely to commit it. As stated above, part of this work was orientated towards drawing out some of the implicit beliefs and theories held by officials and it is interesting to note that while the officials I interviewed generally saw suicide research and theories of suicide as useful for suicide prevention, they were resistant to the suggestion that theories of suicide had any relevant application to their work. However, it was apparent from some of their replies that in fact they do develop common-sense theories of suicide which, it is reasonable to suppose, guide their investigations.

The following extracts, taken from conversations with coroners' officers illustrate first, the resistance to any suggestion that they had preconceived theories of suicide and second, how in response to problems they do in fact 'theorise' about suicide. I asked a number of officials if, for example, there were any situations commonly associated with suicide and received replies such as, 'Well, you can't really standardise'; another replied that, 'It could be any cause really, I wouldn't like to cut anything down to sort of central causes'; another replied that he didn't think that there were particular recurring situations, and that 'every case was individual, and every one's got to be treated as individual'.

Sometimes, I would ask officials to comment upon particular theories of suicide:

ST   Sociologists have argued that being integrated into society, into a social group tends to protect people from suicide. Would you agree with this? . . . What I mean is that lonely, more isolated people are more likely to commit suicide.

CO(1)   Well . . . I wouldn't like to commit myself on that.

CO(2)   I don't think you can generalise like that, each case is dealt with on its merits . . . as an individual . . . there's not a definite pattern to them.

CO(1)   Yes, I don't think you can say a group of people are more likely to commit suicide than another. I wouldn't agree with that.

CO(2)   I mean this year the suicides we've had range from 13 to 70 [i.e. years of age].

CO(3)   Only the other week an old woman killed herself because her husband had died, and she felt she couldn't go on without him. But that dosen't mean all lonely old widows are going to kill themselves, far from it.

ST   Yes, um, not all lonely people kill themselves obviously, but studies have found a strong correlation between social isolation and suicide.

CO(2)   I still think it goes back to the individual.

CO(3)   Some people are naturally 'loners' and they can exist far more happily by being what we would term 'lonely' than other people who could not exist this way.

CO(1)   Well, I can't recall many recluses commiting suicide.

CO(3)   You know the old hermit type of thing, and there's still a lot about.

CO(1)   I don't think you can generalise on these sort of things.

The above extract was taken from a conversation with the three coroner's officers at the office where I did the participant-observation study (with their approval I would normally tape these conversations). I asked similar sorts of questions of other officials I interviewed, and the replies were relatively consistent. When I asked them *specifically* what sort of people they felt tended to commit suicide, what sort of situations were most frequently associated with suicide and so on, the most common response was something to the effect of: you cannot generalise, each case must be treated on its merits, they are all individual, and one should have an open mind and *not begin investigations with preconceived notions*.

However, in response to other questions, and sometimes even after stating that one cannot generalise, or theorise, officials would go on *to do precisely that*. For example:

ST   What sort of people are most likely to kill themselves?

CO   [Laughs] A question . . . Well, anyone! Literally anybody. Anybody who's under stress and strain . . . Let's put it like this, most suicide people, people with suicide tendencies, if they could only talk to somebody . . . doesn't have to be a qualified person, but somebody who'll listen to them, someone with a bit of common sense . . . its a matter of talking . . . If you could get someone who wants to commit suicide, talk to them and find out why, you could talk most of them out of it. But most people now are too busy to listen . . . people are too busy with their own lives . . . You got, what shall I say . . . more of a family feeling years ago, where you know . . . in our family if we'd got any problems we'd discuss it with Father. He was the head of family, and if you'd got problems you'd discuss it with him . . . People haven't got that now, it's all television. There's no family life as there used to be, and the stress, you know of your company directors, your young executives . . . They're so fighting to get to the top, climbing over everyone else's back to do it, and the stress builds up inside them, and then all of a sudden they're made redundant. Their life is finished, as far as they are concerned . . . and they perhaps haven't got anyone to turn to.

In this extract the officer moves through a number of positions. First, anyone can commit suicide. Then it is argued that people are more likely to resort to suicide if they have those tendencies, and if they feel that they have no-one to talk to, i.e. they feel *isolated*. These sorts of situations are on the increase because in the modern world most people are concerned with their own lives and interests; there is, for example, 'no family life as it used to be'. *More* people are isolated, thrown back on their own resources in times of crisis or, in Durkheim's terms, are placed in situations of '*egoism*'. This officer (and many of the others I spoke to who expressed a similar point of view) felt that suicide is associated with (among other things) a lack of supportive social ties. Therefore it seems logical to suppose that in the investigation of sudden deaths that 'could be suicides', he would look for (among other things) a lack of supportive social relationships and, if this was found, it may be interpreted as (further) 'evidence' of suicidal motivation. My own investigations would seem to confirm this. In a passage quoted earlier an officer, when asked about investigating a drowning, stated that he would be interested in finding out how the deceased '*fitted in*'. Similarly, and more significantly, evidence of strong supportive ties, other things being equal, would mean that death was *less likely* to be suicide. In the case referred to earlier concerning the young man found dead in his car in the garage, the fact that he did have strong, apparently 'healthy', social ties appeared to incline investigations *away* from suicide.

It was argued above that officials were interested in evidence of problems, particularly relatively recent problems, that could be discovered in the biography of the deceased. Such problems may be seen as evidence of suicidal intent. Again such investigation seems to be prompted by the officials' 'common-sense theory' that, sometimes, problems may 'trigger off' suicide. This may be seen in the following reply to a question about situations commonly associated with suicide.

> CO   Well . . . obviously depression is common . . . and if you say depression, that takes in money problems, marital problems, then, of course, you've got disgrace about something being found out about you . . . er . . . in the cases the person who's sort of sent to coventry and gets unbalanced that way . . . it could be any one of a number of causes really . . . loneliness . . . someone may lose their life's partner, and perhaps depression builds up from there.

Here is a common 'theory', that people kill themselves because they are depressed, cannot cope with life, etc., and that there are *certain situations, or problems, which give 'clues' as to why the deceased might have been depressed, and in turn can serve as 'clues' of suicidal intent.* One of the most common situations is one where an individual is faced with some great change, or disaster, which he does not feel he can cope with; therefore, suicide seems a way out. This is similar to Durkheim's notion of (acute) 'anomie', and more recent conceptions of 'status change'. Evidence of status change, such as bereavement, financial problems, some impending disgrace and so on, are particularly significant 'suicidal cues'; and again, these stem from officials' implicit 'common-sense theories' of situations typically associated with suicide.

Asked whether or not he found suicide research helpful to him, a coroner's officer replied that he did, but added, 'but basically we're here to try and find out how a person came by his death *and the reasons why only come second*'. However, the logic of the present discussion suggests that 'reasons', or motives, that can be discovered in the deceased's biography (data rejected by Durkheim and others) are in fact *central* to a death being defined as a suicide.

Balancing Intent

The discussion above has drawn attention to the importance of establishing a suicidal motive for a death to be recorded as a suicide, but it would be something of an oversimplification to imply that suicide verdicts are necessarily brought in when the circumstances of death suggest suicide and a suitable motive can be found. In practice a decision as to whether or not a death is suicide is often made by *balancing* this evidence against contra-indications, or life cues. For example, coroners are generally reluctant to attribute suicidal intent to young people. Therefore, even when a person dies in circumstances suggestive of suicide and there is evidence of say, depression in the biography, the deceased's youth may incline the verdict away from suicide towards accident or, more likely, an open verdict.

It is often assumed that the open verdict is used when there is a *lack* of relevant evidence. However, often there is *contradictory* relevant evidence and the decision-making process is complicated, in particular by the fact that many serious suicidal acts, let us refer to them for the moment as 'acts of self damage', fit comfortably neither the suicide nor accident categories. They appear to be undertaken with ambivalent intentions with the individual not so much seeking death as rather gambling with death. The 'risk-taking' nature of many suicidal acts is discussed in some detail in Chapter 7, but the question here is whether or not such acts, for example taking an overdose of barbiturates in circumstances where there is a strong, but not a certain, possibility of 'rescue', or a game of Russian roulette, are classified as 'suicides'. In attempting to set down some specific criteria in this area the SPC team suggested that: 'When people gamble with death, at what odds should the line be drawn to decide between suicide and accident? We believed that to take a needless chance of one in six for death was suicidal.'[24]

My own researches suggest that the risk-taking nature of many suicidal acts and more important, the *recognition* by officials that they may be some dramatic 'appeal' to one or more others, provides an additional and important source of bias in the official rates. For example, suicidal acts undertaken in a relatively 'integrated' situation, or carried out by those who are relatively young and healthy, etc., are more likely to be interpreted as a 'cry for help'. Even when there is quite strong evidence of intent, this may be reinterpreted as some temporary turmoil as the following case illustrates:

Tragedy of a schoolgirl's guilty secret. Sex case schoolgirl M.H. was in torment. She was being quizzed by the police about her relationship with a thirty-year-old man. Finally she took an overdose of drugs . . . and died. But the move may have been meant only as a cry for help, a coroner said yesterday. Recording an open verdict, Michael Collcut told a Northampton inquest, 'I find it difficult to believe that she really thought at the time that she was likely to be dead in a matter of hours.'

M.,14, wrote her parents a note saying: 'I cannot go through with any more questions.' And asked them not to blame the man she said had made love to her. Then she swallowed some of her father's anti-depressant tablets.

Mr. Collcut said: 'One would call her note a suicidal note. But it is a tragic, pathetic note, and I feel the action she was taking may have been a cry for help.'[25]

Coroners generally appear to be quite well informed about the literature on suicide and it was quite clear from my discussions with them that they were familiar with the research that has argued that many suicidal acts (including some which end in death) are attempts at 'communication', 'cries for help', etc. This means that in some cases, even though the act of self damage may be 'known' to be self inflicted, a death is not necessarily suicide if the background circumstances are not suggestive of suicide and/or there is some evidence that strongly mitigates against suicide.

In this context, in my interviews with coroners, I asked them if they would comment on some specific cases that I described to them. In one I outlined the case of a girl who had died from an overdose of barbiturates (taking two-and-a-half times the prescribed dosage) but had left the door of her room open when there was someone else in the house and had telephoned others the same evening (including her doctor) to tell them of her depression and suicidal feelings. I then asked them whether or not it was suicide. In describing the case in this way (which was in fact that of Marilyn

Monroe) I anticipated that the coroners would not actually give a decision; indeed, this is why the case was so described, for I was interested in their reasons for *not* being able to give me a decision; in short, what *additional* information they would require to determine whether or not it was suicide. In fact two coroners did offer tentative opinions. One thought it would 'probably be suicide', while the other said, 'From what you've said and, of course, coming to decision in court I would want to know much more, but from what you've said, I would think probably misadventure'. The others expressed themselves reluctant to comment on 'hypothetical' cases and did indeed say that they would wish to know much more, for example:

> What you would try to find out is whether she'd got a clear intention of killing herself when she took the tablets . . . For example, when she phoned the doctor did she say she was definitely going to kill herself or, in his opinion, was it an attempt to draw some attention to herself? Had she tried to kill herself before? Had she got a mental condition associated with suicide and so on.

It is interesting that even in a 'case' where the officials 'knew' that the victim took the overdose that killed her, five out of six were reluctant to infer suicide without considerable additional evidence. One of the problems raised in the previous chapter was the amount of discretion that officials have to allow their own views to prevail. For example, in the case quoted above the officials have more discretion than in a case where the deceased was seen to shoot himself in the head and had left notes making clear that suicide was his intention. It appears that there are at least two trends which are giving officials increasing scope for the interpretation of biographical data. One is the tendency for increasing numbers to commit acts of self damage by poisoning which often means that due to the period of time between ingestion and death there is the potential for rescue, which may actually be seen as the deceased's 'true' intention. The second is the great output of recent research into suicide and attempted suicide which, amongst other things, has provided coroners with explanations as to why someone could, for example, accidentally hang himself (masochistic sexual activity) or accidentally poison himself (automatism). Furthermore, the literature on the 'appeal', or 'manipulative', quality of some suicidal acts has given support to the idea that even when the act of self damage is believed to be intentional, there may be some end other than death in view.

Conclusions

For a death to be recorded as a suicide, intent must be proved beyond reasonable doubt. If it is felt that it has not been so proved there may well be an appeal. Thus, of the deaths which 'could be suicides', it is only those cases where the officials feel, from *both* the circumstances of death and the biography of the deceased, that the evidence for suicide is more or less conclusive, that a suicide verdict can be recorded. This research has suggested there may indeed be sources of systematic biases in the statistics which could well provide alternative explanations of the positive correlations so commonly found by students of suicide rates. For example, the importance officials attach to the discovery of mental and/or physical illness, problems such as marital or financial difficulties, evidence that the deceased did not 'fit in', indicators of emotional 'instability' such as coming from a broken home, alcoholism and various forms of deviance, etc., in reaching a verdict of suicide means that there could be considerable discrepancy between what is presumed by the theoretical category 'suicide' and what in practice is actually recorded as 'suicide'.

These observations may be taken as further confirmation of the Douglas–Atkinson thesis that students of suicide rates have been discovering not the causes of suicide, or factors associated with the causes of suicide, but rather the criteria used by officials to decide that a death was in fact a suicide. However, this is perhaps reading rather too much into the present results, for one cannot simply assume that revealing the theories and beliefs of those who compile the data and noting how they correspond to expert theories derived from the data, necessarily 'explains' the data. There has been a tendency amongst some societal-reaction theorists to assume that the 'discovery' of 'folk theories' on the part of those who produce the rates, for example police thinking that young blacks are more criminally minded than young whites, provides a convincing explanation of those rates, for example a higher proportion of young blacks arrested. Clearly, further research is necessary to try to demonstrate this point. Atkinson, in his study, compares seventy cases that had been recorded as suicides with seventy that had been recorded as accidents and found that some of the familiar variables typically associated with suicide were far more prominent in the suicidal group.[26] It is difficult to see, however, how this takes us very much further for, as Atkinson himself notes, the same data is open to different interpretation; either it can be seen as further evidence of the causes of suicide, or it can be seen as evidence that these factors lead officials towards classifying a death as 'suicide'.

The position taken here is that further research, rather than starting with deaths that have already been classified, should attempt to follow through a number of cases from their starting point with the death of a person to the verdict in a coroner's court, in order to see as far as possible how the officials' beliefs and theories are realised in practice. Thus in the example given above, in order to prove, or at least more plausibly argue, that the policemens' belief that young blacks are more criminal than young whites actually influences the statistics, the researcher must not only demonstrate that policemen have this belief but also, crucially, that they have the opportunity and inclination to use such discretion and that it is significant. That is, they must try to demonstrate that, other things being equal, blackness is a 'factor' in the apprehension of juveniles.

A similar principle must be applied to a study examining the social construction of suicide rates. For a death to be recorded as a suicide intent has to be proved, and the hypothesis offered here is that a death will not be recorded as a suicide, even if the circumstances of death strongly suggest suicide, unless officials can uncover 'reasons' for the suicide in the biography of the deceased and in this context the officials draw upon their own theories, assumptions, etc., regarding suicidal individuals and situations.[27] If this is the case, the implications for theories of suicide based on such official data are clear. The problem, however, was to devise a methodology where the circumstances of death were held more or less constant in order to try to clarify the effect of secondary cues on classification. The following chapter documents the results of such an attempt.

5

Persons under Trains

Background

The problem in this part of the research was to try to hold one set of variables, the circumstances surrounding the actual death, constant in order to explore better the effect of those relating to the history of the deceased. This meant examining a number of cases where the manner of death was more or less the same. A number of ways of dying could be excluded: drowning for example, because where the deceased was discovered, whether or not he could swim, the time of the year, etc., mean that, from the circumstances of death, some cases will look more like suicide than others. Similar problems hold with barbiturate poisoning, different types of drugs, different levels of dosage, etc., which means that a sample of deaths by barbiturate poisoning will, at the outset, be seen differently in terms of intent.

Finally, it was decided to study the inquests on a number of people killed under London Transport trains. On average, over the past few years, about five people a month have died this way. London Transport keep quite detailed records of each case and they are filed under *Persons under Trains*. Originally, it was suggested to me that I might like to study these files for some further data on my researches, but on examining them it occurred to me that this manner of death might be suitable for the research problem outlined above. This indeed proved to be the case and the main reasons are summarised below:

(1)   It provided a manner of death strongly suggestive of suicide.
(2)   The circumstances of death were essentially similar in all cases.
(3)   In many cases there were no independent witnesses, and often

when there were, statements were not very concise, typically including phrases such as, 'saw a man in mid-air in front of the train', 'seemed to dive under the train', etc.

(4)   Deaths are referred to various coroners' courts, in fact the cases I studied were heard in eight different courts and it was thus possible to compare, to a certain extent, the work of different coroners.

(5)   In such cases the pathologist's report usually has relatively less influence. Whereas, in a shooting for example, the pathologist can state whether or not the entry and exit holes of the bullet are consistent with a self-inflicted wound and so on; in cases of death under trains, however, all they are normally called upon to say is whether or not injuries are consistent with being hit by a train.

(6)   Cases of death on the railway have to be heard before a jury and this had the advantage, from my point of view, of producing much more detailed summaries of the evidence for the benefit of the jurors by the coroners, particularly in pointing out to them some of the most important indicators of suicidal intent.

The initial part of this research involved examining London Transport records of previous years' deaths under trains. These reports consisted of some brief details of the deceased: age, sex, etc., when and where the death occurred, a full statement from the motorman (driver) and any other London Transport (LT) employees, various technical details relating to delays, etc., and finally, the date, place and verdict of the inquest. It emerged that just over half these deaths were recorded as suicides.

It was decided to follow through all deaths under LT trains over a period of one year from the initial report of the death to the inquest verdict: the object of the exercise being to try to discover how it was that starting from, as it were a common denominator, a corpse under a train, some deaths were recorded as 'suicides', others as 'accidents' and others as 'open' verdicts.

Post cards were left with the Operating Manager of LT (Trains) and one was sent to me each time someone was killed under a LT train. The card contained the name of the deceased, the station and the date. From the analysis of previous years, it was relatively easy to tell at which court the inquest was likely to be heard. Deaths in central London were normally dealt with by Westminster coroner's

court, deaths in the north west by St Pancras and so on. I would contact the relevant coroner's court, ask when the inquest on Mr X was
being heard and attend at the appropriate time. In the early stages
of the work I simply asked for the time and date of the hearing, but
as I came to 'know' the chief coroners' officers (particularly at the
two courts where most cases were heard) I asked for additional
information about the circumstances of death and relevant evidence. This was particularly useful because a number of cases had to
be excluded from further consideration, and it was a great help to
know, if possible, which ones these were in advance. Bearing in
mind that the objective was to get a sample of cases where the circumstances of death were strongly suggestive of suicide and more or
less similar to each other, cases were excluded where, for example,
a suicide note was discovered with the body or had been left some-
where else, or where there was more than one independent witness
willing to testify that the deceased 'jumped', 'accidentally fell' or
whatever. Such cases were excluded because it was felt that (as with
an excessively high overdose of barbiturates, for example) there
would be more evidence from the circumstances of death to point
the officials towards one verdict or the other. Similarly, cases were
excluded when there was virtually no evidence at all from the scene
of death – for example, a body being discovered in a tunnel –
because such cases were much more likely to produce an open
verdict.

In all during that year there were sixty-one deaths under LT
trains, thirty-seven resulted in suicide verdicts, thirteen in verdicts
of accidental death, and eleven as open verdicts.[1] For the reasons
given above, twenty-nine cases were excluded from further consideration and of the remaining thirty-two, seventeen were suicide
verdicts, five accidental deaths were recorded, and ten were open
verdicts.[2] All the remaining thirty-two cases were essentially similar
in terms of the reports of the circumstances of death, and the purpose of this part of the work was to discover the sort of evidence
which appeared to be important in reaching the various verdicts.

The thirty-two cases were similar in terms of circumstances of
death because first, the cause of death, being struck by a train, was
similar; second, the evidence from the main witnesses the motormen, was generally the same; and finally, evidence, if any, from
other witnesses was inconclusive. (Cases where evidence from eye
witnesses was relatively conclusive, such as a case where six inde-

pendent witnesses stated that the deceased ran across the platform and jumped in front of the train were excluded from further consideration.)

Statements from the motormen varied in terms of the extent to which they were able, or perhaps prepared, to commit themselves as to whether or not the deceased jumped in front of the train. Many statements were inconclusive, for example, 'I felt a bump', or, 'I saw a shadow fall across the track', while others used terms such as 'dived in front of the train', or 'appeared to jump in front of the train'. In other cases the motormen only noticed the deceased when he was actually on the track and were obviously unable to state whether he jumped or not. The important thing here from our point of view is that evidence from the motormen, even if it states that the deceased 'dived' or 'jumped' in front of the train, is not a *sufficient* indicator of suicidal intent. (Although, as I shall illustrate, when there is other evidence strongly supportive of suicide, a motorman's testimony is often taken as further evidence to 'clinch' the matter.) *Thus suicidal intent in all the cases must be established by evidence other than that from the scene of death;* although that evidence itself may be strongly *suggestive* of suicide, it is insufficient to (legally) 'prove' suicide. This is explained very carefully to juries by coroners in most cases, and the following comments by a coroner are fairly typical, and worth quoting at some length to clarify this very important point:

C   What I have to do now is to tell you about the function of juries when they sit for a coroner at an inquest. And what we have to do is perhaps more limited than you might imagine. First we are concerned with identity . . . then we are concerned with how, when and where the deceased came by his death. Well, in this case he's gone under a tube train . . . Well, with due respect to London Transport, drivers nearly always say he jumped. Whether he did or not, we have only one witness to say, and even, um, if you take that view of the affair . . . the courts of England are a bit reluctant to accuse a man of committing suicide, after his death on just, you know, one statement. *So without some other evidence of his being disturbed in his mind or acting funny, or having threatened to take his own life which we haven't got, suicide would, I think, be an unsafe verdict to return.* Commonly, as far as deaths of this nature are concerned, accidental, er, covers it quite nicely; but if you reckon you haven't heard enough evidence to come to a definite conclusion, you're perfectly entitled to say, we'll leave the matter open . . . so you have those choices, and I'll leave the matter to you on the facts as you've heard them this morning. [my emphasis]

The question in this part of the work revolves around the 'other evidence' that is necessary to bring in a verdict of suicide. It is partly answered by the coroner himself in the quotation above and has also been examined in the previous chapter, but this research aims to examine, under more 'controlled' conditions, the reconstruction of an appropriately 'suicidal' biography. The thirty-two 'identical' cases are examined in terms of the criteria outlined in the previous chapter – state of mind prior to death, mental and physical health, social problems and life history – around which were built, it was argued, some of the most important components of a suicidal biography. Of course, in practice these criteria are interdependent and interrelated, but for purposes of clarity I examine each separately and I shall discuss another cue which only emerged as important during the LT study, that of 'normality of place'.

Before beginning the analysis, however, it might be first useful to illustrate the research problem a little further with reference to the 'immediate circumstances of death' of a couple of cases. The first case in the year I undertook this study occurred on 2 January at Finchley Road tube station and the deceased was a 40-year-old man of Portuguese birth. There were no independent witnesses, and the statement from the motorman said that, 'I then saw a man walk towards the edge of the platform, and when the train was almost level with him, he suddenly dived towards the track and disappeared from view beneath the train'. The second case was that of a 31-year-old man killed at Woodford station on 19 January. Again there were no independent witnesses, and the statement of the motorman claimed that 'a man stepped forward to the platform's edge . . . and with arms by his side rolled in front of the train'. In the first case a verdict of accidental death was returned on a Mr G and in the second, a verdict of suicide on a Mr K. As the circumstances of death were practically identical, the aim was to examine the sort of evidence which inclined the officials towards or away from suicide.

State of Mind Prior to Death

In cases where suicide is suspected the coroner's enquiry is essentially concerned with discovering whether or not the deceased was in a state of mind where he had suicidal intent, and, of course, all sorts of evidence ranging from that relating to the location and circumstances of death to evidence concerning whether or not the deceased had mental problems, social problems and so on is directed towards this end. However, what we are specifically concerned with here is evidence, usually impressions and opinions regarding the deceased's state of mind from those who were close to him before his death. The coroner is interested, therefore, in whether or not the deceased has made any suicidal threats, previous attempts, if he was depressed, anxious, withdrawn and so on.

This evidence concerning the deceased's state of mind – let us, for convenience, call it 'evidence of association' to distinguish it from 'professional evidence' – normally comes from the deceased's significant others, (i.e. one who had close and apparent personal ties with the deceased). However, if the deceased has no close ties, or has not been seen by members of his family for some time, as in the case of people working away from home or students, this evidence (or part of this evidence) might be given, for example, by landladies, work-mates, casual acquaintances, college tutors, and so on. 'Evidence from association' regarding the deceased's state of mind may then come from 'significant others' or from 'distant others', or possibly, from a combination of both.

In an inquest usually only one, or sometimes two, witnesses are called to give this sort of evidence; although, possibly, many more witnesses will have been interviewed in the enquiry. It is thus difficult to specify exact proportions with confidence, but of the cases examined, in twenty this evidence was given by 'significant others', in nine by 'distant others', and in three cases by a 'significant' and a 'distant' other.

Reconstruction of the deceased's state of mind is the result of *negotiations* between the officials and the various witnesses. In cases where suicide is suspected the officials will want to know if the deceased was depressed, threatening to take his own life and so on. The officials then, with these sorts of questions, are suggesting (possible) suicidal intent, and affirmative answers to these questions clearly give more support to the possibility of suicide. However, as

others have pointed out, there is considerable potential for concealment of evidence in these negotiations: notes can be destroyed,
threats of suicide 'forgotten', depression played down, etc. What is
equally important, although less commonly realised is that not only
may the imputation of suicidal intent be resisted *negatively* (for
example, 'no, he wasn't depressed'), but it may also be resisted *positively* (for example, 'he was really looking forward to his daughter's
wedding', etc.).

We may argue, along with Douglas, that if the deceased is in an 'integrated' situation and this evidence is given by significant others,
that there is more likelihood of attempted and successful concealment (i.e. 'positive' and 'negative') than in cases where this vital evidence is given by 'distant' and 'disinterested' others. However,
though this may well be the case, it was argued in Chapter 3 that the
varying rate of concealment hypothesis is virtually impossible to
prove. What does emerge from analysis of these thirty-two inquests is
that *in some cases 'witnesses of association' were clearly attempting to
resist the imputation of suicidal intent, while in others they were not*. It
is suggested, therefore, that 'resistance' is a more fruitful, though ad-
mittedly less ambitious, hypothesis than that of 'rate of
attempted concealment'.

We may hypothesise that first, there is more likelihood of resistance to the imputation of suicide when evidence regarding the
deceased's state of mind is given by a 'significant' rather than a 'distant' other; and second, in cases where there is resistance to the
imputation of suicidal intent by the witness, or witnesses, giving evidence on the deceased's state of mind then, other things being
equal, there is less likelihood of a suicide verdict being returned.

The cases studied tend to give some support to such a hypothesis.
Of the thirty-two cases, there were ten where there was evidence of
resistance to any (implicit or explicit) imputation of suicidal intent;
and in *all* these cases 'evidence from association' regarding the
deceased's state of mind was given by 'significant others', for example a parent, child, spouse, sibling, or other relative if they were living with the deceased. Whether or not the imputation of suicide was
'resisted' is a result of the judgement of the observer, but I found
that it was quite apparent whether or not 'resistance' was taking
place.

This, and other relevant points, may be more usefully illustrated
here by comparing cases where there was obvious 'resistance' to the

imputation of suicidal intent to cases where there was not. The first witnesses in inquests are identity witnesses and they are first asked in court to confirm that the deceased was in fact X and the same witness is then normally asked for evidence relating to the deceased's state of mind. However, this is not always the case. For example, when a student from a city in the Midlands was killed under a London Transport train, evidence of identity was given by his father, but as he had not been home for a couple of months, evidence of 'how he was' was given by another student.

In his examination the coroner will have the witness's statement in front of him and he will read out parts asking for the witness's confirmation in court; he will also ask questions suggestive of possible suicidal intent and often, this will be simply confirmed, or rejected, by the witness. (A useful analogy, I think, is the game of whist; the coroner will ask his questions rather like putting a card down on the table and the imputation will either be confirmed or rejected in a manner similar to winning or losing a 'trick'.)

We look first at an extract from examinations of a witness where there is some resistance to any imputation of suicidal motivation. It is important to stress that there is no suggestion that the witness is 'lying' or concealing important evidence; the important fact, from our point of view, is that the examination provides the coroner with no (further) 'evidence' of suicidal motivation. In this case the deceased was a 51-year-old man killed at Warren Street station, the witness is his brother:

C   And when did you last see him alive?

W   Three weeks ago [i.e. a week before his death].

C   And how was he then?

W   He looked very well.

C   Was there anything, er, preying on his mind?

W   No. Nothing I know of.

C   How was his health?

W   Well, it was quite good. He had some heart trouble, but he had had this for some time . . . It didn't seem to be causing him much bother.

C   And he wasn't working?

W   No, he hadn't been working for a couple of years because of his heart.

C   How was he keeping himself?

W   Very well . . . He was always very clean and tidy.

C   Had he any friends?

W   Yes. He had a number of very close friends.

C   And none of them said anything to you that might throw any light on this?

W   No sir. Nothing.

A similar lack of 'confirmatory evidence' emerges from the following exchange between a coroner and the father of a young man, Mr H, killed under a train.

C   When did you last see your son?

W   About a fortnight ago.

C   How did he seem then?

W   He was very well . . . Quite cheerful.

C   Now he had been having some treatment as an outpatient at the X mental hospital . . . but his doctors had said he was well enough to go away to college.

W   Yes, he was a lot better.

C   Had you heard from him since seeing him?

W   Yes, er, we had a letter.

C   Had he been keeping up with his studies?

W   Yes, he'd been doing quite well.

C   Had he ever talked at all about ending his life?

W   No, sir.

In these extracts, questions which raise the *possibility* that the deceased was in a suicidal state of mind receive no confirmation from the witnesses. In other cases, however, the witnesses seem to have decided for themselves that death was suicide, and there is no such resistance. Here, for example, is an extract from the inquest on a young man, aged 27, between the coroner and one of the deceased's flat-mates:

C   And you saw the deceased regularly?

W   Yes.

C   Was his health good?

W   His health was good, but recently he'd been eating less, getting thinner and drinking more.

C   Were there any signs of depression?

W   Yes.

C   Such as?

W   Well, he didn't like his work, but couldn't see himself doing anything else.

C   What was his job? [looking through the papers in front of him]

W   Window dresser.

C   Ah yes, and how long had he been in this job?

W   Since he left school.

C   What else could he do?

W   He didn't know. He couldn't think of anything else he could do.

C   Did he have any hobbies? Any outside interests?

W   Not really . . . no.

C   When did you last see him?

W   On the morning of the sixth.

C   How was he then?

W   Much the same, he said he was going to the doctor's for some tablets.

C   Did he in fact go to the doctor's?

W   Yes, because when I got back that evening the tablets were on the table.

C   But he wasn't in the house?

W   No.

C   Had he, to your knowledge, made any previous suicide attempts?

W   Yes, once he took an overdose.

C   And was he treated by a doctor?

W   No.

C   How was this attempt treated?

W   I found him, made him drink salt water and he was sick.

C   Did you call a doctor?

W   No, I didn't.

C   Thank you Mr X, I'm obliged to you.

In the above extract we see the coroner looking for the familiar 'suicidal cues' such as health, depression and so on; here, however, the imputation, 'was the deceased in a state of mind that might have led to a suicidal action?' is not contested. Indeed, *both* coroner *and* witness seem to be confirming that he was in such a state. For example, a previous attempt is an important indicator of suicidal intent. All the coroners I spoke to had some familiarity with the important literature on suicide, and one would expect they were familiar with the findings of Stengel and others that a sample of attempted suicides were eight times more likely to kill themselves than a 'normal' population.[3] In this case, however, as the previous attempt was not referred to the local doctor or a hospital, it could have quite easily been concealed had the witness been resisting the imputation of suicidal intent. There are other occasions when the witness volunteers information relevant to suicidal intent. The coroner asks about the deceased's health, as poor health can be a 'motive' for suicide. The witness replies that his health was good; but then, *without being asked*, volunteers the information that 'he'd

been eating less, getting thinner and drinking more'. Other imputa-
tions of intent raised by the coroner are not contested – the witness
says that the deceased was depressed because he did not like his job
(in other circumstances this would hardly be seen as indicative of
any suicidal intent, but in this context, coupled to the rest of the
evidence, it becomes 'significant'); furthermore, it is confirmed that
the deceased had 'no outside interests'. Is it really possible for someone to have *no* interests? The point was not taken further because
the imputation of suicide was not being contested. In other circumstances, however, 'interests' might have been 'found'.

Douglas and others have concentrated upon 'evidence' of suicide
being 'concealed'; equally important is *evidence being offered as to
why the deceased would not take his own life* (what I termed 'positive
resistance' above). 'Had the deceased got reasons to kill himself?'
and 'had he got reasons to stay alive?' are two sides of the same
problem. In the cases studied there was positive resistance only in
cases where 'evidence from association' regarding the deceased's
state of mind came from a significant other.

An example of positive resistance, pointing out what the
deceased had to live for, can be seen from the following exchange
between a coroner and the wife of a man killed under a train:

C   Was he depressed at all?

W   No, not at all.

C   Did he ever talk of ending his own life?

W   No . . . He was looking forward to [their daughter's] wed-
     ding. He had been saving for a deposit for a house for them.

Here the witness states that the deceased had not threatened suicide
and then proceeds to reinforce this with 'evidence' as to why he
would not have contemplated suicide. This may be compared to the
previous case quoted where the deceased was said to have 'no outside interests' and no evidence as to why he should *not* have killed
himself was offered.

The second part of the hypothesis outlined above suggested that
in cases where there was resistance to the imputation of suicidal
intent there would be more likelihood of a suicide verdict not being
returned, other things being equal. Officials, as has already been

shown, must find reasons, or 'motives', that make a verdict of suicide intelligible (the deceased was depressed, insane, etc.). Some of the most important evidence is provided by those who were close to the deceased just before death. Sometimes this provides a great deal of evidence of suicidal intent, sometimes it does not. When it does not, evidence is more likely to have been given by a significant other of the deceased and when evidence of intent is not forthcoming from these witnesses, it is much more difficult for a coroner to 'prove' suicide and there is correspondingly less chance of a suicide verdict being returned. In fact, in this study, in the ten cases where there was resistance, eight resulted in 'non-suicide' verdicts (two misadventure and six open verdicts) where as the other (non-resisted) twenty-two cases produced fifteen verdicts of suicide.

In summary, the evidence from the London Transport study suggests that when the evidence of the deceased's state of mind is given by a significant other of the deceased there is more chance of resistance to the imputation of suicide (resistance being defined here as either the failure to produce confirmatory evidence (negative resistance) and/or the attempt to provide evidence as to why the deceased had definite reasons not to commit suicide (positive resistance)). In cases where there is resistance from witnesses of association, there is correspondingly less likelihood of a suicide verdict being returned. These observations again underline the importance of establishing a 'plausible story' for a verdict of suicide and suggest an alternative explanation for the habitual sociological finding that suicide rates consistently correlate inversely with rates of social integration and positively with social isolation, 'twilight' and 'disorganised' zones.

Of course, it must be remembered that reconstruction of the deceased's state of mind is *negotiated*, and the outcome of negotiated situations is to a certain extent dependent on the *power* of the interested parties, in these cases the power of the deceased's significant others. In cases where suicide is suspected, the scope for resistance will vary in relation to the strength of other evidence. If, for example, the deceased has been found shot with his prints on the gun and has written several notes making clear his intent, then there is obviously little scope, and probably little inclination, for resistance. The deceased's significant others, even if they wished for a suicide verdict not be returned, have little power to resist such an imputation. Similarly, even in more equivocal cases, such as deaths under trains, other background evidence, such as recent admission to hospital for depression, will affect the potential for (successful) resistance. Thus, although in the ten cases where there was resistance, evidence of the state of mind prior to death was given by significant others, there were still thirteen cases where significant others gave this evidence and made no attempt to resist the imputation of suicide.

In an attempt to examine the resistance hypothesis in more detail and under more controlled conditions, I undertook a second study of deaths under trains, this time holding not only the circumstances of death constant, but also *excluding* cases where there was clinical evidence of mental or phsyical illness. Between 1976–7 I examined ten such cases, five of which were recorded as suicide.[4] In the four cases where there was definite resistance, evidence was given by a significant other and a non-suicidal verdict was returned. Obviously, the results of such relatively small samples have to be interpreted with caution but, as far as they go, they do seem to illustrate how resistance can produce important systematic biases in the statistics.

However, as I suggested above, both the inclination and the scope for resistance will be dependent on the relative strength of other evidence typically seen as important in the reconstruction of a suicidal biography. Thus, while what those who last saw the deceased *say* about his state of mind is important, officials have other important sources of information which provide them with evidence of suicidal intent. Perhaps the most important of these relate to evidence of mental illness, and it is to this cue that I now turn.

Mental and Physical Health

Most of the officials I interviewed stated that suicide was usually the result of some form of (possibly temporary) mental illness; those most commonly associated with suicidal risk being endogenous and manic depression. (Curiously, chronic depression does not normally produce much risk of suicide as the individual is often too apathetic to engage in any sort of wilful activity – the most dangerous stage in such illnesses is when patients are 'recovering' and reach the stage where they may see suicide as a solution to their problems, whereas previously they may have been, ironically, 'too depressed' for suicide.)

In the London Transport study there were eight cases where individuals had been patients in mental hospitals, and of these seven were recorded as suicides and in one case which was not recorded as suicide, the woman had not received any treatment for several years. Another six cases had either received, or been receiving, treatment for some mental or emotional troubles, either as out-patients or from their own doctors, and four of these were recorded as suicides. Thus, while there was history of mental troubles recorded in only 44 per cent of the cases, in 65 per cent of those recorded as suicides there was a history of mental troubles (and of those where there was evidence of hospitalisation for mental problems there was an 85 per cent suicide rate recorded).

It was argued in the previous chapter that coroners, as part of their decision making, provide an 'explanation' as to why the deceased might have had reason to kill himself. A history of mental illness provides a *basis* for such an explanation. This may be clarified by examining an example of such a case. A 44-year-old man was killed by a train at Piccadilly Circus, there was no note on the body and there were no independent witnesses. Identity was confirmed by a younger sister, the deceased's wife having been in hospital for some time with what was described in court as 'a severe psychological breakdown'. There were apparently no other relatives. The sister could give little evidence relating to the deceased's state of mind as she 'didn't see him very often' and 'hadn't seen him for some time'. It was established that he had been a barrister but had not practised for some time as a result of psychological problems following a car accident. There was no 'resistance', but there was little evidence regarding the deceased's state of mind prior to death as the witness had not seen him recently:

C   Was he depressed about this? [That is, about not working.]

W   Yes, he had been treated for depression.

C   Did he ever say anything about harming himself?

W   No, not to me . . . But then I didn't see him very often.

The despression cue was followed up in questions to the next witness, the deceased's psychiatrist:

C   What was his illness?

W   He was a manic depressive . . . the depression seemed to have followed an accident in which he had sustained a severe fracture of the skull . . . and since then he had been drinking very heavily.

C   In bouts, or continually?

W   More or less continually.

C   How did he progress since his admission in July?

W   Well, we managed to get him off the alcohol . . . but he was still depressed . . . He had treatment with anti-depressants . . . he then became manic.

C   Is suicide a complication of manic depressive illness?

W   Yes, it's common.

In his summing up to the jury the coroner mentioned that Mr O had a 'long history of mental illness', that he 'had trouble with drink and was unable to work'. He continued:

C   And we have heard the driver say that as the train was coming into the station he saw the man crouch down and jump in front of it. The driver has stated that, in his mind, it was a jump, and not a fall . . . We have further heard Dr G say that self destruction is a common problem in manic depressive illness . . . His wife had also been in hospital, in fact still is in hospital after a mental breakdown. If you think that this was a deliberate act, then you should return a verdict of suicide. If you feel that it was not, or that it is not clear whether or not it was, then you should return a verdict of accident, or an open verdict.

Although the jury here are formally being given the 'option', they are in fact being 'directed' to return a verdict of suicide (which they did); from our point of view, it is important to note how a *plausible explanation* for the deceased's action is built up. Here is a picture of an intelligent man, a barrister, unable to work due to an accident; he had become depressed and had been drinking heavily for several years. It was established that suicide was relatively common in those suffering from his illness, and further 'proof' of intent was given by the driver's evidence stating that the deceased 'jumped' in front of the train. (This last piece of evidence is interesting, because sometimes, as I have already noted, when there is relatively little evidence of intent from the life history, jurors are instructed to 'ignore' the driver's assertion that the deceased 'jumped' in front of the train.)

Similarly, severe physical illness can serve as an indicator of suicidal intent. There were two cases of individuals suffering from severe physical illnesses and both were recorded as suicides (as both were also suffering from depression they have been included in the previous set of figures).

One case concerned a young girl, 24, who had been suffering from multiple sclerosis. As she had been living away from home for some time, evidence regarding state of mind was given by 'distant' others. There is little point in reproducing extensive extracts in order to duplicate points raised earlier; but, it is important to note how the illness, and the deceased's understandable concern and depression about it forms the focal point of the examination. The coroner does not pursue other areas (hobbies or whatever) because here is an 'explanation' for the death. The witness being examined in the following extract is an employer and friend:

C   And you are not related to the deceased?

W   No sir, I have known her for about six years. She was my secretary, and visited my home many times and was a close friend of my wife and myself.

C   Had you noticed any changes in her recently?

W   Yes, since it was established that she suffered from multiple sclerosis, she had become depressed. Sometimes she was bright and cheerful, and at other times very depressed and withdrawn.

C   What were the obvious problems that she faced as a result of her illness?

W   Trouble with walking and eyesight.

C   So there were problems of co-ordination of movement?

W   Well, just with walking mainly.

C   And she was having treatment for depression?

W   Yes.

C   Did it continue?

W   Well she seemed better, then it would return.

C   When did you last see her alive?

W   About two weeks ago.

C   How did she appear to you then?

W   Slightly depressed.

A statement from another witness, another friend, was read out in court, and this confirmed much of the previous evidence, also adding that the deceased had taken an overdose about six months previously. In his summing up the coroner mentions the driver's 'clear evidence' that the deceased 'dived . . . like someone going into a swimming pool', and goes on to say that:

C   There is no doubt in my mind that this was a deliberate act. We have heard medical evidence to the effect that she was diagnosed as suffering from multiple sclerosis, as a result of which she experienced some bouts of depression. As such, one can question the state of her mind at the time of the act with particular reference to the depression induced by the knowledge that her illness had no known cure and would get progressively worse, so encouraging her to take the tragic vital steps to end her own life – therefore killing herself.

In both these cases, and in several others, the deceased's mental, or mental and physical illness, provides a cornerstone of the coroner's explanation and decision. To return to our original formulation of the problem, one manifestation of a 'typical suicide' is the suicide of one suffering from a mental disorder, particularly depression. Here is a source of evidence which, when supported by other evidence of intent (for example, the manner of dying) is often sufficient to 'prove' suicide.

Past or present evidence of a mental condition associated with suicide does appear to have a particular bearing on the inclination for resistance, irrespective of who gives the evidence regarding the deceased's state of mind. As well as the fourteen cases from the original study where there was some evidence of mental and/or emotional troubles that were being medically treated, the second study, although concerned with a different part of the problem, in fact involved attendance at a further seven such cases. In all I examined twenty-one cases where there was some clear clinical evidence of mental instability and in only five was there evidence of resistance and there was no attempt at resistance in any of the cases where the deceased had been hospitalised. It seems that widespread belief that suicide (and particularly spectacular and violent methods of suicide, such as jumping under a train) is usually related to some form of mental disturbance which acts as a cue not only to the officials, but *also to the witnesses* who appear more ready to accept that suicide has taken place. Indeed in two such cases, the witnesses (significant others) giving evidence regarding the deceased's state of mind did not merely accept suicide, but clearly wanted it established so that proper responsibility could be allocated. For example, in one case it emerged at the inquest that the deceased woman had been suffering from mental troubles for a number of years and this had resulted in bouts of very erratic behaviour. The husband had obtained a divorce and had custody of the three children. The witness giving evidence about her state of mind was one of her brothers with whom she had been staying.

C   And can you think of any reason why she might have wanted to end her own life?

W   Yes, because he [pointing to the husband] wouldn't let her see the kiddies . . . That's why she done herself in!

C   That is for the court to decide.

From the evidence provided by this part of the study it seems hardly surprising that students of suicide rates find they correlate positively with forms of mental (and physical) illnesses. This is not to dispute that suicide is associated with various forms of mental disorder, but simply to argue that the official rates are systematically biased in that direction.

Social Problems

The participant-observation study revealed the importance of social problems as a suicidal cue. However, while it is often important in the investigation, evidence of for example, homosexuality, marital infidelity, etc., is not necessarily brought out in open court. It is probable, therefore, that a study confined largely to inquests, as the LT study had to be, underestimates the importance of social problems in providing officials with a motive for a death which appears to be suicidal. In all the deaths recorded as suicides there was some evidence of problems. If the deceased was in a state of mind where suicide was likely, depressed, anxious or whatever, then there *must* be 'things' (problems to him) about which he was depressed or anxious. On the other hand, evidence of such 'problems' in the deceased's history such as financial problems, marital difficulties, etc., are not, in themselves, evidence of suicidal intent (though they are cues) for there must also be evidence (i.e. about his state of mind) that he worried or was depressed about these problems. To a certain extent then the deceased's concern about his problems can be *negotiated* as, for example, in one case where a witness insisted that the deceased was 'not worried' about a forthcoming prosecution. Thus although the coroner may have *objective* evidence of problems, he still has to have some confirmation of the deceased's *subjective* concern about them in contrast to evidence of mental instability which is taken as evidence of the deceased's subjective state and, such is our faith in psychiatry and medicine, as an objective fact.

Concern here is with specific *social* problems which, when seen in conjunction with other pieces of evidence, become suggestive of suicide. There are two 'types' of problems particularly associated with suicide, 'social failure' and 'social disgrace' (or impending 'social disgrace'). The importance that officials attach to this evidence was illustrated in the participant-observation study and confirmed, to a certain extent, in the London Transport study. Social failure and social disgrace were present in many of the cases where the deceased was said to have been suffering from some form of mental illness, but there were other cases where there was no (clinical) evidence of mental illness or depression and where social failure and/or social disgrace formed the basis of the explanation for the verdict of suicide.

There have been many sociological works built around explaining the observation that loss of status (and/or reputation, etc.), downward mobility, professional failure, etc., and suicide are positively correlated. It may result, for example, in 'anomie', 'frustration' and (internally directed) 'aggression' or loss of self concept.[5] However, as was illustrated in the previous chapter, as the officials who compile the data operate with more or less similar theories, this seems an important influence on the official statistics. It may, for example, help to account for the positive correlations between suicide rates and economic slumps. While the suicide of one who is mentally ill is fairly 'typical', so too is the suicide of one who feels a 'social failure', or one who feels 'disgraced'; these too are sometimes 'adequate motives' for establishing suicidal intent, providing there is also evidence of the deceased's great concern over these problems.

An example of 'failure' may be given by the case of a woman of Australian origin in her early forties, who had been a relatively successful jazz singer. The first witness was the landlady of the boarding house at which the woman had been staying for some time, she was also a good friend. After some perfunctory questions about identity and recognition of the deceased's handwriting (there was no note as such, but there was a kind of journal which was used in the evidence and passages from it were shown to the jury) the coroner mentions the deceased's problems:

C   She was a singer.

W   Yes.

C   Did she go away much?

W   Yes she did, but not much recently . . . in the last eighteen months.

C   Was she married?

W   No.

C   Now recently, she'd been having some problems. She'd been finding it difficult to get work.

W   Yes.

C   Had she any relatives in this country?

W   Not as far as I know . . . No.

C   Now, about a month before her death she had been offered work, hadn't she?

W   Yes sir . . . But it hadn't worked out . . . She was very disappointed.

C   Was she depressed about this?

W   Yes sir, very.

C   Did she ever talk of killing herself?

W   No, not really . . . Not in so many words.

C   And you last saw her the day before she died.

W   Yes sir.

C   How was she?

W   Well . . . like always, I suppose.

In this case there was no medical evidence of any mental problems, no visits to her doctor and, from the pathologist's report, it emerged that she had been perfectly healthy. The verdict of suicide which was returned appeared to hang on the deceased's concern with her failing career. It is worth pointing out here, in reference to the point raised earlier in this chapter, that evidence regarding the deceased's state of mind was crucial in this case. It was given by a 'distant other' and the imputation of suicide was not resisted. It was thus established that the deceased was depressed about her 'failure'. In this context other pieces of evidence made sense, completed a pattern. For example, extracts from the journal which were considered 'important' were shown to the jury. (Notes, etc., are not normally read out in court, but as I knew the coroner's officer quite well by this time I was shown this evidence.) One extract referred to the job mentioned above and went: 'losing the job at [a well-known London club] is the last straw'. This is hardly a suicidal statement but, taken in conjunction with other evidence, and more importantly the *interpretation* given to this other evidence, which in turn is a result of a general belief in western culture that 'failure' can lead to suicide, was taken as 'further evidence' of suicidal intent. Again, as with other cases we have looked at in this section, a plausible *story*, an explanation which makes death by suicide intelligible, is built up. In this case it is the story of a once successful singer who was finding it difficult to get work, who was reaching middle age, and who did not have the support of marriage and family to encourage her through difficult times. All these points were raised by the coroner in his summing up and a verdict of suicide was returned. In this case, the deceased's 'failing career' was the key to her state of mind and was consequently a focal point for the investigation, the explanation, and the verdict. In another case, where again, there was no medical evidence of 'mental illness', the deceased's declining business interests (which had led, among other things, to his wife leaving him) and his great concern over an impending court case (for fraud), evidence of which was given by a friend, provided an explanation from which another verdict of suicide was returned.

In the investigation of the life histories of individuals suspected of having committed suicide officials work with a 'common-sense' notion in many ways similar to 'anomie theory'. As one coroner's officer put it to me simply, 'sometimes people get themselves into situations they feel they can't cope with . . . With the pace of life today, everyone wanting to get on, there's more people getting themselves into this sort of mess.' Officials therefore tend to look for such things as status loss, personal disorganisation and so on; if there is positive evidence of such problems, then this provides an explanation as to *why* someone might have killed themselves, they are then 'typical suicides'. As there is more chance of such deaths being recorded as suicides, it is hardly surprising that students who study suicide rates find suicide to be positively associated with status loss and personal and social disorganisation.

Life History

The participant-observation study and the interviews demonstrated that there were important 'suicidal cues' in the general life history of the deceased such as a 'broken home', inability to form lasting social relations, general 'deviance' such as drug taking, crime and so on. Also, a history of mental instability is an important indicator of 'a potentially suicidal person'. Such evidence is not 'proof' of suicidal intent, but it is important in so far as it alerts officials to the greater likelihood of possible suicide, and may also tend to *confirm* a suspicion that suicide had taken place.

Such factors, while they are important in the enquiry into deaths which it is felt could be suicides, are not always mentioned in inquests and it is difficult to assess their influence as a source of bias upon the cases studied in this part of the research. However, in the preliminary reports of cases which were given to the coroner (and I only saw some of these) sometimes facts about the deceased's criminal record, or childhood circumstances were included; for example, in one case that the deceased was 'brought up in an orphanage', and in another, that the deceased 'had a brother who committed suicide'. In one case where the deceased had served a term of imprisonment for manslaughter, evidence was given in court from his prison record which claimed that he was 'emotionally immature and psychologically unstable'. In general, however, the London Transport study was not able to throw much light on the importance of life history in the investigation and classification of unnatural and sudden deaths, mainly because it was confined to the inquest, which is not the process of enquiry but the final stage of the process of enquiry.

Normality of Place

Coroners attach great importance to reconstructing a person's habits, and in general suicide is seen to be more likely when either the deceased was doing something out of the ordinary and/or he had no apparent reason for being where he was at the time of his death. Officials investigating deaths under trains are therefore interested in whether or not the deceased had a ticket (or a pass) and if so, had he some 'valid' and apparent reason for travelling to where his ticket suggested he would be going, for example going home from work or whatever. If the investigation suggests that the deceased had no discernible reason for being at the station at which he was killed, that is a further piece of evidence suggestive of possible suicide. In the inquests coroners were therefore very keen to try to ascertain, normally from the witness(es) giving evidence regarding state of mind, why the deceased would have been at that particular station; in short, *had he an 'appropriate reason' for being where he was at the time of his death?*

One immediate implication of this is that there is a greater possibility of deliberately 'disguised' suicides, i.e. on the part of the perpetrator, being successful. Thus an individual not wanting death to look like a suicide may, for example, 'arrange' to die behind the wheel of a car. Behind the wheel of a car, as opposed to say, lying on the floor with one's head in an oven, is an 'appropriate', or 'normal', place to be in so far as there are numerous (i.e. non-suicidal) explanations and there is less chance of such a death being investigated as a 'possible suicide'. However, more pertinent to our concerns here, particularly in cases where there is resistance to the imputation, are others who could account for the reasonableness of the deceased's presence at the place where he met his death. An example of this may be seen in the following exchange between a coroner and the father of a young man killed on the Underground.

C   Can you suggest why your son was at X station? [He did not live in London.]

W   Well . . . not really . . . But he did have several friends in London, I assume he was going to visit one of them . . . He quite often went up to London.

Having first said that he was not sure why his son was in London, the witness then suggests an explanation and this is reinforced by another statement suggesting that he was in the habit of going to London, i.e. there was nothing strange, unusual, out of the ordinary in him being there. On the other hand, if no one, or at least no one who could be traced, had seen the deceased relatively recently prior to his death, the place of his death is not necessarily 'inappropriate'. Rather 'inappropriateness' of place occurs, becomes significant regarding possible suicide, when there is evidence to suggest that the deceased 'had no reason' to be where he was at the time of his death, i.e. was breaking a habit, etc.

Significantly, deaths of London Transport employees on the Underground, and there were four in the year I undertook this research, were not recorded as suicides. I attended two such inquests (they were not included in the thirty-two cases) and it was clear from the inquests that neither death had been investigated as a possible suicide. An interesting example of a person being in the 'appropriate' place (i.e. where he ought to be, where you would normally expect him to be) when he died and thus not having his death investigated as a possible suicide occurred in the tragic Moorgate tube disaster. On the morning of 28 February 1975, a tube train did not slow down on entering Moorgate station and ploughed into the buffers killing forty-two passengers and the driver. It took several days to cut through to the front of the train to reach the bodies and during this time there was speculation as to whether the driver had been drunk. Had the driver been ill, then the 'dead man's handle' would have automatically stopped the train. The subsequent enquiry revealed that there had been no mechanical fault either in the train or the signals, and that there was no evidence that the driver had been either ill or drunk. It was only at this point, i.e. when the more apparent and obvious explanations had failed, that the possibility of suicide by the driver was considered. The subsequent report of a team headed by the Chief Inspecting Officer of Railways stated that: 'the possibility the collision was the outcome of a deliberate suicidal act cannot be ignored although there is no positive evidence to support it'.[6] It was only then seen as relevant that the driver had been described as 'a lonely man', that he was deaf in one ear and that he had been to see his doctor a few weeks before the crash and complained of being impotent. The interesting point here, regarding the notion of normality of place, is that as the driver was where he rightly belonged at the time of his death, the possibility of suicide was not even raised until a variety of alternative possibilities had been found to be invalid.

As another illustration of this point it may be useful to look briefly at a case in which resistance to the imputation of suicide and the idea of normality of place are combined.

> *Couple's ocean death fall to stay a mystery.* The mystery disappearance of a young couple at sea may never be solved. The couple were lost overboard from a luxury liner that docked in Southampton yesterday . . . Teacher Valerie Y and Raymond T vanished from the 24,000 ton *Ellinis* as it was crossing the Atlantic from Australia to England. When the liner docked the possibility of a suicide pact was firmly discounted by Valerie's 25-year-old sister Jennifer L 'Valerie had so much to live for', she said. 'She was a well balanced, sensible, happy girl, and was loving every minute of the voyage . . . We shared a cabin and there were no secrets between us. We were very close and I know she would never have taken her own life. She was getting over a broken romance which she had ended herself back home in Australia. But she was not broken hearted about it.

Valerie, a teacher in Victoria, met Raymond at a late night swimming party aboard the Ellinis eight days out of Tahiti.

Said Jennifer, 'He was a happy fun-loving guy and was the life and soul of ship-board parties. Like Valerie he had everything to live for.'

The couple were last seen alive at 5 a.m. by Jennifer, 'They came to my cabin and seemed fine', she said. 'They said they were going for a walk round the deck to watch the fabulous Pacific dawn. I never saw them again.'

There was a full scale sea search but no trace of the couple has been found.[7]

In this extract there is not only clear resistance to any imputation of suicide because the deceased people were 'happy and fun loving', etc., but also because they had a good and proper, i.e. 'appropriate', reason to be *where* they were *when* they died – they were on the deck of the ship in the early hours of the morning because they wanted to watch the dawn.

Not only, therefore, is state of mind to some extent a negotiated outcome, but also, in some cases the reasons *why* the deceased was *where* he was *when* he was is a result of negotiation. Other things being equal, suicide is less likely to be recorded if some 'good' and 'proper' reason can be established as to *why* the deceased was *where* he was at the time of his death.

Conclusions

This chapter has been concerned with how (some) deaths under trains become recorded as suicides. Verdicts of suicide are brought in, not simply when suicide is suspected, but when it is felt that suicidal intent can be proved in a court of law. For a verdict of suicide to be returned, not only must the death 'look like a suicide' from investigation of the circumstances of death, but such a verdict must also be made intelligible by the reconstruction of an appropriately suicidal biography. The London Transport study, holding the circumstances of death constant, examined some of the most important areas in the negotiated reconstruction of these biographies. It was argued that a verdict of suicide was more likely when witnesses of association giving evidence regarding the deceased's state of mind were not attempting to resist the imputation of suicidal intent, when there was evidence of mental illness or emotional problems, evidence of concern about social failure or disgrace and when the deceased died in a place where there was no good and proper reason for him to be. These reconstructions clearly reflect officials' beliefs and ideas about suicide (as well as those of other interested parties in the negotiations) but this is not to imply that the statistics are *reducible* to those beliefs and negotiations. The official statistics are rather the product of an organisational process of knowledge production which is determined by a theoretical system of concepts. The 'problem of official statistics' is not whether or not they are **'accurate' (i.e. the extent to which they reflect the real, or true,** rates(, or that they are 'unacceptable' because they are the result of human judgement, background expectancies, etc., but whether or not a correspondence has been established between the researcher's use of some set of statistics and the nature of those statistics. The present research has attempted to show that there is no such correspondence between official suicide statistics and researchers' use of them, and that their 'findings' may be more usefully explained in terms of collection procedures.

None of the four positions on official suicide rates which were outlined in Chapter 3 then appear to be satisfactory although, for practical purposes, in this case a rejectionist position is most acceptible. This is not to imply a complete acceptance of rejectionist arguments, nor does it mean that research has come down on one side or the other in a meaningless debate between advocates of 'quantitative' and 'qualitative' methodologies. One should not be either for or against the use of statistical materials, but those using them must demonstrate that they fulfil the function assigned to them.[8] In the case of suicide research, this is clearly not the case.

Part III

The Social Context of Suicidal Actions

6

Individualistic Approaches to Suicide

Suicide-Prone Populations

In Part II it was argued that official suicide rates do not provide a source of data which is suitable for the sort of suicide research typically undertaken by sociologists. In the quest for alternative approaches this chapter, under the rather arbitrary label of individualistic approaches, examines first, some avenues explored by more 'psychologically orientated' students and second, some studies by those who favour more 'interpretative' methodologies.

It is something of a paradox that while suicide has become a classic subject in sociology, relatively few sociologists have attempted research in that area and *very* few of those have either studied actual cases of suicide or attempted to extend and clarify their knowledge of the phenomenon.[1] Therefore, the sociologist wishing to know more about the subtleties and complexities of suicidal behaviour has to turn to the more 'clinically' and 'psychologically orientated' works of the 'suicidologists'.[2]

However, although psychiatrists and psychologists have generally been much more interested in the study of suicidal behaviour than sociologists, it would be a mistake to posit some fundamental distinction between sociological and psychological approaches. While the latter contains a wealth of descriptive material, some of it excellent, which is lacking in the former, the dominant body of more recent explanatory 'psychological' studies is informed by the same conception of knowledge and employs an essentially similar methodology to 'social-factor' and more recent 'sociologistic' studies of suicide rates. That is, these works are based on the ontological assumption that all concepts originate in sensory perception and the epistemological position that the *only* certain knowledge is that acquired through observation (i.e. sensory observation). In the study of suicide they have classified phenomena in terms of observable similarities ('suicidal', 'non-suicidal'; 'fatal suicidal attempt', 'non-fatal attempt', etc.) in order to discover which particular 'factors' are 'significantly' related to various suicidal populations.

In the discussion of the study of suicide rates in Chapter 2 it was noted that sociologists had tended to move away from general and abstract theories of suicide towards examining instead how particular aspects of 'social structure' were related to the volume of suicide. In the 'psychologically orientated' studies of suicide a similar movement can be discerned in which students have moved away from concern with general theories, such as those of Freud,[3] Menninger[4] and Von Andics,[5] towards the more detailed 'testing' of particular associations. Most of these associations are not connected in terms of some rational theory, as they were in Durkheim's work for example, but are pursued for their own sake, as independent bits of knowledge which it is supposed will contribute in some way to an eventual explanation of the phenomenon.[6] 'Psychologically orientated' studies of suicide have in fact produced far less 'theory' than 'sociologistic' works. Lester explains that:

> There are no psychological theories of suicidal behaviour that compare with sociological theories of suicide. No psychological theory of suicide exists that explicitly states an initial series of postulates, derives predictions from these postulates, operationalises the variables involved, and then tests these predictions in a variety of situations. Psychological theories of suicide are most often simple hypotheses of an important factor in the development of suicidal tendencies or a suggestion that a particular variable might correlate with suicidal tendencies. Such simple notions hardly merit the status of theories.[7]

The general concern of these works has been with the discovery of 'factors' that make some individuals relatively more predisposed, or prone, to suicide. In short, what is it that distinguishes the 'suicidal' from the 'non-suicidal' individual? Detailed consideration of this voluminous literature would take us too far from our present concerns, but a few examples may serve to illustrate this general point.

Many studies have examined the relationship between suicide

and mental disorders.[8] It used to be believed, as was observed in Chapter 2, that all individuals who behaved suicidally were mentally ill. Today, few students accept that assumption, rather they are interested in the extent to which particular 'illnesses' are related to suicidal actions. As Lester has observed: 'the question of whether all suicidal individuals are psychologically disturbed or not has been replaced by a different question: what are the rates of completed suicide in different diagnostic groups?'[9]

Thus students have examined samples of suicide and attempted suicide for incidence of mental illnesses;[10] they have examined the incidence of various suicidal behaviours in different diagnostic samples[11] and attempted to construct rates for particular categories such as hysterics,[12] schizophrenics[13] and psychotics,[14] and have compared 'suicidal' and 'non-suicidal' individuals within particular diagnostic categories.[15] Similarly, students have been interested to know if (and the extent to which) various phsyical illnesses predispose individuals to suicide[16] and they have also tried to find factors which distinguish 'suicidal' and 'non-suicidal' amongst the terminally ill.[17]

There has also been a good deal of work (carrying on a long tradition in the social sciences)[18] examining whether or not 'suicidal' individuals are actually different from 'non-suicidal' ones. Students have examined (without any positive results) whether or not suicide is related to physical size[19] or shape[20] and, more recently, if 'suicidals' differ physiologically from 'non-suicidals'.[21] Those social scientists who have begun to look with renewed dread upon 'physiological' and 'genetic' attempts to explain human behaviour may take some comfort from the fact that, in suicide research at least, results have proved most inconclusive.[22]

Another area of great interest to students of suicide (particularly those trained in psychology) is the extent to which 'factors' in the mind, or personality, might predispose individuals to suicide. A great deal of research was generally stimulated by Bowlby's original conclusion that disrupted relationships in childhood (particularly disruption of the mother–child relationship) made an inability to form lasting relationships in later life more probable and the prospect of anti-social or deviant conduct more likely.[23] Students of suicide have been especially interested in the possible causal relationships between childhood experiences and suicidal behaviour. Broadly, this concern has taken two main forms. While some students have attempted to reconstruct the childhood experiences of particular suicidal individuals,[24] the majority have constructed 'suicidal' and 'non-suicidal' populations and 'tested' each for incidence of 'factors' such as 'family disorganisation',[25] sibling position,[26] child-rearing techniques,[27] and most of all, parental deprivation.[28] Although such work has tended to produce contradictory and inconclusive 'findings', it is nevertheless generally accepted by researchers that childhood experiences must influence proneness to suicide.[29]

A related, but generally more psychoanalytically orientated, body of research has examined personality differences between 'suicidal' and 'non-suicidal' individuals. For a long time the empiricist-orientated school of suicide research tended to dismiss psychoanalytic theories as 'intuitive', 'subjective', 'non-scientific', etc.[30] However, in recent years it has looked with more favour upon this avenue of enquiry since students have attempted to objectify and develop quantitative 'measures' for aspects of personality, such as 'internal–external orientation (MMPI scale),[31] 'anomie'[32] 'extroversion',[33] and 'neuroticism'.[34] Some of this research has suggested that suicidal groups tend to score higher, for example, on scales of 'dependency' and 'resentment',[35] 'aggression',[36] 'neuroticism',[37] 'anxiety',[38] 'negative self attitudes',[39] 'hopelessness',[40] and 'isolation and powerlessness',[41] although there are considerable variations in both the quality and results of this research. 'One of the most interesting lines of enquiry – originally pioneered by Ringel in his classic studies of 'pre-suicidal moods'[42] – is the hypothesis that one of the major variables distinguishing 'suicidal' from 'non-suicidal' individuals is that they tend to have different structures of thought.[43] One approach to documenting and exploring this problem has been the comparison of genuine and simulated suicide notes; Shneidman and Farberow, for example, argue that genuine suicide notes are characterised by a 'destructive logic',[44] while Tripodes has suggested that genuine notes reflect a distinct type of personal disorganisation.[45]

Neuringer, one of the leading exponents of this line of enquiry, applied a number of tests to 'suicidal' and 'non-suicidal' populations in a series of studies aimed at comparing differences in the structure of thought ('cognitive coding systems').[46] He argued that 'suicidal' individuals are characterised by more dichotomous thought (greater rigidity and polarisation of extremes), less use of imaginative resources, and more constricted and 'present-orientated' thought.[47] Ringel's work – which was firmly in the European psychoanalytic tradition – was orientated towards understanding the 'phenomenology of the pre-suicidal syndrome' in which:

> A person is overwhelmed by a given situation in which he feels helpless; the circumstances involved, however, appear to be overpowering and far beyond his influence. Thus extensive spheres of life are placed outside the realm of the feasible and realizable as though they were not accessible to the person involved.[48]

Neuringer, in contrast (like most suicide researchers), is concerned with the reduction of the phenomenon to particular variables, the incidence of which can be quantitatively analysed.[49] However, despite the apparent precision of his findings, there are certain problems with Neuringer's methodology which may be briefly outlined, as similar ambiguities are to be found in a great deal of recent 'psychologically orientated' research.

First, in attempting to establish whether or not individuals had 'dichotomous thought structure', for example, Neuringer simply asked his respondents to rank a list of objects on a scale of preference ranging from 'very good' to 'very bad' (the idea being that those who express a higher proportion of extremes are those ones with greater 'dichotomous thought').[50] One problem with such a method – a problem not even referred to by Neuringer and others – is that predetermined choice categories such as 'like very much', 'quite like', etc., might have very different meanings to the individuals being studied.[51] Thus in opposition to this type of research some students have argued that, as far as possible, the observer must apprehend and appreciate the meanings of human actions in terms of the contexts in which they are made.[52] There is, however, very little of this type of work in suicide research.[53]

Second, a majority of 'psychologically orientated' studies, Neuringer's included, are carried out under experimental, or 'laboratory', conditions; that is, in the absence of laws, the experimenter controls by empirical power. However despite a superficial similarity, there are fundamental differences between the artificiality of the scientific experiment and the artificiality of the empiricist experiment. Whereas the scientist uses abstract rational laws, the empiricist *induces* from the experiment, a procedure that is not really justified as he cannot assume that his findings will be duplicated in the real world. The problem is that even if a pure causal association is found in the 'experiment', it must then be fitted back into the web of causes from which it was taken if it is to be put forward as causal explanation.[54]

Third, Neuringer does not specify whether the association between, for example, dichotomous thinking and suicidal behaviour is because they are both effects of some other cause (for example, 'loss' or 'crisis') or because there is a direct cause–effect relationship. The implication of Neuringer's works is that the latter is the case and in this context he could have attempted to reconstruct the life styles or early experiences of his subjects in order to see if particular situations, or social contexts, were commonly associated with 'dichotomous structures of thought'. Suicide researchers have by and large tended to dismiss this type of research as 'subjective', 'intuitive' and 'non-scientific' and they have confined themselves to 'hard', 'objective', 'measurable', data.[55] However, it should be noted that, despite the apparent scientific precision of many of these 'findings', in many cases assignment to various categories was solely on the basis of the subjective opinion of the observer or the subjective response of the subject.

I have been discussing here studies which have compared 'suicidal' to one or more 'non-suicidal' populations, in order to uncover the factors that make some individuals particularly 'suicide prone'. There have also been a number of complex variations on this theme: for example, comparisons between 'completed' and 'attempted' suicides,[56] 'high' and 'low' risk attempters,[57] 'high' and 'low' suicidal thinkers[58] and detailed consideration would take discussion too far from its present concern with the sociology of suicide. The more limited aim of this section has been to show that, despite apparent and superficial differences (supposedly 'internal' versus 'external' explanations, for example) the majority of 'psychologically orientated' works on suicide are in many important respects similar to social-factor and more recent sociologistic studies of suicide rates. The majority of works in both approaches tend to favour a narrow empiricism which is suspicious of both abstract theoretical analysis and studying human behaviour as essentially meaningful social action. In opposition to this latter doubt are those who object in general to the assumption that the methods of the natural sciences may be imported into the study of humanity and in particular, to attempts to quantify human actions. These students stress the differences between the natural and the cultural sciences and argue that the latter must be concerned with the use of 'interpretative' methodologies to examine the situational and problematic nature of the meanings actors give to their own conduct.[59] The following section examines some 'interpretative' approaches to suicidal behaviour.

Interpretative Approaches

Interpretative approaches are in the tradition of the Romantic vision of individuals as essentially active creators of their own social reality.[60] Human action is *purposeful*, and therefore its meaning demands to be understood in a manner which clearly differentiates it from the mere explanation of natural phenomena.[61] This general position covers a variety of differing views on how (and indeed, if ever) the study of human action can become scientific.[62] However, we may say that interpretative approaches are bound together by the conviction that attempting to explain human activity cannot be divorced from grasping the meaning that actors give to their own conduct.

While interpretative, or subjectivist, approaches provide the main alternative to traditional, positivist, hypothetico-deductive studies, other familiar sociological perspectives such as the ecological approach,[63] exchange theory,[64] and learning theory have been applied to the study of suicide. They are not considered in detail here because they do not, except in the most superficial sense, provide any alternative to 'conventional' sociological explanations. In the application of learning theory, for example, Akers argues that a person may learn that suicide offers a solution to his problems either by developing a pattern of suicide attempts or (indirectly) simply by participating in everyday life.[65] However, presumably all members of a social group learn about definitions of suicide whether or not they contemplate, or commit, such an action themselves, and when Akers comes to the crucial problem of why *some* people kill themselves he merely falls back on the familiar sociological explanation that suicide is 'related to the degree of social integration'.[66]

In the interpretative studies we may distinguish between interactionist and neo-phenomenological approaches; the former is predominantly concerned with the *reaction* of a specific respondent or general audience to the subject's critical situation, suicidal threat, etc.; whereas the latter is initially concerned with, as far as possible, trying to reconstruct the meaningful world of the suicidal *subject*.[67]

Relating interactionist theory to suicide, Rushing argues that deviant behaviour such as alcoholism, mental illness or economic failure may result in a significant loss in social interaction which, in turn, makes suicide more likely.[68] In this formulation suicide is presumably a kind of 'secondary deviance', a kind of protective response that an individual makes to societal reaction to his primary deviance.[69] The hypothesis is extremely general and, as Rushing acknowledges, 'remains to be tested'. In its present form questions such as how in some cases stigmatisation and societal rejection become translated into suicidal meanings, or why suicidal meanings can arise outside this process, remain unanswered.

Breed, in a more detailed and systematic attempt to apply symbolic interactionist theory to suicide, criticised the 'reductionist' tendencies of conventional sociological and psychological explanations; that is 'if a sociologist is talking, suicide comes from malintegration, when the psychologist or psychiatrist replies, suicide is attributed to depression, narcissism, dependency, an oral fixation, or other traits 'under the skin' of the individual'.[70] Breed argues that both approaches are incomplete, and a more satisfactory explanation would take into account the individual, the situation and his response to the situation.

From this basis Breed develops a 'suicide syndrome' consisting of firm *commitment* to a particular self concept; a *rigid* inflexibility to change; *failure*, especially in occupational roles for men and sex roles for women;[71] the response of *shame* to the role failure and *isolation*, especially from the approval of others. Breed argues that this syndrome 'proceeds well beyond the Freudian and Durkheimian notions' and in cases of suicide one would expect to find all, or most of these characteristics.[72] However it is hard to see how the 'advance' over existing 'reductionist' approaches that is claimed by Breed can be substantiated. It seems that Breed *thinks* he has made some advance over a Durkheimian notion because he depicts a crude caricature of it.

If we look at Breed's concept of 'rigidity', for example; it is claimed that this 'suggests the dynamics of "anomie" lacking in

Durkheim's formulation, and its relevance as felt by the individual; *with the society unable to supply regulation over him, he responds with excessive self regulation*'.[73] Such a criticism, however, is not really applicable; for, as the quotation above demonstrates, Breed is assuming a *division* between 'the social' (forces) and 'the individual' (forces) which is *not present in Durkheim's work* (although Durkheim has been continually 'accused' of making such a division, or separation). Rather, it is *Breed* who has explicitly claimed that there are 'external' and 'internal' explanations of suicide and that his model has reconciled the two to a certain extent. In fact he has produced, as might be imagined, a logically contradictory position. In suggesting that 'with the society unable to supply regulation over him, the individual responds with excessive self regulation', Breed is mistakenly likening 'regulation' to some totally external, *physical* force, which weakens (sociological influence) and is then replaced by self regulation (individual influence). Durkheim, however, did not see 'regulation' as some 'external' force 'out there' in the society, rather he argued that 'society' was in the consciousness of the individual.[74] Where, we may ask, does this self regulation come from? Breed says from the individual (forces), but this is inconsistent: either 'society' does influence individuals or it does not. We can argue that 'the states of different social environments' do differently 'regulate' individual actions (as seen for example by differing suicide rates), or we can argue that this is not the case and that suicide is in fact caused genetically or whatever. What we cannot argue is that 'society's influence' can be 'turned off' like a tap, and that in some way an 'individually based' regulation takes over. In contrast, Durkheim's explanation is quite consistent: 'excessive self regulation' is socially caused; that is, it is a result of the individual's relationship with his social environment, and that even if the individual becomes a recluse and apparently 'regulates' himself in isolation, 'society', so to speak, is still 'living in' him, and is thus a source of his action.

Breed's claim to have made an 'advance' on Durkheim rests on his caricaturisation of him as a social determinist. A more accurate assessment of Breed's syndrome would be to see it as an elaboration of the 'reductionist', 'psychological' or 'sociologistic' explanations of which he is critical. Breed is not providing an 'alternative explanation', rather he is attempting to reconcile the 'individual' and the 'social' by taking into account 'the individual's response to his situation'. It is providing scope for additional description. For example, it is argued that individuals who are more 'committed' to a particular self concept are more prone to suicide. We are not told, however, the sources of this commitment. It could be inherited (genetic theory), or developed through child-rearing/socialisation techniques (personality theory) or it could be more common, or typical, in particular social environments (sociological theory), etc. In so far as the student is interested in an explanation, he apparently has to fall back upon one or other of the reductionist explanations criticised by Breed. Breed's theory therefore is essentially as 'strong' or 'weak' as the ('reductionist') explanations of the causes of suicide upon which it must implicitly rest as it is unable to generate an explanatory theory. Breed's syndrome, however, might be a useful elaboration of existing explanations. It might be, for example, that some social groups, say a military society, produce individuals with a high commitment to a particular self image, that these individuals have a rigid personality, are particularly vulnerable to failure feeling great shame, they are then ostracised by a society intolerant of failure and are consequently more likely to see suicide as a solution to their problems. Such a process could be seen as an elaboration of Durkheim's notion of altruistic suicide, but Breed's model does not in itself constitute an alternative approach.

Ironically, the most persuasive illustration of the societal-response approach to suicide came not from a sociologist, but from two psychiatrists, Kobler and Stotland, who documented a 'suicide epidemic' in a mental hospital.[75] I shall examine this work in more detail in a later chapter, but it may be noted at this stage that Kobler and Stotland were particularly critical of concepts of mental illness which located the causes solely within the (deviant) individual. According to Kobler and Stotland:

> Our conception views suicidal attempts and verbal or other communications of suicidal intent as efforts, however misdirected, to solve problems in living, as frantic pleas for help and hope from other people . . . Whether the individual then actually commits suicide . . . seems to depend to a large part on the nature of the response by other people to his plea.[76]

Kobler and Stotland's work attempts to show that the 'epidemic' of suicides in the hospital was, in part, a result of the negative responses that patients received from staff to their pleas for help and hope.

Clearly, the nature of the response by others to suicidal communications, threats and attempts is a particularly important area of analysis and, in some cases, may be a crucial influence in determining whether or not a 'serious' suicidal act occurs. However, even if one accepts Kobler and Stotland's analysis of the suicide outbreak, there remains the problem of why some individuals begin to define their problems in terms of suicide, and why some still seek suicide in spite of others' caring and interested responses. Other students of suicide, adopting a neo-phenomenological approach, have sought explanations for suicide in terms of the suicidal meanings the actor 'constructs' for his suicidal action.

Jacobs, in his study of suicide notes, examines the processes whereby individuals justify to themselves the violation of the sacred trust of life.[77] For an individual to commit suicide, not only must he be faced with an intolerable situation to which death is the only solution, but he must also justify his action by defining the situation as not 'really' of his making. In this way the constraint against suicide is overcome. Jacobs illustrates this process in 'first form' notes (which reveal the entire process) and to a lesser extent in 'illness', 'forgiveness', 'accusation' and 'instruction' notes. He concludes that most people prefer the uncertainties of life to the uncertainties of death because they have defined for themselves the possibilities of things happening. However, the individual whose view of life excludes uncertainty and can only see things getting worse, 'might better try the uncertainties of death for its very ambiguity allows for either'.[78] Jacobs concludes by arguing that 'a fuller understanding of suicide will emerge only if one's procedures for "transcending the data" do not end by ignoring it, and that the "data" transcended ought to have some direct relation to the real life phenomenon under study, i.e. suicide'.[79]

Jacobs is surely right that one does not transcend the data by ignoring it, but from his analysis it is doubtful if he wants to 'transcend' the data at all, for he talks of 'explanation' being 'derived from' and 'validated' by the data and of fuller understanding of suicide 'emerging'. Explanation, however, neither emerges nor is derived from data, it has to be *invented*. By confining ourselves to the data, as Jacobs suggests we should, we become trapped in a world of descriptive particulars. In short, it is impossible to explain *without* transcending the data; though one does not explain merely by ignoring the data. In the following chapter, with reference to this point, I shall attempt to illustrate first, how researchers who have not made a detailed study of the phenomenon, particularly sociologists, have seriously misunderstood its nature on certain crucial points and second, how researchers who have 'confined' themselves to the data, i.e. the 'observable' properties of the phenomenon, have been inclined to separate things that belong together and conversely, lumped together things which are really (i.e. logically) different.[80]

Perhaps the most comprehensive set of prescriptions for an alternative sociological approach to suicide has come from Douglas.[81] Like Weber, he accepts that social action must be defined in terms of the subjective meanings of the actors involved.[82] Thus actions which appear to be identical to an observer but which have different meanings for their actors are in effect different things.[83] Consequently, Douglas argues that the researcher's first task is to study the 'situated', or concrete, meanings of suicidal actions through biographical data such as suicide notes, diaries, interviews, reports of case histories, etc.[84] This analysis will reveal certain common, or typical, 'patterns of meaning' that actors 'construct' for their suicidal actions. According to Douglas the most prevalent meanings in the western world are those involving 'revenge', 'the search for help', 'escape', 'repentance', 'expiation of guilt', 'self punishment' and 'seriousness'.[85] Suicide is to be explained in terms of the meaningful 'constructions' of actors. Of course, they do not just construct any meanings for their actions; meanings are related to social situations and are developed in terms of (or are constrained by?) generally shared values and meanings or, in Douglas's terms, general dimensions of suicidal meanings. These general dimensions of suicidal meanings in the western world indicate that there is something fundamentally wrong with the actor and his situation, which means that suicidal actions can be used reflexively by the actor to show, for example, that someone is to blame for his situation (i.e. revenge meaning).[86]

This approach, Douglas argues, can be used to study the suicide process by which he means, not the crucial stages leading up to a suicidal act, but rather studying the communications and interactions that lead to the construction of specific suicidal meanings by individuals. This analysis is not really taken very far, although

Douglas notes that threats from those who have previously attempted suicide are more likely to be given a suicidal meaning by others, and that certain situations, such as ones of great loss, are more often given a suicidal meaning.[87]

For Douglas, the detailed analysis of situated meanings of suicide is prior to the construction of more general theories; just as those engaging in social-factor studies of suicide rates argue that careful observation of statistical associations is necessary before any general theoretical considerations are possible. The only difference is what constitutes 'proper' data: whereas the positivist gathers the 'hard' data of experiment and statistics, Douglas and others stress the importance of understanding the meanings that actors give to their behaviour in their 'natural cultural habitat' as opposed to the 'fictions' obtained from the arbitrarily imposed categories of experimental and statistical studies.[88] This approach still maintains the importance of 'grounding' theory in observation and experience. Douglas makes this perfectly clear: 'we must work from clearly observable, concrete phenomena upward to abstractions about meanings in any culture'.[89]

However, such emphasis on the 'purity', or 'real-world' nature, of careful observation of actors' meanings (i.e. as opposed to data which is refracted unfaithfully through the scientists' categories) implies that such descriptions are, in some mysterious way, independent of some structuring of order by the observer. As those engaged in the debate with hermeneutics have long realised, understanding is achieved through *discourse*.[90] Any attempt to understand meaningful human activity presupposes not the 'recreation' of raw experience, but some prior understanding on the part of the observer of what is to be interpreted.[91] The idea, therefore, that the 'real world' is in some way given to us if we are diligent enough in searching out its meanings is hardly tenable.

Second, as Giddens has observed in his discussion of the construction of suicidal meanings by actors, Douglas 'holds that the causal influences involved in the events leading to suicide operate solely . . . through the actors involved in the situation'.[92] However, if suicide is to be 'explained' in terms of the meanings of those who perpetrate it, then it becomes not a unitary phenomenon, but whatever individuals make it. If one accepts this point of view,[93] then there is little point in attempting to 'classify' the social meanings of suicide in the hope of building up to a more general theory of explanation. For if suicide is not a unitary phenomenon, i.e. it is many different things albeit 'wrongly' described by the same word, then it does not constitute a field of study (particularly via case histories collected with some definition of suicide in mind) and, logically, there is no more reason why different 'suicides' should be studied together than there is for studying chalk and cheese as though they were one thing.

Clearly the subjectivists are correct in criticising the assumption of sociologists and others that suicide can be understood without recourse to the careful study of the micro-social contexts of suicidal acts; but in so far as one's goal is classification and explanation, the student must have some unitary conception of the phenomenon which transcends the specific meanings of individual actors. In short, we cannot begin to classify the meanings of a phenomenon (or anything else about it) until we have some conception of what that phenomenon *is*. The first section of the following chapter is therefore devoted to establishing a conception of the suicidal act.

Conclusions

Although students of suicide sometimes make a crude distinction between studies of suicide rates (which are seen to be 'social' in orientation) and experimental, or case-study, approaches (which are seen as 'individually' orientated), in fact many of the 'clinical' and 'psychological' studies of suicide adopt the same positivist philosophy and methodology that is employed in 'social-factor' and 'sociologistic' studies of suicide rates. The main alternative to this approach comes from various subjectivist works which stress the necessity of interpreting the subjective meanings of suicidal actions (or the responses to suicidal actions and threats) in the social contexts in which they occur. Both approaches, however, share the same positivist view of science,[94] and in both we find the conviction that 'true' knowledge can only come from experience and observation though there are considerable disputes as to how this 'true' knowledge is to be obtained. Consequently, proponents of both approaches share the same mistrust of Durkheim's highly abstract theory of suicide. However, while critics such as Jacobs are quite correct in observing that Durkheim was wrong to ignore the actor, his meanings and the immediate social context of his act, later sociologists have made little progress in that direction. Many still confine themselves to suicide rates, while most 'alternatives' are not so much 'new' approaches to the study of suicide, but are the application of favoured perspectives to the 'known facts' about suicide. In particular most sociologists who have studied suicide (through the statistics or other means) have confined themselves to completed, i.e. fatal, suicidal acts and have been working with a conception of 'suicide' which does little justice to the complexities of the phenomenon. I shall argue in the following chapter that the distinction commonly made in the sociological literature between 'successful' and 'unsuccessful' suicides is entirely misleading and that, for reasons that will be obvious as the discussion progresses, the scope of study must not confine itself to completed suicide (i.e. acts which end in death) but must include a variety of suicidal behaviours.[95]

7

Suicide and the Gamble with Death

Suicide: the Gamble with Death

Despite the shortcomings and ambiguities in Douglas's own attempts to analyse the social meanings of suicide, he was quite right to stress the importance of more descriptive material on suicidal actions, communications, etc.[1] This is not to concur with the view that there are on the one hand (legitimate) descriptions of 'real world' phenomena and on the other (illegitimate) 'fictional' descriptions obtained through predefined 'scientific', or bureaucratic, categories; but simply to make the obvious assertion that one understands more about a chosen field of study first, by reading the relevant academic literature and second, if possible, by examining the writings, statements and other communications of those whose behaviour one is seeking to explain. On both these counts most sociologists who have tried to explain suicide, including Durkheim, have a poor track record.[2] Perhaps, like the criminologists castigated by Matza, an overemphasis on cause and correction has impoverished description and appreciation.[3] Whatever the reason, the fact remains that most sociological students of suicide, whether or not they use the official statistics, work with a conception of suicide that does little justice to the complexities and subtleties of the phenomenon.

The traditional sociological perspective on suicide has always assumed (and its proponents still tend to assume) that a clear-cut distinction can be made between the 'genuine' suicidal act (i.e. aimed exclusively at death) and various other ('false') non-suicidal acts (i.e. aimed at survival) and consequently, all the major works in this perspective have confined themselves to those who have died (i.e. as a 'sample' of 'genuine' suicides).[4]

However, examination of the social contexts of suicidal acts renders such an assumption untenable. Detailed research into cases of suicide and attempted suicide has drawn attention to the hair-breadth differences that frequently separate death from survival. Ettlinger and Flordah, for example, from a study of 500 cases of attempted suicide, found that while only 4 per cent could be regarded as in any sense 'well planned', only 7 per cent were more or less 'harmless'.[5] Arieff, McCulloch and Rotman investigated a sample of attempted suicides in Chicago, and concluded that, 60 per cent could have met with death';[6] while Rains and Thompson argued that 'what appears to be a suicidal gesture can in a consider-able percentage of cases, miscarry and end in actual death'.[7] Stengel has argued that even with fatal suicidal acts, few are carried out in such a way that death is inevitable or almost inevitable.[8]

In most self-destructive (or potentially destructive) acts, there can also be found life-preserving and contact-seeking tendencies.[9] For example, most suicidal acts are initiated in a setting[10] and often employ a method that makes intervention from others quite possible,[11] and most are preceded by a number of warnings and threats from the individual regarding his intentions.[12] Often before (and sometimes after) initiating an act of potential self destruction an individual will *communicate* his intention either with direct 'threats' or with more indirect 'clues', such as 'significant passages' marked in books which are then left open in 'obvious' places, 'ambiguous' telephone calls 'just to say goodbye', 'pointedly' giving away treasured possessions and so on.[13] (The 'communicative' aspect of suicidal actions will be discussed more fully in the follow-ing chapter.) Stengel has thus argued that in many cases: 'survival, then, depends on the life-preserving and contact-seeking tendencies prevailing over those of self-destruction'.[14]

Stengel,[15] Weiss,[16] Litman and Farberow,[17] Futterman,[18] Lester and Lester,[19] amongst others, have argued that the majority of 'serious' suicidal acts are *literally gambles with death*, the outcome, or 'result', usually depending upon factors outside the individual's control. For example:

A man ingested barbiturates and went to sleep in his car which was parked in front of his estranged wife's house. A note to her was pinned on his chest indicating his expectation that she would notice him when she returned home from her date with another man. This possibility of being rescued, however, was obliterated by a dense fog which descended around midnight.

A woman took a considerable quantity of barbiturate tablets at 4.30 pm and fell asleep on the kitchen floor in front of the refrigerator. She knew that every working day for the last three years her husband came home at 5 pm and went straight to the refrigerator for a beer. There was thus a strong possibility that she would be rescued. However, her husband was delayed and did not reach home till 7.30 pm.[20]

In his study of the Polynesian island of Tikopia the anthropologist, Raymond Firth, discovered that one way in which an individual commonly attempted to resolve a seemingly irreconcilable crisis in life, usually a family problem, was for a woman to swim, and a man more often to canoe (forau), out into shark-infested waters.[21] Once news of the trip became known, rescue fleets were organised and, if the individual was saved, he was welcomed back into the society, and every effort was made to assist him with his troubles. From his observations, Firth concluded that:

[in many cases] there may not be a clear-cut line between the categories of suicide and non-suicide, between intending to kill oneself and not. There may be instead a scale of intention-cum-risk-taking. At one end, no intention to lose one's life, and little risk, at the other end, the intention to kill oneself and the most grave risk of accomplishing it, or little risk of being prevented. In between there may be many degrees of partly formed intention mixed with reluctance to die and hope of being saved, with yet enough resolution to face the risk and abide by the outcome.[22]

Social processes broadly similar in form to those described by Firth can be found in contemporary western industrial societies. An anthropological student of industrial society (unacquainted with the 'conventional' notions of suicide) might observe that: 'It is not uncommon for a minority of natives occasionally to commit a deliberate act of self damage (usually poisoning) which, while rarely inevitably leading to death, nevertheless puts their lives in great danger. If the "clues" they have left (their life lines) are recognised and acted upon, the alarm is raised and the rescue procedures (usually expert medical services) go into action and every effort is made to save the individual's life.' In this context Jensen and Petty have observed that: 'equivocation (on the part of anyone given the opportunity to intervene or interrupt will change his function from rescuer to pallbearer'.[23]

When suicidal acts are seen in their social contexts the apparently clear and 'obvious' distinction between genuine suicidal acts (where the unambiguous purpose is death) and 'false' suicidal acts, 'cries for help', 'gestures', etc., collapses. Of course, there are suicidal acts where the individual is unequivocally seeking death and there are suicidal 'gestures', etc., where the individual certainly does not want to die (termed 'pseudocide' by two authors[24] and 'parasuicide' by another)[25] but the assumption that all (or most) 'suicidal' acts will fit into either one or other of these categories – a belief apparently held still by most sociologists – is no longer valid. It appears that *most* suicidal acts are gambles with death, and *most* suicidal acts are undertaken with ambivalent intentions. This clearly has important implications for theorising about and attempting to explain suicide.

Stengel, on the basis of data gathered from decades of careful research into suicide and attempted suicide, has argued that most suicidal acts are 'Janus-faced', orientated towards *both* death and destruction and life and survival.

> Most people who commit acts of self damage with more or less conscious self-destructive intent do not want either to live or to die, but to do both at the same time – usually one more than the other . . . Most suicidal acts are manifestations of risk-taking behaviour. They are gambles. The danger to life depends on the relationship between self-destructive and life-preserving, contact-seeking tendencies, and on a variety of other factors, some of which are outside the control of the individual. *Uncertainty of outcome is not a contamination of the genuine suicidal act, but rather one of its inherent qualities.*[26] [my emphasis]

Similarly, Litman and Farberow have noted:

> Destructive behaviour is often undertaken with ambivalent feelings. The wish to die is balanced by the wish to live and to be

rescued and reunited with their loved one . . . on the other hand, in many of these gambles with death, death wins.[27]

Interviewing 106 suicide attempters, Kovacs and Beck found that fifty per cent stated that they wanted to live and die at the time of the attempt.[28] This ambivalence is then likely to be manifested in the (risk-taking) nature of the suicidal behaviour. Stengel points to the death of Marilyn Monroe as a typical example:

> She had made several dangerous suicidal attempts before. She poisoned herself with narcotics in her home during the night. There were no signs of precautions against survival. On the contrary, her housekeeper was at home and might easily have come into her bedroom before it was too late. Marilyn Monroe was found dead clutching the telephone. Shortly before she took the poison she had had a talk with her doctor over the phone telling him of her depression and anxiety. She had been in the habit of doing this, with or without suicidal threats. On many previous occasions the doctor had come to her house during the night and managed to calm her down. That particular night he tried to do so by talking to her over the phone and made various suggestions for what she could do to get over her acute depression. He was criticised for not having gone to her house on that occasion as he had often done previously.[29]

It appears, then, that we must widen the familiar question 'why do people kill themselves?' to include the broader question: 'why do so many people engage in acts of self damage which may result in death?' The sociological approach to suicide, however, has no place for risk-taking in its conception of the phenomenon.[30] Most sociological students of suicide have either slightly modified, or simply accepted Durkheim's definition of suicide as 'applied to all cases of death resulting directly or indirectly from a positive or negative act of the victim himself which he knows will produce this result. An attempt is an act thus defined but falling short of actual death.[31] Most students have used a concept of suicide built around the individual's deliberate and unambiguous attempt to die; 'attempts' are those acts which are 'accidentally' forestalled. The suicidal act may thus be separated from other acts which *may* result in death. Durkheim, for example, recognised that there were acts 'closely akin' to suicide which carried not the certainty, but the probability of death. He argued that such acts formed 'a sort of embryonic suicide', and that it was 'not methodologically sound to confuse it with completed and full suicide.[32]

The assumption is thus that there are two 'separate orders' of acts, 'proper suicides' (with which sociologists have exclusively concerned themselves) and various other acts which may 'resemble' suicides in so far as they are 'destructive' and death is possible, but are nevertheless, *not* suicides. In the following chapter I shall attempt to demonstrate why this is a mistaken distinction and *how* in fact seemingly disparate destructive behaviours can be understood and related in terms of an overall structure of suicidal actions. The implication for the 'sociologistic' approach to suicide of the foregoing observations, however, is that sociology should either include some notion of 'risk' in its conception of suicide, or, if it insists on using some kind of Durkheimian definition (and the distinction this implies between 'proper' suicide and other 'related', but 'non-suicidal' acts) then it must find some ways of confining its attentions to the minority of suicidal actions where precautions taken against discovery, or the methods used, mean that death is more or less inevitable once the act is initiated. It should be noted that this would almost certainly exclude the use of official suicide rates where many actions which would not fit a Durkheimian definition (and would not 'really' be 'proper' suicides) do in fact get recorded as suicides.[33]

In contrast, a more general conception of suicide is employed here, one which it is felt more accurately reflects the complexities and variety of forms of the behaviour. The term suicidal will be used to refer to *any deliberate act of self damage, or potential self damage, where the individual has to await an outcome, and cannot be sure of survival.*[34]

In the light of this more recent work into the social contexts of suicidal actions some writers, as noted above, have likened many suicidal acts to 'gambles with death', games of 'Russian roulette', and so on. Classification however, has been confined to the suicidal act itself and more particularly, the observable properties of the act. That is, it has been noted that some suicidal actions are more 'dangerous', or 'lethal', than others. Researchers have then attempted to develop some criteria for classifying suicidal actions in terms of 'dangerousness', 'lethality' or whatever. For example, attempted suicides may be asked, 'did you really want to die?'; or researchers might decide for themselves from the available evidence that X per cent of a sample of attempted suicides were 'serious' while the rest were not. Alternatively, the observer may classify acts in terms of the degree of 'hazard' to life (threat to bodily functions, place where the act was initiated, etc.). The sample is then divided into categories: for example, 'very dangerous', 'moderately dangerous' and 'not dangerous' and the different groups may be examined for the prevalence of particular factors and this may reveal that certain factors are perhaps, 'significantly' related to 'very dangerous' attempts but not to 'moderate' and 'not dangerous' attempts and so on. As in most suicide research, actions are classified in terms of *observable common properties* (such as degree of 'danger') and the resulting groups are thus taken to be homogeneous categories of human action suitable for comparative analysis. The search then begins for 'significant' factors, and explanations may be induced from these findings, or they may simply be advanced as more knowledge (facts) about suicide.

In a pioneering study pursuing this line of enquiry, Weiss classified a sample of attempted suicides in terms of 'expressed suicidal intent'.[35] Those who said that they had felt certain they would die as a result of their action (23) were called 'aborted successful attempts'; those who were uncertain as to whether or not they would die (113) were called 'true suicidal attempts' and finally, those who were quite sure that they would not die (20) were classified as 'suicidal gestures'. Some later studies, however, have tended to confine themselves more strictly to the overt behaviour of the subjects. Schmidt *et al.* distinguished between 'high' and 'low' level attempts by placing into the 'high' (i.e. serious) category those acts 'in which the patient has done to himself enough damage to put him in serious medical or surgical condition . . . or in which the psychiatrist was convinced that the patient had fully intended to commit suicide'.[36] Dorpat and Boswell evaluated 121 suicide attempts and rated them on an ordinal scale of 'seriousness' of attempt from one to five based on the degree of risk taken by the subject: thus a rating of one was a suicidal gesture, three an ambivalent attempt, and five a serious one.[37] Lester argued that suicidal actions should be seen in terms of a 'continuum of lethality',[38] and in an attempt to operationalise this, Worden devised a 'Risk–Rescue Rating'.[39] The 'Risk–Rescue Rating' is an attempt to 'measure' (in fact 'scale' would be a more accurate description)[40] lethality, examining what a person did to himself (i.e. the extent of the physical damage) and the context in which he did it (i.e. assessing the probability of intervention). It is based on 'external' criteria and explicitly excludes the statements, beliefs, etc., of the attempter. The scale scores five factors of 'Risk' (agent used, degree of impaired consciousness, level of physical damage, reversibility and level of treatment required) on a three point scale; and five factors of 'Rescue' (location of act, person initiating the rescue, the probability of discovery by any rescuer, accessibility of the person to be rescued, and delay until discovery) also on a three point scale. From this scale Worden divided a sample of forty attempted suicides into three categories of lethality: 'high', 'moderate' and 'low'. (Although, given the purely behavioural orientation of the research, 'Hazard–Rescue Rating' would have been a more accurate term, because the *intention* of the subject (i.e. to take a risk) is deliberately excluded from analysis.)

In general in these studies, it is hypothesised that suicidal actions differ in terms of lethality, risk or whatever and that the different categories of attempts may be usefully compared. Thus, for example, in their comparison of high and low-level attempts, Schmidt *et al.* found that 'high-level' attempters tended to be older, had different psychiatric diagnoses, and different life problems.[41] Dorpat and Boswell found high attempts to be positively associated with males, age and psychotic diagnosis.[42] Such findings tend to confirm some of the factors which often distinguish 'completed' from attempted suicides, for example that more men than women kill themselves, but that more women attempt suicide, that the peak age for suicide is 55–64, and for attempted suicide 24–44.[43]

There has, however, been relatively little attempt to explain the risk-taking aspect of suicidal actions,[44] and it is to consideration of this problem that the present work now turns. However, to state the problem in this way is to assume *neither* that *all* suicidal acts are manifestations of risk-taking behaviour, *nor* that one must devise one set of explanations for risk-taking suicidal actions and another for completely purposive acts. The purpose here is to develop a theoretical framework which attempts to explain the relationships between varying types of suicidal behaviour. While the type of research outlined above has been concerned with trying to scale the 'danger' or 'lethality' of suicidal acts, which is then taken as a reflection of the degree of risk, the position taken here is that a classificatory scheme of suicidal actions (or any other type of behaviour) must account for the meaning the act has for the actor. While the actor's subjective meaning for his action is not the cause of that action, one does not reach those causes merely by 'bypassing' the actor. Laing has argued that behaviour which society labels as 'mental illness' may also be understood as 'a special strategy that a person invents to try to live in an unliveable situation'.[45] Similarly, suicidal actions may also be usefully conceived of in one sense as 'strategies of escape' from unliveable situations. Theories of suicide must identify and explain these strategies.

The Game of Suicide

It was argued in the previous section that uncertainty of outcome is a common feature of most suicidal acts, many of which may usefully be likened to an *ordeal,* using the word in its medieval, ritual sense; a dangerous test, or trial, to which the individual submits himself (or is submitted to), the outcome of which is accepted as a 'judgement'.[46] Stengel, the first student to develop this idea in relation to suicidal actions, observed that it is not uncommon for survivors of suicidal attempts, when asked whether or not they really wanted to die, to reply that they 'didn't know', 'didn't care' or wanted to find out if they were 'meant to go on living'.[47] For example:

> A 40-year-old male schizophrenic left home in a state of depression. He was brought home by the police; though watched, he slipped away and locked himself in the lavatory. He opened the door only after his wife had implored him to do so. He had a towel round his neck soaked in blood; there were two long cuts under the skin. He declared that he had made the suicide attempt 'as an act of faith, to prove whether God wanted him to live or die'.[48]

One of the most interesting observations provided by studies of suicide attempters, especially in long-term 'follow-up' or 'cohort' studies, of which there have been several, is how rare it is for survivors of even the most dangerous attempts to try to kill themselves again at the first opportunity.[49] Re-attempts, certainly in the short run, and surprisingly often in the long run, are relatively rare.[50]

'Survival', Stengel has observed, 'is usually accepted without demur'.[51] For example, Lonnqvist and his associates found that from a sample of a hundred attempted suicides, only four had committed suicide eight years later, giving an annual suicide risk of 0.5 per cent.[52] Similar relatively low rates have been observed in other follow-up studies;[53] while Dorpat and Ripley, from a review of the available literature on follow-up studies, estimated that only between 10–20 per cent of attempters go on to commit suicide at some later time.[54] In many cases this may be due to the 'appeal quality'[55] of the suicidal act actually changing others' attitudes towards the attempter and producing increased sympathy and concern for him.[56] Indeed, some students have argued that *all* suicidal acts are appeals, and the determining factor as to whether or not they are repeated is the response of others to the 'cry for help'.[57] However, this is a view I would wish to argue against, as I shall show later in the chapter, because there are some suicidal attempts which simply do not fit this pattern. In some cases simply having survived a 'death' in 'coming through' an ordeal may provide the individual with some feeling of rebirth, or renewal – a chance to start again psychologically. As I shall illustrate, 'surviving suicide' may well produce significant changes in an individual's orientation to life, even in cases where there is no direct 'appeal' to others.

There are many reports illustrating that surviving some traumatic and dangerous ordeal (even if the individual did not deliberately put himself at risk) can give rise to feelings of life being renewed. In some cases subjects express feelings of having 'died' and then emerged reconstituted. For example, interviewed in a documentary about Nazi war crimes, a survivor from a concentration camp said: 'I bless every day that I continue to live. Every day is profit. I could say that I am 27 years old. The years before don't count. I was not alive in the camp. I died, then I was reborn.' It is part of my argument that such observation about 'coming through' an ordeal provides insight into the ordeal character of suicidal actions, and the ways in which they are subsequently evaluated by the survivors.[58]

Rosen interviewed seven of only ten known survivors of jumps from San Francisco's Golden Gate and Oakland Bay bridges and found that all of them had 'experienced transcendence and a spiritual rebirth phenomenon'.[59] One explained that:

When I hit the water I felt a vacuum feeling and a compression like my energy displaced the surface energy of the water. At first everything was black, then grey–brown, then light. It opened my mind – like waking up. I was very restful. When I came up above water, I realised I was alive. I felt reborn. I was treading water and singing. I was happy and it was a joyous occasion. It affirmed my belief – there is a higher spiritual world . . . in that moment I was filled with new hope and purpose of being alive.[60]

Often a decision to go on living and the realisation that death provides no 'answer' to one's problems results, not from changed life circumstances, but from a conviction that a 'death' has in fact taken place and that 'someone different' has arisen from the ashes, that the 'self' that the individual sought to kill has indeed 'died'. Rebirth may not necessarily have been sought by the act, but, as in other 'non-suicidal' ordeals, may have followed as a *consequence* of survival. Another Golden Gate Bridge survivor recalled that:

It was strange because I thought suicide was the right thing to do. Before I jumped I was agnostic – no real belief in God. After the jump I became fully Christian; I believed in God and Jesus Christ. Christ became a living reality for me. It is still going on. I'm now in a period of painful growth – of being reborn.[61]

Of course, these are 'spectacular' and most unusual survivals, and in many cases the experience of having died and been reborn may be far less optimistic and exhilarating, but none the less equally profound. A more detailed example is provided by Alvarez's account of his own suicide attempt and what followed:

[Suicide] was the one constant focus of my life making everything else irrelevant, a diversion. Each sporadic burst of work, each minor success and disappointment, each moment of calm and relaxation seemed merely a temporary halt on my steady descent through layer and layer of depression, like a lift stopping for a moment on the way down to the basement. At no point was there any question of getting off or of changing the direction of the journey. Yet despite all that, I never quite made it.[62]

The row which led to his wife's departure and precipitated the attempt seemed to him merely an 'excuse' for the act. He swallowed forty-five sleeping tablets and, although there was the possibility of rescue, it was clearly a very serious attempt with the odds weighted heavily in favour of death. Writing about the attempt ten years later he said that he had never contemplated suicide since. This was not because his life situation had altered dramatically for the better – indeed, his marriage finally broke up a few months after the attempt – nor because he found some 'fulfilment' in some hitherto neglected sphere of his life, but rather because *he* came to see *himself* in a different way, as a different person. No longer having the same 'high' expectations from life, he was no longer vulnerable to the same frustrations and despair. Thus when his marriage did break up, although he went through 'the expected motions of distress', in 'his heart he no longer cared'. He reflects that:

> The truth is, in some way I had died. The over-intensity, the tiresome excess of sensitivity and self-consciousness, of arrogance and idealism, which came in adolescence and stayed on and on beyond their due time, like some visiting bore, had not survived the coma. It was as though I had finally, and sadly late in the day, lost my innocence . . . as the months passed I began gradually to stir into another style of life, less theoretical, less optimistic, less vulnerable. I was ready for insentient middle age . . .
>
> It seems ludicrous now to have learned something so obvious in such a hard way, to have had to go almost the whole way to death in order to grow up. Somewhere I still felt cheated and aggrieved, and also ashamed of my stupidity. Yet, in the end, even oblivion was an experience of a kind. Certainly nothing has been quite the same since I discovered for myself, in my own body and on my own nerves, that death is simply an end, a dead end, no more, no less. And I wonder if that piece of knowledge isn't in itself a form of death. After all, the youth who swallowed the sleeping pills and the man who survived are so utterly different that someone or something must have died. Before the pills was another life, another person altogether, whom I scarcely recognise and don't much like – although I suspect that he was in his priggish way, far more likeable than I could ever be.[63]

For Alvarez, the feeling of having emerged from death a different person followed as a consequence of having 'experienced', yet survived, death. However, in other cases – the ones I shall be concerned with in this section – the desire to 'experience' and 'come through' death, to renew one's life by risking it, seems to be a conscious motive, or precipitating cause, of the act. Death is summoned and challenged in order that life may continue. Such actions are literally confrontations with death. However, as there are numerous non-suicidal motives for confronting death, I have used elsewhere the more precise term 'thanatation'.[64]

It is important at this stage to make two conceptual distinctions. First, it is important to stress that discussion here is about 'risk-taking' actions. 'Risk' is used here to refer to the individuals *subjective* awareness that he is gambling with death, risk being defined by Cohen as 'embarking on a task without being certain of success'.[65] This may be contrasted to 'hazard' which will be used to refer to the degree of *objective*, or actual, danger into which the individual places himself. Although, as Stengel has said, most suicidal acts are 'characterised by uncertainty of outcome' (i.e. hazard), we cannot simply assume that they are necessarily manifestations of 'risk-taking' behaviour (though it may be strongly inferred). Second, in this context, I shall make a distinction between suicidal acts where the 'risk', or the 'gamble with death', is a consequence of, or contingent upon some other purpose (for example, communicating unhappiness), and those where it is central to the meaning of the act. Thanatation refers to these latter types of acts.

In many suicidal acts, whether or not the individual dies, he will have *communicated* to others something of the extent of his misery and unhappiness.[66] In thanatation, however, the 'payoff' is *simply* the thrill, the wonder of still being alive. The gamble with death is merely a *characteristic* of most suicidal acts, arising out of the unhappy individual's desire to be both dead and yet alive; but in thanatation, the gamble with death is the very essence of the act. In most suicidal gambles others, usually significant others, are given the opportunity to 'rescue' the individual by recognising and acting upon 'suicidal clues'. Thanatation, in contrast, is usually a more 'self-contained' and private act and typically others are excluded from possible intervention. The individual is not gambling upon others' sensitivity and responsiveness, but playing a 'game' of 'pure' chance.[67]

Such action may, for example, enable an individual to 'escape', not necessarily from life itself, but from the clutches of boredom and fatigue with life. Life is risked in order that it may be confirmed and

reinvested with meaning and purpose. Graham Greene, in his autobiography, describes how, in his youth, feelings of suffocating boredom and inertia were at least temporarily dispelled by playing
Russian roulette.

> Now with the revolver in my pocket I thought I had stumbled on
> the perfect cure. I was going to escape in one way or another . . .
> The discovery that it was possible to enjoy again the visible world
> by risking its total loss was one I was bound to make sooner or
> later.
>   I put the muzzle of the revolver to my right ear and pulled the
> trigger. There was a minute click, and looking down the chamber
> I could see that the charge had moved into the firing position. I
> was out by one. I remember an extraordinary sense of jubilation,
> as if carnival lights had been switched on in a dark drab street. My
> heart knocked in its cage and life contained an infinite number of
> possibilities. It was like a young man's first successful experience
> at sex – as if amid the Ashridge beeches I had passed the test of
> manhood . . .
>   This experience I repeated a number of times. At fairly long
> intervals I found myself craving for the adrenalin drug, and I took
> the revolver with me when I returned to Oxford.[68]

Thanatation may also serve as a way of exorcising death and, in
the short run at least, give the individual a feeling of having con-
quered it. The poet, Sylvia Plath, for much of the later part of her
life experienced the feeling of being stalked by death. She survived
one serious suicide attempt in her youth, and years later, confessed
to a friend that a recent car 'accident' she had survived had been
quite deliberate. She had driven off the road knowing full well that it
might kill her. However, having survived, she was then able to write
freely about the act because it was behind her.[69] The car crash, like
the previous suicidal attempt, became 'another death' that she had
'come through'. She felt that death was something that had to be
confronted periodically, and Alvarez observes how one of her
poems captures the feeling of triumph in her survival:

> And I a smiling woman
> I am only thirty
> And like the cat I have nine times to die.[70]

For Plath, being alive meant to survive, but in turn survival incurred a debt to death which had to be paid every decade. Alvarez writes of Plath that: 'In order to stay alive as a grown woman, a mother and a poet, she had to pay in some partial, magical way with her life . . . Suicide was not a swoon into death . . . it was something to be felt in the nerve ends and fought against, an initiation rite qualifying her for a life of her own.'[71]

Greene describes how, when the 'drug' of Russian roulette had worn off, a series of hazardous expeditions served to stave off the same feelings of boredom.

A kind of Russian roulette remained too a factor in my later life, so that without previous experience of Africa I went on an absurd and reckless trek through Liberia; it was fear of boredom which took me to Tabasco during the religious persecution, to a leproserie in the Congo, to the Kikuyu reserve during the Mau-Mau insurrection, to the emergency in Malaya and to the French war in Vietnam. There, in those last three regions of clandestine war, the fear of ambush served me just as effectively as the revolver from the corner cupboard in the life-long war against boredom.[72]

The fact that, for Greene, these dangerous expeditions functioned periodically to renew commitment to life, as the games of Russian roulette had once done, suggests a link between certain 'risk-taking' suicidal actions and other dangerous, or 'daredevil', pursuits not normally associated with suicide.[73] That is, there may be important similarities in the *form*, though not necessarily the *content*, of these social actions.[74] The small community of Formula One motor-racing drivers, for example, does not have the sort of life style normally associated with suicidal situations – despair, isolation, disenchantment with life, etc. On the contrary, they urgently, almost obsessively, believe that life must be lived to the full, to its 'outer limits'. This 'living on the edge' involves periodic confrontations with danger and the possibility of death. Because of this, life takes on a heightened intensity. Jackie Stewart, three times World Champion and winner of a record twenty-seven Grand Prixes, claims that: 'People who are allowed to live life to its outer limits are a blessed group. I think I have seen more corners and crevices of life than almost anyone my age. So many highs and so many lows.'[75] By living 'on the limits' of life more experiences are somehow crammed into each moment. Stewart talks of having to 'speed up his capacity to enjoy life' since he became a motor-racing driver: 'The pleasure is just that I perhaps get greater pleasure out of one day's holiday than some people get out of ten'.[76] People who live 'on the limits' tend to develop a philosophy arguing that it is through the confrontations with death and danger that life is realised.[77]

This is not to imply some agreement either with those who see risk taking as the manifestation of some 'death instinct',[78] or with those who claim that 'dangerous risk taking' represents some homogenous category of action. With reference to the latter point, Shneidman has lumped together the Russian roulette player, the inexperienced pilot and ledge walker under the category 'death darers',[79] while Neuringer has used the term 'probability suicides' to include activities such as Russian roulette and driving a racing car.[80] This is clumsy reasoning, for the notion of a 'suicidal' act becomes generalised out of useful existence. There are important differences between the suicide (even the thanatationist) and the daredevil that cannot be overlooked. For the former, the 'payoff' as has already been suggested, is simply the *intrinsic* satisfaction of survival, whereas for the latter there are also *extrinsic* satisfactions, such as demonstrating skill and courage, public acclaim, financial reward and so on. (Indeed, for some daredevils, certain criminals for example, risk may not be so much sought after, as endured for the sake of financial gain.) A second important distinction is that during what Goffman has called the 'determination phase' of the action,[81] the daredevil, though certainly 'riding his luck' (the racing driver, for example, is dependent upon the mechanical efficiency of his car), is also exercising skill and judgement and thus has some *control* over his situation. An individual engaging in a suicidal act, however, makes a *total* commitment to chance, and once the 'play' has begun, can only *passively* await the outcome.[82] (Those cases where an individual having initiated an act of self-damage with suicidal intent then intervenes himself and calls for help may, if the intervention is successful, be referred to as self-aborted suicides, and if unsuccessful, failed aborted suicides.) We may say then in summarising this point that the daredevil engages in a *contest* and the suicide in a *gamble*.

However, despite these important distinctions, it is still possible to gain some useful insights into the ordeal character of suicidal actions by examining the experiences of those who periodically and quite deliberately seek out danger and 'lay their lives on the line'. In both contests and gambles 'something of value to be staked comes up for determination'.[83] For both daredevil and suicide, the stake is life itself. People who habitually engage in dangerous pursuits often explain their activities in terms of a desire to 'test' themselves. The notion of pushing one's skill, courage and endurance to their very limits as a test of 'character' is constantly recurring in the writings and comments of racing drivers, stuntmen, round-the-world yachtsmen and mountaineers.[84] Christopher Brasher, for example, wrote of the mountaineer, the late Dougal Haston:

> After all these years and from amongst all the many thousands of words that were spoken into the homes of millions of viewers that weekend in August 1967, one sentence only remains in my memory and I seem to recollect it was the only sentence spoken by Dougal. I asked him why he climbed and he said: 'To know myself.'[85]

But why are such 'extreme tests', or 'dangerous games' needed to provide an answer to the question: Who am I? Some insight into this question has been provided by an article on sport in which Ashworth argues that games can be conceived of as 'idealised forms of social life which establish identity with a consensual certainty that in social life itself is not always possible'.[86] For an individual to find out what he is necessarily involves comparisons with others. Thus human identities develop and bring each other into being, self knowledge deriving from knowledge of others. For example, he is rich because he has more money than others, but the others must be there with their 'lack' of money for his 'richness' to come into being. However, while individuals are required to make such comparisons in order to try and establish identity, in western society at least, such comparisons can rarely be accepted as 'definitive of being'. For example, a poor man may accept that acquiring wealth is evidence of 'intelligence', but he may well be reluctant to admit that *he* is less 'intelligent' than a wealthy man and claim that he did not have the same 'opportunities' as the rich man:

If this is the case, then how do people compare themselves and thus know themselves at all? Western thinking puts man in a terrible dilemma of identity. Western society requires the individual to make comparisons, indeed it is only via comparisons that identity is acquired and sustained at all, but it creates conditions which render comparison well nigh impossible.[87]

Scientists resolve this dilemma by experimentation carried out under controlled conditions and Ashworth argues that the game can be compared to a simulated experiment, 'an experiment in living that enables men to see what they are under conditions that satisfy the comparative, experimental method'. In the game all start equal, rules are agreed upon, and 'outcomes can therefore be mutual and not individual'.[88]

In a sporting match it is essential that the outcome is not known in advance. A 'test' must be involved. Knowing beforehand makes it unnecessary to gain knowledge. Being uncertain, however, makes a test essential, and the 'outcome' is taken to 'prove' something that was not 'known' before. Sport, therefore, may be conceived of as 'symbolic dialogue with the universe', and in western society it 'symbolises the strict requirements of how a dialogue should be conducted'.[89]

Ashworth's notion of sport as 'symbolic dialogue with the universe' may also be usefully applied to other dangerous *contests*. Goffman has argued that by voluntarily exposing themselves to 'fateful moments' individuals gain information about their own character.[90] Going 'where the action is' is a way in which people demonstrate (to themselves and others) courage, gallantry, composure, etc., by trying to manage 'fateful moments'. The more uncertain an individual becomes about the 'results' of his attempts to establish identity with some certainty, then the more likely it is that he will resort to some 'extreme' form of 'game', or 'test'. The type of action referred to earlier as thanatation may also usefully be conceived of as a 'game', but one that has gone beyond 'conventional games'; in fact the last possible 'game' left to the individual. Those who engage in such suicidal confrontations are in the common state where the uncertainty they are faced with cannot be resolved *unless* such risks are taken. Conventional means of validation (including contests) have proved non-revelatory, and no longer can anything in *this world* validate what they are. Therefore, something *outside* the self is consulted in an *ordeal* to determine whether or not that self has any validation in life: 'the world', 'fate', 'chance', 'luck', or 'God' is *provoked* into making a decision one way or the other. As noted above, it has been observed that sometimes survivors of suicidal attempts, when asked whether or not they intended to kill themselves, make statements (such as 'I wanted to see what would happen', or 'I wanted to find out if God wanted me to live') which express the desire to *gain knowledge* about one's self. In such cases individuals – usually privately – expose themselves to death thus relinquishing, not life, but their hold on life, their 'say' as to whether or not they go on living, in order to find out *whether or not they are meant to go on living*. It was observed earlier that the 'outcome' (of most suicidal acts) is usually accepted in the short run; it is hypothesised that in thanatation the outcome would *always* be accepted in the short run, because an 'answer' has been provided. The idea of a 'test' to find out whether or not one is meant to go on living, is nicely illustrated in a passage (apparently based upon a real life incident) from Hardy's *Jude the Obscure*:

> Jude . . . came to a large round pond. The frost continued though it was not particularly sharp, and the larger stars overhead came out slow and flickering. Jude put one foot on the edge of the ice, and then the other: it cracked under his weight; but this did not deter him. He ploughed his way inward to the centre, the ice making sharp noises as he went. When just about the middle he looked round him and gave a jump. The cracking repeated itself; but he did not go down. He jumped again, but the cracking had ceased. Jude went back to the edge, and stepped upon the ground.
>
> It was curious, he thought. What was he reserved for? He supposed he was not a significantly dignified person for suicide. Peaceful death abhorred him as a subject, and would not take him.[91]

It was observed above that classification here would not be in terms of the 'dangerousness' or 'lethality' of the behaviour, but rather in terms of the common logical properties of the actor's 'strategy'. Thus the common feature of the acts that I have called thanatation is not some necessary and objective level of 'danger' or whatever, but that the individuals who engage in such acts are faced with an *uncertainty about themselves* which is (a) intolerable, and

(b) can only be resolved by a 'judgement' from death. All such actions are by definition 'risk taking' and they are quite likely to be 'hazardous' (in the sense that the individual might die); but they are not necessarily 'characterised by uncertainty of outcome' (i.e. from an observer's point of view). They may be quite lethal as the following example illustrates.

> Devoted churchgoer Denys Christian believed that God would save him in a leap from his thirteenth floor flat . . . So despite warnings from his wife he went ahead with the ultimate test . . . and died. [His wife] told an inquest at Southwark, London, yesterday that her 26-year-old husband stepped on to a balcony and balanced on a six inch ledge . . . She said: 'Four days before his death he said he would jump to prove his faith in God. He told me nothing would happen to him' . . . A parishioner friend said 'We never thought he would go to these lengths to prove his faith.'[92]

Conclusions

Recent research has revealed that most suicidal acts are characterised not by the certainty of death, but by the possibility of death, and the majority of these are 'risk-taking' acts. The position taken here is that such actions *are* suicidal. Most research in this area has attempted to distinguish between 'genuine' (serious) attempts, 'ambivalent' (moderate) attempts and 'gestures' (not serious) or have used some logically similar scheme. Two interpretations are put upon such research; either it is argued that one is dealing with two separate but overlapping populations (those who die and those who survive),[93] or that suicidal acts should be classified in terms of some continuum of 'danger', 'seriousness' or whatever.[94] In both cases, however, types of suicide are derived solely from the observable properties of the acts themselves, and students in this field have taken it for granted that acts which look the same (for example, 'moderately serious' attempts) are the same and are also different from acts which look different (for example, 'very serious' attempts). As these types of suicide are different, they require different sorts of explanations. One of the problems with such an approach is that the more 'facts' that are discovered about suicide, the more explanations must be devised to account for them. To question such an approach, however, is neither to underestimate the value of such careful descriptive work nor to imply that one should instead play 'eureka games' and search for the *one* key cause of all suicidal actions. The recent rich and detailed literature on suicidal actions has clearly shown that the phenomenon is far more complex and varied than many of the early 'one cause' theorists imagined. Explanation has to transcend descriptive particulars, and the view taken here is that rather than confining analysis to suicidal behaviour (and asking for example, was it fatal or non-fatal?, 'serious' or not?, etc.) explanation must incorporate the meanings of the social actors. Such an approach has been attempted here and it has been argued that while Greene, Plath and Christian all had different conscious motives for engaging in suicidal actions (escape from boredom, desire to 'defeat' death and need to prove faith in God), all – as I have tried to show with the concept of thanatation – were engaging in the same type of social action; they were in a common state of mind where their existence in the world could *only* be confirmed in this way. More importantly, had their actions been classified in terms of 'danger' or 'lethality', etc., they would have been placed into *different* categories because, in terms of that criterion, their actions all *appear* different (Christian was virtually certain to die, Plath had a high probability of dying, while Greene had a six to one chance of survival).

Researchers such as Worden who quite explicitly do not concern themselves with 'the phenomenology of the attempter' and adopt a behaviourist position,[95] nevertheless at some time have to impute meaning to human actions (either explicitly or implicitly) or their results are literally '*meaningless*'. In the study of this area of suicide researchers have simply assumed that in 'dangerous attempts' the individual 'really wants to die', in 'moderate' attempts he is 'ambivalent' and so on. The logic of the argument offered here suggests, in contrast, that the assumption of a clear-cut correspondence between 'risk' and 'hazard' is unwarranted and that, while actors' meanings, or 'motives', are not 'explanations' of their conduct, at the same time those meanings and experiences cannot merely be 'reduced' to the subjects' behaviour.[96]

8

The Ordeal and the Sacrifice

A Structural Approach to Suicide

This chapter is concerned with the development of an alternative social-psychological approach to suicide. Typically sociological approaches have been associated with the analysis of suicide rates, while the few alternative critical studies have tended to be neo-phenomenological, or 'interpretative', thus reflecting a more general debate in the social sciences between 'positivism' and 'subjectivism'. What is common to both parties in this dispute is the acceptance of a positivist account of natural science, the point at issue being whether or not it is applicable to the study of the social world. In contrast, the structural approach developed here is based upon a *realist* view of natural science which rejects the positivist ontology of nominalism, its empiricist epistemology and its general belief in an absolute unity of scientific method. For the realist, science involves the explanation of observable phenomena through the discovery of underlying, unobservable structures and causal processes.[1]

Of course, descriptions of philosophies of science in the theoretical literature usually refer to idealised typifications to which, in practice, authors commit themselves to a greater or lesser extent. In this context the analysis of *Suicide* is particularly interesting for throughout the work there is an unresolved tension between positivism (expressed for example in Durkheim's 'inductive' methodological exhortations and the nature of claims of statistical 'proof' for his theory)[2] and the realism which is to be found in his theoretical analysis of suicide rates.[3] As I have shown earlier, the students who 'rediscovered' *Suicide* for American sociology emphasised its positivist possibilities for generating 'useful' hypotheses about the relationship between 'social' factors and 'individual' action. From the positivist point of view Durkheim has been widely criticised as 'unscientific', 'metaphysical', 'essentialist', etc., for positing the *existence* of unobservable entities, and even his 'followers' have been inclined to 'explain away' his realism as the product of unnecessary and aggressive polemics. Analysis from a realist standpoint, however, gives more or less the opposite view of an essentially scientific theory of suicide handicapped by a crude, empiricist epistemology. That is, it is not 'unscientific' for Durkheim to try to show that the presence of unobservable phenomena may be established by reference to the observable phenomena they generate; but for Durkheim then to claim that society exists (and is constraining) because we can *experience* its effects is quite inconsistent with his general theoretical position.[4]

In *Durkheim's* analysis of suicide there is no absolute and necessary relationship between suicide and objects,[5] but rather a rational relationship of a universal kind between suicide and interrelated states of meaning. It follows, therefore, that no specific empirical association (such as a low suicide rate in Protestant England) can refute the theory; but by the same criterion, empirical associations *in themselves* cannot 'prove' the theory. The theory is dependent on its logical, rational relationship to observable phenomena. This does not make it 'unscientific', or 'irrefutable' (as I shall try to show in the following section), but it does differentiate it from positivism.[6] While I argued the case in Part I for a realist interpretation of *Suicide*,[7] there are those who quite wrongly apply the term 'positivist' to any student interested in making the study of society scientific.[8] However, whether or not we actually end up labelling Durkheim a 'positivist' is of secondary interest to one of my main concerns in this work which has been to show how Durkheim's approach to suicide differed in important respects from those of later students. It is surely curious that in *Suicide*, supposedly one of the founding works of modern positivist sociology, we do not find, for example, the fact–value dichotomy that characterises positivism; indeed Durkheim, like some of his statistical predecessors, was concerned with establishing a science of moral order; nor do we find in *Suicide* the positivist ontological distinction between theoretical and observational categories, while we do find Durkheim concerned with the analysis of essentially meaningful, as opposed to physicalistic or purely behavioural, social life. Nevertheless, in

English-speaking sociology at least, the positivist interpretation of Durkheim (and *Suicide* in particular) persist,[9] and one has to look to the French structuralists, particularly Lévi-Strauss who declares himself to be in the 'Durkheimian tradition' and acknowledges a specific debt to Mauss,[10] for the development of some of the realist possibilities in Durkheim. However, while realism presupposes some notion of structure, a structural approach does not imply a commitment to realism. Both British anthropology[11] and American structure-functionalism,[12] for example, employed the notion of structure in a positivist sense in that they sought to examine the invariant relations between the observable parts of a social system. A realist approach, in contrast, looks for the structures that lie behind observable phenomena,[13] and I shall use the term 'structure' here to refer to this latter approach. While Durkheim is normally associated with (positivist) structure-functionalism, his work has much more in common with modern structuralism. Whilst acknowledging the considerable gulfs amongst structuralists themselves (including whether or not there is a structuralist approach as such)[14] and the reservations some of its most able proponents have against both Durkheim's 'globalism'[15] and his 'collective consciousness',[16] there are important common elements in the work of both Durkheim and modern structuralists on which I shall attempt to build a structural theory of suicide.

First, there is the ambition to make objective, law-like statements about a *meaningful* and essentially ideal social world, which distinguishes both Durkheim and the structuralists from subjectivists (who are interested in meaning but exclude science) and the positivists (who are interested in science but exclude, or have difficulty in accounting for, the meaning of behaviour). Second, there is the ontological assumption that the explanation of observable phenomena involves the search for 'deep', or underlying, structures which are discovered not by observation, but by the theoretical work of logic and deduction. Thus Chomsky's notion of 'deep structure' to explain linguistic 'competence', for example, was the product of theoretical reflection, not observation and induction.[17] Third, Durkheim and structuralists study social phenomena not as a mass of separable events and sequences, but in terms of general theoretical structures whose concepts express the *relations* between constituent elements (often developed in terms of binary opposition and association).

Both Durkheim and some modern structuralists are sometimes accused of failing to give sufficient weight to human subjectivity.[18] To concur with this view is not to imply acceptance of the various empiricist notions of subjectivity, but merely to state that the rules, or laws, of social life, whether we locate them in collective social life, the organising properties of the human mind or wherever, unlike the laws of nature, operate only through the conscious, intentional and reflective activity of individuals. It seems reasonable to suppose, therefore, that any student of human behaviour should, as far as possible, examine both the intentions of social actors and the details of the social contexts in which they act, for it is precisely these that we seek to explain.[19] In this respect the present work has criticised Durkheim and most other sociological students of suicide for assuming they could by-pass this area of explanation and consequently mistaking the nature of many suicidal acts and ignoring, for example, the risk-taking component of suicide.

From this point of view our approach to suicide should involve the study of the contextualised meanings of suicidal actions as they appear to the actor. However, it is argued here that this understanding comes not from some sort of attempt at 'immersion' in, or 'reconstruction' of, the 'lived-in world' of the subject, but by attempting to explain his particular experiences in concrete situations in terms of more general meanings of suicide developed through theoretical abstraction.[20]

In this context I shall distinguish between the *performance* of suicide, which refers to the communications, situation, behaviour, etc., of the individual actor and the *production* of suicide, which relates to a structural concern with the discovery of basic, latent rules of suicidal behaviour which produce in individuals a necessary and sufficient cause for suicide.[21] With this ultimate aim in mind, I shall develop an abstract model of suicidal actions which, like Durkheim's, is exhaustive in so far as it attempts to account for all suicidal behaviour.

Most classificatory schemes in suicide research derive types of suicide solely from the *behavioural* properties of the act and, as we have seen, distinguish for example, between degrees of 'seriousness', or 'lethality'. Other students are more committed to the actor's subjectivity, and thus Shneidman, for example, basing his classification on the actor's meaning, distinguished between suicide as 'communication', 'revenge', 'fantasy crime', 'unconscious flight', 'magical revival', or 'rebirth and reconstitution';[22] while Klopfer has argued that students should distinguish between the following phenomenological dimensions of suicidal acts: collective or individual suicide, passive or active suicide, sincere or attention-getting and planned or impulsive suicide.[23] Both types of classification, however, are derived from 'observable' properties of the suicidal act, and the more observations that are made the more concepts have to be invented to describe them. Whereas early studies tended to have very simple classifications, for example between completed and attempted suicides, in more recent studies classificatory schemes have become increasingly complex.[24] Shneidman explains that the researcher has to choose between oversimplified classification and 'complex, but more meaningful classification'.[25] The complexity of the real world must apparently be reflected by the complexity of the student's conceptual scheme. In such an approach data orders theory, with new concepts being invented for 'new' discoveries and each one explaining, or describing, correspondingly less.[26]

In contrast, the conceptual scheme developed here was derived not from observation, but from an abstract theoretical structure which, similar to Durkheim's, is based on an equilibrium notion of 'protection' from suicide resulting from the balance of the binary opposition of interrelated states of meaning. Whereas most theorists have tended to see deviance as caused by 'alien' traits in societies or individuals, Durkheim saw both 'deviant' and 'normal' behaviour emanating from the same sources. Thus in modern research, as I showed in Chapter 6, concepts such as 'anomie', 'alienation', 'frustration', etc., are particular variables which can be 'measured' without reference to other concepts by survey techniques, the hypothesis being that a 'high' incidence is more likely to be associated with suicide and other forms of deviance, and a low incidence with 'normality', well-being and so on.[27] However, for Durkheim, social health and psychological well-being stems from a *balance* between anomie and fatalism (and egoism and altruism). Therefore, for an individual to live normally, i.e. without thoughts of suicide, there must be in his life a balance between uncertainty (i.e. the possibility or prospect of change) and certainty (i.e. a sense of stability and predicatability). If either exists in excess to the detriment of the other then the individual is more vulnerable to suicide. The causal concepts, therefore, only make sense in terms of their logical *relationship* to one another. The framework developed below is similarly built around the idea of a balance between opposities but includes, as central to its analysis, the risk-taking, or ordeal, aspects of suicidal actions which have been completely ignored in the work of Durkheim and most other sociologists.

It must be made clear that the prescriptions outlined in this section are *ambitions* for a structural theory and, while the model outlined in the following sections is intended to show the possibilities of such an approach, it is necessary to point out first, that it is at this stage speculative and incomplete. Second, many of the ideas and arguments advanced, such as the communicative aspect of suicide, are not my discoveries but the result of careful and detailed research by others. One of the claims made for the model is that it helps to explain some common research 'findings' and clarifies some of the most common 'issues' in suicide research; for example, the relation between completed and attempted suicide, 'planned' and 'impulsive' suicide, 'public' and 'private' suicide, etc. More important, however, is the attempt to make suicidal performances more intelligible to the observer through the discovery of the rules of suicidal production. In this undertaking I have used research findings and case histories from a variety of sources, including some from my own current study of adolescent suicide, to try to show how data collected by a number of researchers with different objectives in mind can be incorporated within the scope of the theory.[28]

Submissive Suicide

Although the theory of suicide production is dependent on a concept of total structure, for purposes of clarity, I shall develop each part separately in this discussion and, as in the previous Chapter, I shall employ the metaphor of the 'game' to try to clarify some of the arguments. Social life resembles the game, albeit in a crude, unidealised way, in so far as human action is both *purposive*, in that the individual acts in terms of desired goals, has a margin of choice and feels that various *possibilities* are open to him; and it is *constrained*, for there are rules of social life whereby individuals 'discover', or 'confirm', things about themselves, others, or the world. For the participant, there is both *possibility* (of change, development, etc.) and *certainty* (in that 'outcomes' and 'results' are produced). If we then ask why someone might cease to participate in the game we deduce that, either he has lost all faith in the rules of *this* game and, therefore, in its purpose and outcome, or that he stops playing because the game is over and the 'result' is known. Similarly, we may say that to the extent that an individual feels that the rules of interaction have become ambiguous or meaningless, and no longer provide him with the certain knowledge he requires to establish things about himself, others or the world *or* that these rules have told him *everything* about himself, others or the world and he therefore has no margin for choice or possibility, then suicide is more likely. We may say then that *suicide is more likely in situations of (almost) complete uncertainty where the individual feels that he knows nothing worth knowing or in situations of (almost) complete certainty where the individual feels that he knows everything worth knowing* (see Figure 8.1).

Uncertainty	Certainty
Individual feels that he 'knows' nothing worth 'knowing'.	Individual feels that he knows everything worth knowing. As everything is now 'known', there is no more possibility. After this knowledge, other 'knowledge' is irrelevant.

FIGURE 8.1

Thanatation is a suicidal act of uncertainty: the individual is uncertain about his own identity and the meaning of his own existence and, as nothing in this world (i.e. 'normal' means of confirmation) can validate his existence, he imposes an ordeal on himself in order to try to resolve the uncertainty. He knows nothing worth knowing because, until this uncertainty is resolved, all else is irrelevant. The suicidal actions *produced* by this are *necessarily* ordeals; they are 'game-like' and may be described as 'ludenic'.

Suicidal actions of this nature, described in the previous chapter, may be directly contrasted in one respect with those where individuals resort to suicide from a psychological sense of complete certainty. Such might be the case, for example, for the depressive who now 'knows' that his life is one long, dark tunnel with *no* hope of light at the end, or for one who is chronically sick and realises that he has but a few painful months in which to linger on. For some, there may seem little point in pressing on into a future that is already 'known' and is beyond all doubt. Those in such situations may develop a desire to die arising from a fatalistic acceptance that, to all intents and purposes, life is already over. I have referred to this as *submissive suicide*.[29] Whereas the thanatationist has become uncertain about the rules of the game and its results, the submissive suicide recognises that for him the game is irretrievably over and lost. He therefore knows everything worth knowing because, having established that for him life is over, knowledge that may once have been important (such as the state of his bank balance) is now irrelevant. In submissive suicide the act will therefore be 'serious', or purposive, as opposed to ludenic, and thus more *likely* to be fatal, for the individual is not confronting death in an ordeal to resolve the uncertainty of whether he is dead or alive, but is embracing death because to all intents and purposes he is already dead. Death is not seen as a 'competitor', or a 'judge' as in thanatation, but more of an ally, a friend helping the defeated individual leave the field with a little dignity and grace.[30] While the thanatationist is asking *Who am I?*, the submissive suicide is saying *I am dead*. In performances of submissive suicide, we find the individual expressing defeat, resignation, loss of hope. For example:

A 62-year-old woman dying of lymphosarcoma. During the three weeks prior to her suicide she had repeatedly said, 'I'm through. I'm whipped. This is the end. I can't take it any longer.' During the final week she added, 'I will not die a lingering death'. On the morning of her suicide, she kissed her husband goodbye as he was leaving for work and said to him, 'Darling, this is your last kiss'. She committed suicide later that morning.[31]

Jean Gray, after a somewhat unsatisfactory life with several successive husbands, found herself at the age of thirty-three deserted by her husband, estranged from her parents, and with an adolescent daughter. Cancer developed, and when Mrs Gray could no longer work, her daughter found work which supported them, since relatives refused to assist. . . . When the cancer became serious, she committed suicide, leaving the following letters. 'To My Daughter Alice: Baby please forgive me for not trying to struggle along any longer but I am at the end. It is of no use to try. Please try to live up to my teaching and be a pure sweet girl always and if you love Arthur and he is still willing to marry you, why you have my consent, although I realise that you are very young, but if you had someone to protect you and provide for you it would be a whole lot better for you, as, my dear, you will find this world a pretty hard place to live in, but be brave and make the best of things. I wish I could stay with you a while longer but it cannot be done. With love, Your Mother.' To her doctors she wrote: 'I know you have done all you could to try to save me but I realise it cannot be done. I thank you for all you have done and I know there is no use to try to struggle any longer.'[32]

It is into this context that we can place the activities and demands of those who seek changes in public attitudes and the law regarding voluntary euthanasia. Those who are dying in great pain, it is argued, if they so wish should be allowed to be helped to die without anyone fearing criminal prosecution. The publicised activities of Meg Murray provided a good example of the commitment to this idea. Mrs Murray, a long-time sufferer from multiple sclerosis, decided that when the disease became worse, rather than die slowly and painfully 'by inches in public', she would commit suicide in order to die with a little dignity.[33] For our understanding of submissive suicide and its relation to other types it is important to note that in her comments there was no anger or bitterness; no blame was attached to others, just a simple acceptance that active, useful life was over and death would be a welcome release. The only complaint was that society should make it easier for those who wish for such release. Similar sentiments were expressed by the famous American philosopher and physicist, Percy Bridgman, who at the end of his life had cancer and was in great pain. He was aware that no more could be done medically to halt the disease, the pain was worsening and he wished to submit to the inevitable death. He asked his doctors to end his life but they refused, and his suicide note, sent to the *Bulletin of the Atomic Scientist*, stated that: 'It isn't decent for society to make a man do this himself. Probably this is the last day I will be able to do it myself. p.b.b.'[34]

It is relatively characteristic of the submissive suicide to try to establish that he is not 'really' committing suicide at all, for he is virtually dead anyway. Another characteristic – which I shall discuss at more length later in the chapter – is that the individual does not 'blame' others for his death. The 'causes' are either outside anyone's control, or the individual himself is to blame. Thus, although

Bridgman and Murray might have expressed anger that society refused to help them to die, there is no suggestion that others were responsible for them *wanting* to die. Many suicide notes and other communications from suicides express a concern that others are *not* to feel in any way that they are to blame.[35] It is suggested here that such communications are products of submissive suicides. For example:

> Twenty-three years old, happily married, a young wife took poison and left the following note: 'Dearest love: It is hard to part with you. But I am so ill. Always I am so nervous, and it interferes with everything I want to do. Do not grieve, my love. How can I say what happiness it has been to have known and lived with you these precious years? B.'[36]

> A successful student, member of a well-to-do family, and a fraternity man, found himself unable to adjust to the limitations which his illness set upon his activities, although it completely incapacitated him only occasionally. According to evidence at the inquest, he was often moody and depressed, and very sensitive about his illness, so that other members of the family dared not speak of it in his presence . . . The letter which John Morton left to his parents when he committed suicide reads in part as follows: 'I've tried everything and every plan. Each had its attraction simply because it was different from the rest; but after all, I can't live any of them. I'm only sorry that my condition did not put me in a position where I could show my appreciation of what you were doing for me; for I did appreciate it. I know you have done more for me than the average parents, and I would like to repay you in a small way. I know how grandma fitted into life, a welcome member of the family – but a problem . . . I've thought it all out; I'm not acting on the spur of the moment, or under stress of mind. It is the inevitable end, so why not now. Please let the matter drop as soon as possible by knowing that I am at last happy and contented.'[37]

Such submissive suicides are usually the easiest to reconcile to the idea of normal, understandable behaviour. Most of the officials I worked with or interviewed in connection with the earlier part of the research stated that they thought that most suicides at the time of the act were mentally 'disturbed' in some way or other; however, they tended to make exceptions of those who kill themselves to escape great physical suffering. It is in such cases that the observer often ends up saying to himself, 'well, I might have done the same thing', as the following case illustrates:

> The patient . . . had been admitted following a determined attempt at suicide. A man of about 50, he was destitute, living in a room by himself, and in constant pain and practically unable to eat because of an inoperable cancer of the throat. My psychiatric assessment was brief and to the point: I wrote, 'So would I.' It was significant that that was one of the few occasions in which I was complimented by my medical colleagues for having 'common sense', even though I was a psychiatrist.[38]

However, while many performances of submissive suicide are characterised by a loss of hope related to physical illness and degeneration, this is not a necessary component. One of the determining features (I shall discuss the other later) is the actor's feeling that life is over and cannot be retrieved and this might have a variety of particular manifestations and focal points. For example, while I was undertaking the participant-observation study, there were several cases where elderly people had apparently given up the struggle with life in order to 'rejoin' some departed loved one; one such case concerned an elderly widower who went out for an evening with some friends and, according to a witness had 'a very good time', but even then his suicide notes were already in the post and he returned to his room in an old folks' home and killed himself. Two of the notes to old friends both stated what 'a good life he'd had' and 'how much he had to be grateful for', but he just couldn't continue without his wife (who had died two years previously). He thanked them for all they had done for him but said that 'it was just impossible to go on without Millie' (his wife) so he had 'gone to be with her'. A third note to the Matron of the home apologised for the trouble this would put them to, thanked the staff for their kindness and said he was off 'to be with my Millie'. All the notes, and indeed some of the things the man had said during his last evening, showed that he was very keen to stress that no one was to blame, indeed they had all 'been very kind', 'good friends' and so on, but that life was just impossible without his wife. Without her he *was* dead, so he submitted to the inevitable to 'be with her'.

In another reported case, an elderly man deliberately drank para-quat upon finding out that his wife, to whom he was devoted, had accidentally drunk the same substance.[39] In such situations there often seemed to be a feeling amongst the officers that in some ways the deceased had, perhaps, done the 'right thing'. For example, in the case of the widower, he had nothing to live for, so had tried to reassure those who might be upset, apologised for any inconvenience and, having as it were put his house in order, he had 'gone to be with my Millie'. 'Let's hope he finds her', the sergeant said without a trace of sarcasm.[40]

Submissive suicide then, is *produced* by revelation: all is now known, the individual's existence has been completely demystified and drained of possibility. The world of the submissive is one of constricting horizons; of closing doors, blind alleys and cul-de-sacs. Those is such situations are going to engage in *purposive* suicidal acts, quite possibly well planned, with some precaution taken against discovery. Submissives are also more likely to be elderly and much less likely to try to seek help by 'communicating' their problems to others, and it is interesting in this context that relatively few elderly people contact the Samaritans.[41]

The apparent prevalence of submissive suicide suggests that Durkheim, possibly because of the implications for his own theory, underestimated the importance of fatalism in the causation of suicide. It should also be noted, in relation to Durkheim's theory, that because the theory developed here was constructed in terms of a different notion of suicide, the concept of uncertainty differs in important respects from Durkheim's use of anomie. It is not being asserted here that individuals engage in suicidal actions simply because they are uncertain, in the way that some theories argue that 'deviance' results from 'anomie'. Rather, it is argued that, while uncertainty (or certainty) is *necessary* to produce suicide, it is not *sufficient* to produce it.

The general indifference of sociologists to the study of the microsocial contexts of suicidal actions, which has already been observed, means that their theories have been limited to looking for the relationships between social 'factors', 'structures' or 'meanings' to a uniform type of behaviour, suicide. That is, they have not considered that the social conditions, or social meanings, which they suggest might produce suicide may also be related to the actual performances of suicidal acts. By not moving beyond the social conditions which preceded the act, questions such as, why some suicidal acts are 'gambles' with death while others are 'serious' attempts at ending life in a relatively efficient manner; why some are attempts at 'communication' while others are not; why in some suicidal acts 'blame' is attached by the perpetrator while in others it is not and so on, are not examined. If sociologists consider them at all, they locate such issues in the province of the psychologist, or the 'suicidologist'. The position taken here, however, is that it is precisely these kinds of problems that a social-psychological theory should be trying to clarify.

There is logical ambiguity in Durkheim's (and other theorists') use of anomic which the concept of uncertainty helps to rectify. In many works, including Durkheim's, it has been argued that individuals *purposively* engage in a deviant act, such as crime or suicide, because they are 'anomic'. However, this is a contradiction in terms. For example, if an individual says to himself.'I really don't want to go on living so I am going to kill myself', then (even if he *once* was) he is no longer 'anomic'. He is not seeking the 'unattainable', so he is quite 'nomic'. It is hard to see, therefore, at least in terms of Durkheim's conception of suicide, how an individual could commit 'anomic suicide'. The position taken here is that individuals are more likely to contemplate suicide in situations of great psychological uncertainty. If that uncertainty remains unresolved and the individual finds this unbearable and actually engages in a suicidal act, then that uncertainty will be carried into the act itself, and it will be an *ordeal*.

Ectopia and Symphysis

In the previous section a distinction was made between thanatation and submissive suicide. However, *both* types of suicide are the product of a state of mind I shall refer to as *ectopic*. That is, they are characterised by the individual's sense of detachment from others. Many studies argue that social isolation is *the* key cause of suicides; however, there is a tendency to define this in terms of physical isolation, whereas ectopia refers to the individual's *moral* insulation from others. In thanatation others cannot tell the individual what he most wants to know; while in submissive suicide, others cannot dissuade the individual from what he already knows.

In one of the most famous case studies of suicide, Ellen West expresses this sense of ectopia very strongly:

> By this fearful illness I am withdrawing more and more from people. I feel myself excluded from all real life. I am quite isolated. I sit in a glass ball. I see people through a glass wall, their voices come to me muffled. I have an unutterable longing to get to them, I scream, but they do not hear me. I stretch out my arms towards them; but my hands merely beat against the wall of my glass ball.[42]

Some of the most eloquent expressions of an awareness that the self is somehow beyond the redemption of others is to be found in literary and autobiographical works.[43] Like Ellen West, Sylvia Plath likened her sense of detachment to being trapped in a bell jar, a situation where a confrontation with death seemed to offer the only means of making contact with the world and breaking free.[44] Both the autobiography of Mary Savage and the 'confessional' poetry of Anne Sexton document a long period of detachment from others, a sense of the unreality of the subject's own existence and its relation to suicide attempts.[45] For Sexton, this doubt in her own existence is a major theme in her early works where she likens herself, for example, to a 'plaster doll', or 'watercolour' that easily 'washes off'. As an 'object' she does not have the 'normal' experiences of 'real' people.

Ectopia then, produces in people a psychological detachment from the opinions, actions and feelings of others, and the suicidal performances which arise from such situations are therefore private and 'self-contained'. If others are informed verbally or in notes they are usually told that they are not to blame for the suicidal act is not part of a 'dialogue' with others. As we saw in the previous Chapter, in thanatation the individual resorts to a suicidal ordeal because others can no longer validate his existence. In submissive suicide he resorts to self destruction because nothing others do or say can dissuade him from his conviction that his life is over and death is the only answer. In his study of student suicide, Hendin argued that many of the most 'seriously' suicidal students had 'grown up dead' in loveless, desolate childhoods.[46] They thought of themselves as dead and defied the therapist to convince them otherwise. For example, Hendin writes of Larry, who had barely survived one serious attempt:

He protected himself against letting me know or reach him by attempting to stop any observation or interpretation of his behaviour by quickly saying 'it is possible'. Insisting on the futility of our talking and on the futility of his life, he said he could stand back and listen to our conversation and it was like a Z grade movie. Standing back, listening while grading himself and others were characteristic ways in which he defended himself against involvement. He kept insisting that nothing could change his life to any degree, suggesting a determination to see to it that nothing did.[47]

The process whereby an individual submits to death because he comes to realise he will never be 'really' alive again (or has never been really alive) may be illustrated by the life and writings of Cesare Pavese, who killed himself in 1942 at the height of his literary fame. His is the history of one acutely aware of what he felt to be his inability to establish authentic communication with others and who became, after a long struggle, finally weighed down with his experiences of failure:

Deep anxiety and recurrent crises of self doubt and self contempt were already evident when he was in his teens. Physically he was a weak, clumsy, unattractive young man who suffered from asthma. He was painfully aware that his appearance raised a barrier between him and the world. This sense of physical inferiority became a constant source of insecurity, making its mark on his relations with the opposite sex. It was Pavese's wish to be liked by women for his physical attributes rather than his intellect.

His deep inner torment at an early age can be detected in a poem written when he was eighteen years old and sent to a friend:

'On a December evening I was walking along a small, lonely country road with my heart in turmoil. I was carrying a gun . . . I was imagining the terrible bang it would give out in the night when my last illusions and fears would abandon me and I would stick it against my temple to blow my brains out.'

To this a letter follows:

'By now, I've known myself well in the light of the most recent events: I'm a man good for nothing, shy, insecure, half dead, and never, never will I be able to acquire lasting social standing, that is, as people say, "to be successful in one's life". *Pavese is dead.*[48][my emphasis]

The expansion of his intellectual horizons and his literary success only made him more aware of the vastness of his own feelings of failure to become a 'complete' person by establishing meaningful relations with another. The hope of something better to come in the future, which may have sustained him through his adolescent crises, was rapidly being drained out of the mature man. The *possibility* of a better future was replaced by the certainty that it would never happen. He wrote that: 'Emptiness is no longer made up for by any vital spark. I know very well *I'll never get further and, by now, all has been said*. To wait is still an occupation. To wait for nothing is terrible.' [my emphasis] And his last poem he ended:

Someone has died
long time ago
someone who tried
but didn't know.[49]

Suicides resulting from states of ectopia are 'inner-directed', they are the product of an 'inner debate' in which the individual tries to validate his own existence to himself. Although others may have played a significant part in 'causing' the situation (for example, affectionless parents producing 'dead' children as Hendin has suggested) they are excluded from the 'suicide process'. The individual's sense of detachment from others which makes him question the validity of his own life at the same time means that he is 'insulated' from others' actions and feelings. Others' cruelty or indifference cannot then 'precipitate' such suicidal action and thus, as I observed below, in his suicidal performance the individual does not 'blame' others for his predicament, he does not use the performance to 'communicate' (directly) to others what they have done to him.

The diary of Wallace Baker, which he kept for the year and a half prior to his suicide and which was quoted at some length by Cavan in her study, provides a good example of this 'inner-directed' suicide process. The diary reveals the subject's obsessive and exclusive concern with his own feelings and emotions. Amongst his reasons for suicide, he lists his 'disillusionment' with his own lack of genius;

being 'alone without a home' and having 'no place in the world'; fear of insanity and ungratifying sexual experiences with 'mercenary women'.[50] In her analysis Cavan observes that:

> A dominant characteristic of Wallace Baker was introspection. His attention centred upon his own sensations, moods and reactions. His whole interest lay in the development of certain ideals for his own conduct. In the entire course of the diary he mentions only one person as a friend, outside members of the family: a girl to whom he wrote upon leaving his home to go to Chicago. His recreation had reference only to his own conception of himself; when he read or attended plays it was because he wished to become a writer of plays, not for enjoyment of the play as such.[51]

His submission to death lay in his own realisation that he would never achieve his own cherished ideals of genius and sexual fulfilment, a hope that had sustained him in his early years:

> Up to now this diary does not show the vast progress towards disillusioned manhood I have taken. In reality they are so big that I have at times bridged the gulf and said, 'All is illusion'. I have felt the utter pettiness of this struggle and seen things from the impersonal and even transcendental viewpoint . . . Suicide again presenting itself as the only way out, I was prompted to read over my diaries. True, from my fifteenth year I have been in a bad way, but until several years ago a solution seemed bound to come. Suicide never entered my thoughts in those days.[52]

In ectopic situations the suicide process may be likened to a *monologue*, and suicidal actions are produced either by a profound feeling of uncertainty that nothing worthwhile is *fixed* in the world or a profound certainty that nothing worthwhile is *possible* in the world *and* from a sense of detachment which tells the individual that others cannot help to resolve these problems. In this respect the theory is logically different from those of Durkheim and others who have argued that egoism, isolation, etc., cause suicide. However, individuals do not necessarily kill themselves because they are egoistic, or socially isolated from others; indeed, some live quite happily this way. The position taken here is that while ectopia is a necessary condition for the production of suicide, it is not a *suffi-*

cient cause. Rather, the suicidal actions described above are produced by the *combination* of detachment from others *and* uncertainty about one's existence, or a certainty that one's life is over. This part of the theory may be summarised diagrammatically (see Figure 8.2).

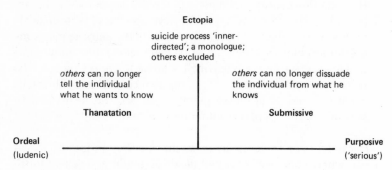

FIGURE 8.2

The second main dimension of the theory distinguishes between the 'inner-directed' suicidal acts described above which are produced by the individual's strong sense of *detachment* from others, and 'other-directed' suicides produced by the individual's overriding sense of *attachment* to others. Therefore: *suicide is more likely to the extent that individuals are either psychologically immune from the opinions, feelings and wishes of others or are psychologically unprotected from the opinions, feelings and wishes of others.* Suicide then is produced in situations of ectopia where others tell the subject *nothing* about himself, or in situations which I shall call symphysic where others tell him everything about himself. That is, without others', or a particular other's, good opinions, love, respect, or even mere presence, the individual feels that his own existence is problematic. He may be said to by symphysic because he has no 'real' existence independent of others' favourable validation of him.[53]

Symphysis produces a particular type of suicidal performance. Whereas ectopic suicidal performances were likened to *monologues*, where the individual debated the meaning of his existence with himself, suicides resulting from a sense of symphysis are part of a *dialogue* with others. The primary characteristic of symphysic suicidal performances is that they are *communicative* and as such, cannot be understood apart from those to whom they are addressed.

Appeal Suicides

The communicative nature of suicide has long been recognised by researchers and those specialising in suicide prevention; and the notion of suicide as an 'appeal', or a 'cry for help' is well known.[54] Many suicidal acts are attempts at communication with a specific other. Shneidman has referred to these as 'dyadic suicides':

> Although suicide is always the act of a single person and, in this sense, stems from within one mind, the dyadic suicide is essentially an interpersonal event. In these cases, the cries refer to the frustration (of love and the search for love), hate, anger, disappointment, shame, guilt, rage, impotence and rejection in relation to the other. The key to the act lies in the unfulfilled need: 'If only he (or she) would . . .' Suicide notes, usually prefaced by the word 'Dear', are typically addressed to a specific person, an ambivalently loved one. Most suicides are dyadic; they are primarily transactional in nature. The victim's best eggs are in the other person's flawed basket. He (and his figurative eggs) are crushed. The dyadic suicidal act may reflect the victim's penance, bravado, revenge, plea, histrionics, self-punishment, gift of life, withdrawal, fealty, disaffiliation or whatever – but its arena is primarily interpersonal and its understanding (and thus its meaning) cannot occur outside the dyadic relationship.[55]

Most people who commit suicidal acts communicate their intent, in one way or another, to others. Stengel has suggested that *all* suicidal acts are communicative,[56] while Kobler and Stotland have argued that all suicidal acts and communications are 'pleas for help and hope' from others, and whether or not suicide actually follows is largely the result of others' responses to this plea.[57] My purpose here is not to try to contradict these views, but rather to *qualify* them. I have shown in the previous sections of this chapter that not all suicides are of this communicative nature; in thanatation and submission the subject is beyond such direct communication with others; that is, although he may inform them of his decision, he is not committing a suicidal act *because* of them. We must therefore distinguish between suicidal acts where the communication of intent is *incidental* to the meaning of the act (as, for example, in 'preparing' others or telling them not to worry) and those where it is at the *focal point* of the actor's meaning. In other words, we must differentiate between communication *about* suicide and communication *through* suicide.

Communication with others *through* suicide is not a characteristic of suicide as such, but rather of symphysic, or 'other-directed', suicide and, just as a distinction was made between 'inner-directed' suicides of certainty and doubt, so a distinction can be made between 'other-directed' suicides of certainty and doubt. Thanatation is an 'inner-directed' suicide of doubt where the individual resorts to suicide because of doubts about himself. Literally, he is asking, *Who am I? Do I exist?* 'Other-directed' suicides of doubt, which I shall call *appeals*, are caused by the individual's doubts about the nature of the other. He is asking others, *Who are you? Do you want me to live?*

The suicidal performances produced by such situations are characterised by direct warnings, pleas, threats and dire prognostications.[58] If both the unbearable uncertainty and the attachment to the other(s) continue, the resultant suicidal act will necessarily be an ordeal. The individual cannot certainly (i.e. 'seriously') kill himself because then he would never find out, but neither can he not kill himself, for other means of 'validation' have failed. He therefore gambles with death with some hope that he might live and yet be responded to as if he had died.[59]

Appeal suicides combine the wish to die with the wish for change in others and improvement in the situation; they are acts both of despair and of hope. This ambivalence is reflected in the suicidal performance and the subject's expressions of intent as the following extracts, taken from my study of adolescent suicide illustrate.

A 15-year-old girl, with a history of 'difficult' behaviour, consumed most of the contents of a 100-bottle of aspirins after her parents, concerned about what they believed to be her sexually promiscuous behaviour, had prevented her from going out in the evening. On being asked her intention at the time of the attempt she said that she 'didn't really want to die' although she didn't know whether or not the tablets would kill her. She said she wanted to 'get back at them' (her parents) and 'show them how fed up I was'. She said that whereas they had never really taken much notice of her up till the attempt, things 'were much better now', and she could talk to her parents whereas before, 'it had just been shouting with no-one listening'.

A 19-year-old youth took a large quantity of valium after a row with his girl friend. He said that everything had got on top of him and he had enough of 'being kicked around all the time by everyone', and that he would 'shake them up a bit'. At the time of the attempt he said he was unsure whether or not he would die, 'but one way or other I was going to get a result'.[60]

Both thanatation and appeals produce ordeals; however, whereas in thanatation the individual is gambling on 'pure' chance, the appeal suicide being addressed to others is dependent on their responsiveness to the communications. The subject gambles on communication by suicide when other means of validating the other's identity have failed. The following case, reported in some detail by the Los Angeles Suicide Prevention Team, further illustrates the communicative nature of appeals:

The autopsy report concerning a 57-year-old female who was found dead in her home indicated that the cause of death was acute barbiturate poisoning. On the face of it the mode of death appeared equivocal and the case was referred to the Suicide Team for investigation.

The victim's physician was contacted and he reported that she had been emotionally upset for several years. She felt her husband's personality had changed and that he was moody and was not spending time or doing things with her. On two occasions she had been severely depressed but seemed to have come out of these moods fairly quickly.

An appointment was made with the victim's husband. He exhibited many feelings of remorse and guilt, with much crying at times . . .

The husband stated they had been married for 25 years; there were no children. From the beginning the marriage had many elements of discomfort in it as a result of his wife's hysterical excessive demands and lack of consideration of their economic situation. After about ten years of marriage, there was a period of separation by divorce, but they came together again and eventually remarried. He first stated that there had never been any prior suicidal attempts or threats, but it later became known there actually had been many. These were described of minimum lethality and had had a dramatic quality to them. For example, she would put a little iodine around her lips and say that she had swallowed some, but when he took her to the hospital iodine was not found in the stomach contents. On a number of such occasions, he had responded with a good deal of anger to his wife's suicidal attempts. Once she had threatened to kill herself with a knife and he had given her a hunting knife, telling her to use it since it was sharper.

The husband stated that during the previous 6 to 8 months he had made up his mind that his marriage would never be successful. He had not communicated this to his wife, because he did not intend to divorce her.

It was felt that the husband was a man who had very marked dependency needs which were not being met by his wife, and that he had reacted to these with a good deal of anger and rejection of her. The wife apparently needed the marriage very much, and she made the suicidal threats and attempts in an effort to bring her husband closer to her. On most occasions, such suicidal attempts or threats brought about a reconciliation. However, at this particular time, the possibility of reconciliation had lessened considerably because of the husband's decision. Whether this decision was based on something specific, such as an attraction to another woman, it is impossible to tell. He denied this specifically, however, without being asked.

At the time of the suicide, the husband, a salesman, had gone to a neighbouring city to conduct some business. His usual practice was to call his wife and tell her the time he would be home for dinner. He tried this but was unable to reach her until late. She was very angry when he arrived home and threatened to leave him. He told her to go ahead, and then went out to a restaurant. Later he returned home and found his wife sleeping on the floor in the hall 'breathing heavy'. Her clothing was not disarranged in any way so he had given no thought to anything like violence being involved, and he supposed she had simply gone to sleep on the floor. He apparently made no attempt to arouse her except to place a pillow under her head to allow her to sleep more comfortably. He then left the house and went to a hotel. One significant fact the husband related was that the night before her death his wife had called her sister and brother-in-law and had made a will, leaving all her possessions to her sister.

The impression made by the investigator was that this was a chronically depressed woman of hysterical type, anxious about the separation from her husband, and that the husband, for reasons unknown had decided not to continue the marriage on an effective basis. What was considered pivotal was the denial by the husband to himself of his wife's desperate situation, which was probably symptomatic of their destructive symbiotic relationship. While unconscious death wishes on the part of the spouse might be inferred, what seemed clear was that the dyadic relationship was one that permitted the rejection of the victim by the potential rescuer. Thus, the victim's gamble with death was lost because the person who could have saved her did not permit himself to receive the intended communication.[61]

Survivors of suicide attempts often acknowledge the communicative aspects of their action. Often the response is, 'I didn't know what else to do', as the following case, again from my own research, illustrates:

A 19-year-old girl became very distressed when a married man with whom she had been having an affair returned to his pregnant wife. She bombarded the man with letters, telephone calls and visits until finally, a court order was placed on her. The following day she took a substantial overdose of barbiturates before wandering out into the street, collapsing and being taken to hospital. Upon being asked whether she intended to kill herself she said, 'I don't know . . . Not really I suppose . . . but *I couldn't see any other way of getting through to him*'.[62] [my emphasis]

Bonnar and McGee from their study of married couples report that:

The suicide attempt as a form of communication is obvious in Group 1 [the suicidal group]. The wives readily admitted that their attempt was a 'cry for help' and that it was specifically directed toward their husbands. Some commented: 'I didn't really want to die; I just didn't know what else to do.' Several said: 'It was stupid. I didn't really want to die; I was just so miserable. We fought all the time and he wouldn't listen to me. I just wanted some attention.'[63]

Stengel was one of the first students to examine the communicative nature and social effects of suicidal actions.[64] In his follow-up studies of attempted suicides, he and his associates found that in many cases the attempt had brought about significant changes for the subject in that the attempt had established the (positive) identity of the other. For example:

> Mrs F.I. was unhappily married to a brutal psychopath. They separated in 1944. In 1946 she learned that he had taken divorce proceedings which, though she wanted a divorce, greatly upset her. She had some time previously started a love affair with a colleague, a married man with one child. Soon after she learned of her impending divorce, her lover told her he did not intend to leave his family to live with her, as she had hoped he would. She became acutely depressed and tried to poison herself with aspirin. She was taken to the observation ward whence she was sent to a convalescent ward after two weeks. Three months after the suicide attempt she resumed work. Her lover left his family after all and at the time of the follow up six years after her suicidal attempt they were living together and both declared that they were thoroughly happy. She thought her suicidal attempt 'had brought him to his senses'.[65]

While appeals are attempts to communicate the 'seriousness' of the situation, a seriousness which the other has not realised, the other is not necessarily held responsible for the situation. For example, an individual may engage in a suicidal ordeal as an act of *repentance* to the other:

> A 27-year-old white housewife was discovered in the act of sexual intercourse with the man who lived next door, by her husband who that afternoon had returned home from work unexpectedly. The wife became very agitated, pleading that this was 'the first time' and that she loved her husband dearly. (The neighbour dressed hurriedly and left.) The husband, shocked, finally told his wife that he was going to divorce her. The wife began to cry and scream, and then ran into the kitchen, seized the bread knife and slashed herself three times across the abdomen.
>
> At the hospital the woman stated that she had thought there was some chance she might bleed to death as a result of her action – that although she had made the attempt in front of her husband, who was likely to rush her to a hospital, 'it might not be in time'.

She said that she would rather be dead than divorced. '*Anyway, it showed my husband how much I love him.*'[66][my emphasis]

Appeals then are attempts at communication through suicide and they are not necessarily produced by any specific act of the other, but rather by the subject's uncertainty about the other and his continuing complete attachment to the other (see Figure 8.3). It is in this context that the nature of the response (and the subject's interpretation of it) is often crucial in determining whether or not suicidal behaviour is repeated. Bonnar and McGee observe that in speaking of 'successful' or 'unsuccessful' suicidal acts, one must not ask, 'Did the victim live or die?' but rather, 'Was the message received?'[67] While this is an important consideration our analysis here would direct us to enquire whether or not the subject's uncertainty had been resolved.

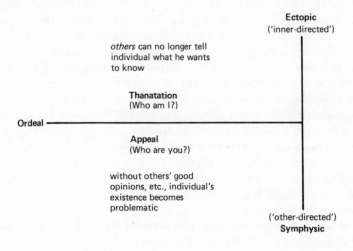

FIGURE 8.3

Sacrifice

Appeal suicides are produced by the individual's desperate uncertainty regarding his symphysic relationship to another (or others) and suicidal performances reflect his growing doubts about the meaning of his existence to the other. However, just as we made a distinction between ectopic suicides of uncertainty and certainty, so too we must separate symphysic suicides of uncertainty and certainty. The latter are produced when the subject's dependency on another (even an abstract other), or others, reveals to him the certain knowledge that he has no alternative other than suicide. Either others' conduct has ruled out the possibility of him continuing to live or his own actions make it impossible for him to continue living because of what he has done or is doing to those with whom he has a symphysic attachment. In all cases the defining characteristic is the subject's certain knowledge of those who tell him *everything* about himself indicating to him (directly or indirectly) that he must die; certain knowledge which the subject, because of his over-attachment to those others, is unable to resist. I shall refer to suicidal acts produced by symphysic certainty as *sacrifices*. Like the submissive, the sacrificial suicide is presented with a situation that reveals to him his life is certainly over and the suicidal performance is, therefore, likely to be 'serious'; however, whereas the former says to *himself* '*I am dead*', the latter informs others '*I am killed*'.

This general cause produces a variety of suicidal performances; the revelation to the subject that his life is over may come quite suddenly, in the case of a dependent individual who has been betrayed for example, or it may develop gradually over a long period of distress and despair (which may include suicidal threats and attempts) in which the individual perceives others confirming (albeit unwittingly) his feelings of despair and hopelessness. Jourard has proposed that people destroy themselves 'in response to an invitation originating from others that they stop living'.[68] It is argued here that this is not a characteristic of suicide as such, but more a characteristic of *sacrificial* suicide.

In some cases the individual may descend gradually into this state of despair as a result of others failing to give appropriate 'recognition' to earlier 'appeals'. As Litman has observed: 'When these potential rescuers are not available or if they fail to respond appropriately, the suicidal behaviour is often repeated until the conversation with the significant others is permanently terminated.'[69] Much of the performance associated with appeal suicide concerns the subject's uncertainty over the identity of the other and his failure to appreciate the gravity of the situation. However, the quality of the responses might leave the subject in no doubt about the identity of the other, they may reveal to him that the other can do nothing for him, or indeed, does not wish him to live. In such situations uncertainty becomes translated into certainty and, providing the attachment remains, this will produce a serious, or purposeful, suicidal act:

> A 40-year-old man returned from the overnight ward of a general hospital after his third serious suicide attempt, to be greeted by the following comment from his wife in the presence of their children: 'Here comes your father; he has never done anything well, even taking his own life'. The wife and children went out to shop; on their return he was dead by hanging.

> An 18-year-old woman decided to kill herself after her husband had deserted her; on awakening from a coma induced by a large amount of barbiturates, she found a guilt-ridden husband who wished for a reconciliation and who pledged fidelity. When his behaviour became errant again, she made a knowingly superficial gesture, quite unlike the previous attempt, but again achieving change in his behaviour. The pattern was then repeated, but finally without reconciliation. Thereupon the woman killed herself.[70]

Similarly Kobler and Stotland argue that the suicide 'epidemic' at a mental hospital they studied was the result of the staff's low moral, fear and sense of helplessness transmitting itself to certain acutely depressed patients who had developed a total dependency on the staff and the hospital as the last hope.[71] However, as a result of the negative responses, they developed a concept of themselves not only as very 'sick', but also beyond 'cure'. According to Kobler and Stotland's analysis, this 'hopelessness' was communicated by the staff.

Other sacrificial suicidal performances manifest themselves in the revenge of the subject, where those clearly 'responsible' for the killing are identified. In such cases the individual makes it quite clear that he does not 'really' want to die, but others have made it quite *impossible* for him to go on living. His death is thus 'retribution' for those who have 'killed' him. Such suicidal performances are invariably 'publicly orientated' as others must be informed, in notes or by other means, of the situation and who is responsible for it:

A young clerk 22 years old killed himself because his bride of four months was not in love with him but with his elder brother and wanted a divorce so that she could marry the brother. The letters he left showed plainly the suicide's desire to bring unpleasant notoriety upon his brother and his wife, and to attract attention to himself. In them he described his shattered romance and advised reporters to see a friend to whom he had forwarded diaries for further details. The first sentence in a special message to his wife read: 'I used to love you; but I die hating you and my brother too'. . . . Still another [note] read 'To whom it may interest: The cause of it all: I loved and trusted my wife and trusted my brother. Now I hate my wife and despise my brother and *sentence myself to die* for having been fool enough to ever have loved anyone as contemptible as my wife has proven to be. Both she and her lover (my brother) knew this afternoon that I intended to die tonight. They were quite pleased at the prospect and did not trouble to conceal their elation. They had good reason to know I was not jesting.'

The brother who is 23 years old spoke frankly to the police about his friendship with his brother's wife. Though separated in childhood when the parents drifted apart, the two brothers had later on become inseparable companions until shortly before the tragedy, when both fell in love with the same girl. The younger man attempted suicide when his love was not returned and upon his recovery, the girl agreed to marry him out of pity – but later on she found she could not live up to her bargain. After a few weeks of married life, the husband discovered the relationship existing between his wife and his brother. He became much depressed and threatened suicide. The day before his death, there was a scene and when assured that the two were really deeply in love with each other, the clerk retorted: 'All right, I can do you more harm dead than alive.' [My emphasis.][72]

In other cases this revenge is extended to include the actual 'execution' of the 'murderer'.[73]

Ernest King, a man of thirty-six, of German parentage, a carpenter by trade, a Catholic, who earned $55 a week and owned real estate, killed himself after some five years of married life. He was separated from his wife, who had started divorce proceedings.

The five years of their married life had been a series of quarrels, and several times his wife had threatened to commit suicide and also to kill him. The final straw was added when he met his wife at her lawyer's. After writing a history of his married life he went to his wife's home, killed his sister-in-law, wounded his wife, and killed himself.

MY WILL AND TESTAMENT

I am alone in my flat. My wife left me and left our child without a cent. (Ten days ago) she started a suit for divorce without reason. I am a sick man with heart trouble. My wife is responsible for my condition. She just nagged me to death. She did not believe I was a sick man and claims everything I earned, worked and paid for as hers . . . I made as high as $160 a week. I gave her all I earned and still she was not satisfied, she wanted more. And I tried to earn more. In the summer I was hurt internally . . . I went to a doctor and he told me . . . that I should rest for one year and I would be well again. My wife did not believe it and I went to work anyhow . . . My wife said I was too lazy to work and she drove me on until I am a physical wreck today . . . I have not long to live so I must write this to let people know my side of things in general. I met my wife at her lawyer's office today and she laughed at me and sneered at me and said all kind of mean things to me, showing that she has no sympathy for anything. When my wife saw me she just laughed at me. She never asked how the baby was. She did not think that much of him . . . All she had in her mind was money and the property. And that she earned it all and I did nothing. Well, I am so sick I do not know what to do; she hounds me to death.[74]

A working man had a sexual affair with a young woman considerably above him in social class. In response to her family's protests, she decided to end the association. This led to some violent quarrels during which he threatened to shoot himself. Finally he appeared to agree to their parting, only to return the following day and shoot her dead and then himself. His suicide note explained that they could not be happy without each other and he had decided to take her with him.

A chronically depressed single man, a foreign refugee in his early forties, had been in hospital several times for investigation of numerous hypochondriacal complaints. He subsequently formed a forlorn attachment to a prostitute, on whom he spent a lot of money. He then became jealous, asserting bitterly that she had wanted him only for money. At the time he was still complaining of insomnia, nightmares, and various aches and pains of nervous origin, for which he was having sedatives from a local doctor. During one night when they were together he strangled this woman and then killed himself with an overdose of drugs, lying down to die beside her. He left behind notes expressing his resentment against her for spurning him, and his inability to face life without her.[75]

In some cases it is the subject himself who feels, or is encouraged to feel, that his own general failings, weaknesses, or even his mere existence, is placing an unnecessarily heavy burden on those to whom he is attached and he sacrifices himself in order to liberate the other(s); the suicide is then a gift of freedom to the symphysic other:

A woman had been chronically bedridden for 20 years . . . Gradually the husband began to express his distaste for his own caregiving role, to blame his wife more and more for the constriction imposed on his own activities, and to voice barely disguised antipathy toward her for continuing to live. He verbally projected the picture of what he would be 'robbed of' in the future, but at the same time expressed concern for her very real physical pain and continued his nursing activities. As the neighbourhood deteriorated over the years, he began to talk of burglaries and purchased a gun which he discharged in a 'how to work it' session; he then left the loaded gun within arm's reach of his bedridden wife. After the demonstration and a particularly bitter soliloquy, the husband went to work. The wife killed herself shortly afterwards.[76]

A man poisoned himself after a night out with his wife and the man she had left him for and wished to marry. He apparently made it clear during the evening that he did not wish to stand in their way and the note he left explained that he only wanted his wife to be happy, and this made things easier for her.[77]

There are also suicidal performances, necessarily publicly orient-ated and usually dramatic, where the subject sacrifices himself for political, moral or religious reasons; suicide here is the communica-tion of an ideal, or cause. For example, the suicide note of a member of the Proutist Universal group who immolated herself explained that:

> This act of self-immolation is my own choosing and planned in secrecy. Divulgence would have meant sure prevention. It grew from a burning desire, an inner need to do something, to help to stop the criminality of our exploited lives on earth. It was inspired by the sacrifice of seven others for the same cause – three from India, two from Germany (one woman) one American and one Swiss woman, whose own sacrifices have not been properly understood by the world.[78]

While many of the ritualised, spiritual, military or political pro-test suicides that are typically referred to as 'altruistic' may be incor-porated within this category, I have tried to show in this section that 'sacrifices' are not the sole prerogative of 'primitive', or 'tradi-tional', societies or groups, but are in fact more widespread in indus-trial societies than is normally supposed, and that such suicides are not necessarily produced by over-integration, but by over-attachment, often to only one other. It is also a mistake to assume that there is a homogeneous category of suicide which incorporates all 'idealistic', transcendental or obligatory suicides. Often political, or protest, suicides begin as appeals, as in the hunger strike for example, where the subject's protest is orientated towards testing the nature of the other(s) by putting the onus on him to perform some act which will *prevent* the death of the subject. Such suicidal performances are *ordeals*, and it is only if death results because of the other's lack of action that they become popularly redefined as sacrifices.

Sacrifices then are not necessarily produced by 'higher' ideals or institutionalised obligatory pressure, but rather by a combination of complete *attachment* to something outside the self, usually one other person, and the certainty that such attachment indicates to them that they have no possible alternative other than death.

The theory in its totality may be summarised diagrammatically (see Figure 8.4 overleaf).

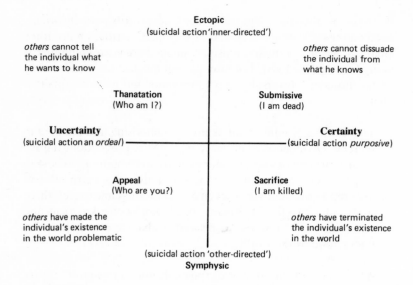

FIGURE 8.4

Conclusions

Earlier in this work it was argued that many students of suicide, particularly sociological students, have tended to underestimate the complexity of the phenomenon they are seeking to explain. However, I also tried to show, with reference to more 'individualistic' approaches, that this complexity will not be explained, but merely duplicated, by a methodology whose logic is to break the phenomenon down into an ever increasing number of discrete empirical categories each of which requires separate analysis and explanation. With respect to this problem this chapter developed a structural theory of suicide which attempts to show how a complex variety of suicidal performances are the result of four general states of meaning produced by a combination of the subject's conviction that either nothing is certain or that nothing is possible in the world and either a profound sense of moral insulation from others or a complete attachment to them.

While the theoretical statement outlined above clearly requires more elaboration and detailed analysis, I have tried to show how such an approach which tries to reveal the underlying rules of suicidal action might help to clarify some of the main problems in suicide research, such as the relation between completed and attempted suicide, the role of others in precipitating suicide and the various communications of suicidal intent, and explain the relationship between, and characteristics of, distinct types of suicide. For example, while some have suggested that *all* suicidal acts are appeals to others (and thus the quality of the response is usually crucial),[79] it has been shown here that this is only a characteristic of *some* suicidal acts. Similarly, there are those who argue that individuals resort to suicide when their horizons become so narrow and 'constricted' that they see no possibility of change and thus, as there is no longer uncertainty in life, they seek instead the uncertainty of death;[80] while others have suggested that suicide results when individuals perceive that they are invited to die,[81] or perceive others defining their situation as 'hopeless'.[82] However, it has been argued that none of these are characteristics of suicide as such, but rather of particular types of suicide (i.e. submissive and sacrifice).

Furthermore, I have tried to show here how the social-psychological preconditions for suicide might be related to the nature of the suicidal acts themselves. For example, those who engage in suicide from a sense of detachment and uncertainty do so by means of an ordeal from which others are excluded. In this context we may also make the general observation that perhaps social scientists have been mistaken in viewing a submission to fate, or the sacrifice and ordeal as characteristics only of primitive, or traditional, societies. On the contrary this discussion suggests that industrial man, although living in a 'disenchanted' world, is rather closer to his 'primitive' ancestors than many would like to believe.[83]

General Conclusions

The research undertaken in this book has suggested, in opposition to Durkheim and the sociological tradition apparently following him, that official suicide rates are a most inappropriate source of data for suicide research and that suicidal actions will not be satisfactorily explained without reference to the actor's intentions and the micro-social context of his action. However, this view of sociological studies did not lead to an acceptance of what may be termed 'individually orientated' approaches, one variety of which locates the causes of suicide in factors physically 'inside' the individual as opposed to 'outside' in his environment, while another argues that suicide has to be 'understood' in terms of the meaning that the individual 'constructs' for his own action.

The respective debates based on these views between 'internal' *vs* 'external' and 'positivist' *vs* 'subjectivist' explanations are largely irrelevant and trivial, and this may be seen by examining them in relation to Durkheim's work. Critics argue that Durkheim's opposition to psychology was such that he and his followers ignored the importance of 'individual factors', such as personality, in the causation of suicide. Thus in the literature a distinction is made between 'social' explanations (studying suicide rates) and 'individual' explanations (studying cases, experiments, etc.). However, this distinction (and the solution based upon it which advocates uniting the 'social' and the 'individual') is misleading because, as I observed in Chapter 2, studies of suicide rates, even by sociologists, are not following Durkheim in that they are seeking order at a nominal and phenomenal level and indeed, reject his social realism. In this respect, as I showed in Chapter 6, they are far closer to the positivist studies of the 'clinical' and 'psychological' students. In short, there is nothing 'Durkheimian' (or sociological) about studying suicide rates and, as I have demonstrated in the concluding Part of this work, nothing 'un-Durkheimian' (or un-sociological) in studying case histories.

Some students, who would agree with this general 'bracketing together' of 'social' and 'individual' approaches, would go on to argue that their shortcomings derive from their attempts to apply the methods of the natural sciences, whereas in fact the study of social life requires its own 'interpretative' methods. For these students then the crucial division is between 'positivist' and 'interpretative' methodologies. However, this distinction also tends to mislead and we may illustrate this by again turning to Durkheim who, although popularly placed firmly in the positivist camp, was in important respects *outside* this debate. For Durkheim, approaches which view social phenomena as either a mass of separable components or the subjective meanings of individuals are individualistic, and therefore incapable of producing scientific understanding; for while the latter reduces social reality to the subjectivity of the actor, the former reduces it to the subjectivity of the observer. Contemporary studies of suicide, whether analyses of suicide rates by sociologists, examinations of suicide-prone personalities by psychologists, or phenomenological interpretations of actors' meaningful 'constructions', share a common commitment to the observed, phenomenal world. In this respect they may be differentiated from Durkheim who argued, against both positivism and subjectivism, that the nature of social reality is not given to us by our participation in it as members of society and those who confine themselves to the observable world build their explanations on the shifting sands of passing empirical associations. For Durkheim the study of social phenomena involved trying to discover the underlying mechanisms that caused the relations between observable phenomena. His causal concepts were thus real (i.e. as opposed to being mere descriptions of real things such as industrialism, urbanisation, etc.) and yet not given by sensory perception. As I have tried to show, the heirs of a Durkheimian approach are neither the positivists nor the functionalists, but structuralists who, like him, adopt a realist ontology.

The present work has attempted to develop an alternative sociological approach to suicide derived from certain common elements in the work of both Durkheim and the modern structuralists. Such an approach does not deny the importance of careful observation and description, but it does insist that the question of what exists is distinct from what can be observed and challenges the assumption inherent in most works on suicide that theories are arrived at inductively by moving from particular to more generalised observation. The model of suicide developed here was constructed by theoretical reflection and abstraction and attempts to show how a variety of specific suicidal performances are produced, or generated, by one of four interrelated states of meaning. Of course, once the generative mechanism has been identified then *it* becomes the phenomenon to be explained. From this point of view the essence of science 'lies in the move at any one level from manifest phenomena to the structures that generate them'.[1]

While the approach adopted here is in important and obvious respects both different from, and critical of, that employed by Durkheim, I have tried to show why his work remains so important to our understanding of suicide. In this context it is perhaps a little ironical that a work begun many years ago with, amongst other things, an ambition to 'disprove' Durkheim's 'positivist' study of suicide should end in agreement with many of his fundamental principles especially, that why some people kill themselves while others go on living are not separate questions, but two sides of the same problem.

Postscript

Since the completion of this text, J. Baechler's *Suicides*, which makes an important contribution to the interpretative approach to suicide discussed in Chapter 6, has appeared in English translation (trans. B. Cooper, Blackwell, 1979). Baechler argues that we must begin with the assumption that 'men make their own destinies' and that suicidal actions must be seen as rational responses to life problems: not so much an end, but rather a means to an end. Suicide is thus defined as 'all behaviour that seeks and finds the solution to an existential problem by making an attempt on the life of the subject' (p. 11). For Baechler, the question, then, is: 'what people seek what solutions to what problems by suicide? In this undertaking he adopts the approach advocated by Douglas: that is, examine the situated, or concrete, meanings of suicidal actions in order to reveal more general patterns, or types, of meaning.

From his analysis of case material Baechler claims to have found eleven distinct suicidal meanings which he groups into four general types of suicide. There are *escapist* suicides, where the subject is seeking to flee from an intolerable situation; *aggressive* suicides, directed towards harming, or appealing to, others; *oblative* suicides, which are orientated towards some higher metaphysical or moral state; finally, there are *ludic* suicides, where the subject is gambling with his life in an ordeal or a game. Unlike some who adopt an interpretative approach, Baechler does not assume that suicides are the free constructions of the actors who accomplish them, but, rather, relates his typology to some of the causal factors most commonly associated with suicide. However, this problem is never worked through, and it is somewhat disconcerting for the reader to be suddenly transported from a phenomenological world of meaningful rationality into a positivist environment of causal influence, not only without warning, but also without apparent consideration of the contradictions involved.

Baechler's book has the great merit, in contrast to sociological works in particular, of considering a wide range of suicidal pheno-mena, including Stengel's notion of the ordeal dimension of suicide. The main problem with the typology is that many of the cases pre-sented by Baechler could have been quite conveniently found in categories other than those into which they were placed, and I found similar difficulties relating cases from my own researches to the typology. For example, one of the commonest behaviour patterns in adolescent suicidal behaviour is one where the subject makes threats to others (or a specific other) regarding their treatment of him, or her, and then engages in an act of self-damage where there is the possibility of death. In Baechler's terms, such acts are attempts at *escape* from an intolerable situation; but they are also *aggressive* in the sense that are directed towards others either in blame and/or appeal; they are also *ludic* as the subject is gambling with death.

While Baechler acknowledges that 'the meanings can encroach on each other' (p. 203), it seems that the problem is rather greater than this. The difficulty of fitting cases of suicide into Baechler's scheme leads one to question the value of typology. For example, while the terminally ill patient and the bullied, hounded misfit may both wish to *escape* to death, the meaning of their suicidal actions is essentially different. Whereas the former says to himself 'I am dead', the latter states to others 'I am killed'. Although both acts may, in a shallow sense, be said to be characterised by *escape*, they are examples of different types of suicide. There are similar prob-lems with each type of suicide offered by Baechler, and the general criticisms raised in my own book about inductivist explanations may also be applied to *Suicides*. I have tried to show in my book that we should derive types of suicide not from the apparent and superficial similarities of suicidal performances, but rather from theoretical analysis of the underlying structures that generate them. In this con-text it is both unfortunate and perhaps a little ironic that a French student who pays tribute to Aron should be so casually dismissive of Durkheim. For despite the scholarly approach, the excellent use of data and the catholic interest in a variety of approaches to suicide, Baechler's work, like so many others on the subject, is much the weaker for his conviction that those seeking to unravel the mysteries of suicide have little or nothing to learn from Durkheim. If my book, in some small way, helps to correct some of the most common misrepresentations of Durkheim's *Suicide* and leads to more sympathetic and appreciative consideration of Durkheim's work on the part of both suicide researchers and sociologists, then it will have achieved its major objective.

Appendix: 'Persons under Trains' 1975

Total no. 95 (excluding Moorgate disaster)

		Male	Female
Fatalities	61	44	17
Suicide	37	21	16
Accident	13	13	0
Open	11	10	1

Five of those killed (all male) were employees of London Transport. All were returned as accidental deaths.

Extract from a motorman's statement (these tended to be fairly standard and this is simply taken from the first case that year where in fact an 'accident' verdict was returned):

> As I entered Finchley Road station I saw a man about fifty feet ahead standing approximately three feet from the edge of the platform begin to walk towards the train. When the train was almost level with him, he suddenly dived forward towards the track and disappeared from view beneath the train. I immediately made an emergency application of the brakes and the train came to a halt after travelling another 125 feet.

VERDICTS OF COURTS

	Suicide	Accident	Open
Battersea	4	0	2
Croydon	1	0	0
Epping	1	0	0
Hammersmith	3	2	0
Hornsey	4	3	2
Southwark	3	0	1
St Pancras	4	4	4
Walthamstow	4	0	0
Westminster	<u>13</u>	<u>4</u>	<u>2</u>
	37	13	11

Notes and References

Chapter 1: Durkheim's 'Suicide'

1. T. Morris, *Deviance and Control: the Secular Heresy* (London, Hutchinson, 1976) p. 79.
2. Those who have defended the moral right of the individual to take his own life have included Donne, *Biathanatos* (New York, Facsimile Text Society, 1930); Montaigne, 'A Custome of the Island of Cea', *The Essays of Michael Lord of Montaigne*, translated by J. Florio (Oxford University Press, 1929) and more recently T. Szasz, 'The Ethics of Suicide', in B. Wolman (ed.), *Between Suicide and Survival* (New York, Gardener, 1976).
3. Masaryk, for example, anticipated Durkheim by declaring that, 'To psychologists and sociologists social phenomena are simply facts, just as stellar phenomena are simply facts to the astronomer'. T. G. Masaryk, *Suicide and the Meaning of Civilization*, translated by W. B. Weist and R. G. Batson (University of Chicago Press, 1970) p. 5. Like Durkheim, Masaryk intended his work to be far more than a discussion of the causes of suicide. He claimed that it 'gives in a nutshell a philosophy of history and an analysis of our modern era', p. 291.
4. H. Morselli, *Suicide: an Essay in Comparative Moral Statistics* (New York, Appleton, 1903) p. 1.
5. A view which some writers still hold today. Veith, for example, has claimed that: 'Suicide . . . clearly represents an illness and is, in fact, the least curable of all diseases.' I. Veith, 'Reflections on the Medical History of Suicide', *Modern Medicine* (August 1969) pp. 116–21.
6. See A. Giddens, 'The Suicide Problem in French Sociology', *British Journal of Sociology*, vol. 16 (1965) pp. 3–15. Reprinted in Giddens (ed.), *The Sociology of Suicide* (London, Cass, 1971) pp. 36–51.
7. Some writers have tended to present a much too simple view of this problem by suggesting that one *either* believes in determinism *or* free well. In some debates 'determinism' has been depicted as necessarily conservative, a philosophy of humanity opposed to social change. However, many of the earliest social scientists were arguing that the human condition is only *presently* determined and that, in order to become more free (i.e. more wilful) one must first recognise that one is *not* free. It is a characteristic of these early 'positivist' studies, not that they *simply* saw human action as determined as opposed to willed, but rather that they handled the *tension* between determinism and free will in a particular way. Many of these early studies express the belief that the world can indeed be changed. Masaryk, for example, discussing tendencies for suicide in

modern society, argued that: 'Science gives us the means at hand to protect ourselves from the harmful effects of nature. It teaches us how we can shape to our advantage all the conditions we studied in the chapters on bodily organisation, general societal conditions and psychoses. Why do we not shape them? Because we do not want to.' Masaryk, *Suicide and the Meaning of Civilization*, p. 222.

8. Morselli, *Suicide*, p. 2.
9. A. Lewis, 'Statistical Aspects of Suicide', *Canadian Medical Association Journal*, vol. 74 (1956) pp. 99–104.
10. **For example, M. A. Quetelet,** *Du Système Social el des Lois qui le Régissent* (Paris, 1848); P.-E. Lisle, *Du Suicide: Statistique, Médecine, Histoire et Léglislation* (Paris, 1856); A. J. F. Brierre-de-Boismont, *Du Suicide et de la Folie Suicide Considéres dans leurs Rapports avec la Statistique, la Médecine et la Philosophie* (Paris, 1856).
11. H. T. Buckle, *History of Civilization in England*, vol. 1 (London, Longman, 1871) pp. 12–13.
12. Morselli, *Suicide*, p. 16.
13. Ibid, p. 12.
14. E. Durkheim, *Suicide: A Study in Sociology*, translated by J. A. Spaulding and G. Simpson (London, Routledge & Kegan Paul, 1952).
15. Douglas has argued that '*Suicide* was primarily an attempt to synthesise the better principles, methods of analysis, and empirical findings of the moral statisticians'. J. D. Douglas, *The Social Meanings of Suicide* (Princeton University Press, 1967) p. 15.
16. E. Durkheim, *The Rules of Sociological Method*, translated by S. A. Solvay and J. H. Mueller (New York, Free Press, 1950).
17. See, for example, I. Taylor, P. Walton and J. Young, *The New Criminology* (London, Routledge & Kegan Paul, 1973) pp. 70–3.
18. H. Alpert, *Emile Durkheim and his Sociology*, (New York, Russell & Russell, 1961); R. A. Nisbet, *The Sociological Tradition* (London, Heinemann, 1967).
19. A. Giddens, *Studies in Social and Political Theory* (London, Hutchinson, 1977) p. 29.
20. Ibid, pp. 29–31.
21. C. Bagley, 'Review of A Handbook of Suicide', *The Times Higher Education Supplement* (2 January 1976).
22. Durkheim makes it quite clear in the Preface of *Suicide* that his 'target' is not specifically 'non-sociologists', but rather those 'sociologists' who do the discipline a disservice by mistakenly trying to base it on the psychological constitution of the individual. However, this is not an argument 'for' the case of sociology as opposed to psychology, but an argument against subjectivism.
23. Durkheim, *Suicide: A Study in Sociology*, p. 36.
24. Social facts may be recognised, Durkheim argued, by their constraining effects on individuals. Thus crowd behaviour, currents of opinion and the moralities of law and education, for example, have in common that they are collective phenomena that have an existence *independent* of particular individuals. They thus constitute a distinct area of reality and are consequently deserving of a distinct academic discipline to explain them.
25. R. Bierstedt, *Emile Durkheim* (London, Weidenfeld & Nicolson, 1966) p. 157.
26. As Giddens, amongst others, has observed, *The Rules of Sociological Method* is by far the weakest of Durkheim's popular works. In particular, Durkheim often advocates a crude empiricist epistemology which is clearly at odds with the realist ontology of his major studies. Giddens, *Studies in Social and Political Theory* pp. 291–3. See also P. Q. Hirst, *Durkheim, Barnard and Epistemology* (London, Routledge & Kegan Paul, 1975).

27. Durkheim, *Suicide*, pp. 37–8. For Durkheim, the importance of urging us to treat social facts as 'things' was not that he was advocating 'materialism' as *opposed* to 'idealism', but rather to warn us against subjectivism. That is, as participating members of society, we think we know the nature of social realities, but we must not be misled into thinking that social realities are immediately known to us. Thus socialism, for example, is neither what people who call themselves socialists say it is, neither is it what I, the observer, say it is. However, how one may 'know' the nature of these social realities is a problem that Durkheim himself never satisfactorily resolved. In chapter two of *The Rules of Sociological Method*, Durkheim, in stressing the importance of eliminating *our ideas* from the realm of observation, ends up with an inductive epistemology which he did clearly not adhere to himself and which, as I observed above, contradicts his realist ontology. See the excellent discussion by D. A. Nye and C. E. Ashworth, 'Emile Durkheim: was he a Nominalist or a Realist?', *British Journal of Sociology*, vol. 22 (1971) pp. 133–48, cf. E. Benoit-Smullyan, 'The Sociologism of Emile Durkheim and his School' in H. E. Barnes (ed.), *An Introduction to the History of Sociology* (Chicago, Phoenix, 1948) pp. 500–1.
28. Durkheim, *Suicide*, p. 38.
29. Ibid, pp. 38–9.
30. R. A. Nisbet, 'Sociology as an Art Form' in M. Stein and A. Vidich (eds), *Sociology on Trial* (Englewood Cliffs, Prentice-Hall, 1963) pp. 148–62.
31. 'In terms of sheer bulk of material, suicide was probably one of the most discussed social problems of the nineteenth century. By the time at which Durkheim wrote, a substantial number of correlations had been established linking suicide with a range of social factors.' Giddens, 'The Suicide Problem in French Sociology', in *The Sociology of Suicide*, p. 37.
32. Many writers have argued that it was the fear of the breakdown of society and consequent concern with the 'problem of order' that gave decisive impetus to the genesis of sociology. It is argued that sociology was thus shaped by the 'conservative reaction' to the Enlightenment and the French Revolution and in particular, the desire to restore some form of 'supra-individual' hegemony. See, for example, A. Dawe's excellent discussion: 'The Two Sociologies', *British Journal of Sociology*, vol. 21, (1970) pp. 207–18 and I. M. Zeitlin, *Ideology and the Development of Sociological Theory* (Englewood Cliffs, Prentice-Hall, 1968) pp. 35–82. In this context Robert Nisbet has argued that: 'it was Durkheim's feat to translate into the hard methodology of science ideas and values that had made their first appearance in the polemics of Bonald, Maistre, Haller and others opposed to reason and rationalism, as well as revolution and reform'. R. A. Nisbet (ed.), *Emile Durkheim*, (Englewood Cliffs, Prentice-Hall, 1965) p. 25. In Nisbet's view, Durkheim was thus a positivist and a conservative, an interpretation which does little justice to Durkheim's work. In fact Durkheim was quite explicit that the problems facing modern societies could not be resolved by a return to the autocratic discipline of traditional orders, but rather there had to be a moral consolidation of the differentiated division of labour. As Giddens has observed, in relation to Parsons's claim that all Durkheim's work was an attack on the problem of order, 'the main trend of Durkheim's work is about the analysis of the changing forms of social solidarity over the course of societal development', A. Giddens, *Capitalism and Modern Social Theory* (Cambridge University Press, 1971) p. 106. See also: Giddens, 'Four Myths in the History of Social Thought' in Giddens, *Studies in Social and Political Theory*, pp. 208–34.
33. Durkheim, *Suicide*, p. 35.

34. Ibid, pp. 46–52.
35. Ibid, pp. 133–42. Of course, this 'refutation' would no longer be so valid today where reports of suicide which might influence others to imitation are carried by the mass media. See, for example, J. A. Motto, 'Newspaper Influence on Suicide', paper presented to the Fifth International Conference for Suicide Prevention (1969).
36. S. Lukes, *Emile Durkheim: His Life and Work: a Historical and Critical Study* (London, Peregrine, 1975) p. 205.
37. Durkheim, *Suicide*, p. 146. In this context Jacobs has complained that Durkheim 'abandoned the search for a common denominator to suicide before beginning it'. J. Jacobs 'A Phenomenological Study of Suicide Notes', *Social Problems*, vol. 15 (1967) p. 60 (reprinted in Giddens (ed.), *The Sociology of Suicide*, pp. 332–48).
38. Durkheim, *Suicide*, p. 148.
39. Ibid, p. 151.
40. Described by La Capra as 'Cartesianized neo-Kantianism'. D. La Capra, *Emile Durkheim: Sociologist and Philosopher* (Cornell University Press, 1972) p. 8.
41. Durkheim, *Suicide*, p. 209.
42. Ibid, pp. 152–6. Halbwachs has criticised Durkheim for not attempting to control for urban rural differences, which was important as the latter were predominantly Catholic. M. Halbwachs, *Les Causes du Suicide* (Paris, Alcan, 1930) p. 8. Pope, attempting to control for urbanisation, has argued that, 'for countries high on civilization, it is invariably the Catholic that have the higher average suicide rates': W. Pope, *Durkheim's Suicide: A Classic Analyzed* (University of Chicago Press, 1976) p. 67. Much of Durkheim's evidence for Catholic–Protestant comparisons is taken from Morselli's data, and Pope notes that Durkheim elected not to use that data of Morselli's that contradicted his theory. For example, for the years 1852–4 and 1858–9 the suicide rate (per million) for Galicia (Austria) was 45 for Catholics and 16 for Protestants; for Transylvania, it was 113 to 74; and for Military Frontiers (Austria) it was 28 to 25. In short, the data does not support Durkheim's contention that 'everywhere without exception, Protestants show far more suicides than followers of other confessions'. Durkheim, *Suicide*, p. 154.
43. Durkheim, *Suicide*, p. 168. Durkheim was not the first to argue that an increasingly 'free spirit of enquiry' was linked to increasing vulnerability to suicide. Masaryk also observed that both Protestantism and education, in helping to promote more 'free enquiry' made more people vulnerable to suicide. Masaryk was particularly opposed to what he called 'half education'. In a statement that would please many today, Masaryk claimed that: 'Knowledge which cannot be used makes it possessor a victim of fantasy, of hypercritical nonsense, destroying the desire for useful labour, creating needs which cannot be satisfied, and leading in the end to boredom with life'. Masaryk, *Suicide and the Meaning of Civilization*, p. 68.
44. Durkheim, *Suicide*, p. 189. Durkheim, however, did not explain why in some cases (for example, France compared with Oldenburg) the 'coefficient of preservation' varies with the sexes. As Pope has observed: 'Following up Durkheim's own argument – that the sex with the highest coefficient of preservation for married persons varies from one country to another, and even by region within a given country – centres attention on aspects of the data that may be interpreted as suggesting that his larger hypothesis (relating family size and suicide rates) may apply to men in one country but not to women (France); to women but not to men in another country (Oldenburg). See Pope, *Durkheim's Suicide*.

45. An observation which has quite often been contradicted; for example, Kozak and Gibbs claim that their data shows that 'whatever possible effect dependent children have tends to decrease as the number of children increases'. C. M. Kozak and J. O. Gibbs, 'Dependent Children and Suicide of Married Persons', *Suicide and Life Threatening Behaviour*, vol. 9 (1979) p. 73.
46. Durkheim, *Suicide*, p. 208. A hypothesis confirmed, for example, by Biller's finding that the suicide rate fell for random populations in the weeks following President Kennedy's assassination. O. A. Biller, 'Suicide Related to the Assassination of President John F. Kennedy', *Suicide and Life Threatening Behaviour*, vol. 7 (1977) pp. 40–4.
47. Ibid, p. 209.
48. Ibid, pp. 228–39.
49. Durkheim never managed to document this point adequately. In the first place, he tended to use absolute indicators of a society's increasing prosperity (such as machines) without indicating the *distribution* of this prosperity. Similarly, he observed that low wheat prices (in Prussia) coincided with an increase in the suicide rate without saying anything about, for example, the level of wages during that period. Finally, his observation that the richest departments of France had the highest suicide rates, of course, tells us nothing about the relationship between prosperity and suicide. Ibid, p. 245.
50. Ibid, p. 254.
51. Ibid, p. 258.
52. Ibid, p. 287.
53. See, for example, J. P. Gibbs and W. T. Martin, *Status Integration and Suicide: A Sociological Study* (University of Oregon Press, 1964) pp. 6–7; N. J. Smelser, *Sociological Theory: A Contemporary View* (New York, General Learning Press, 1971) pp. 18–19; R. W. Maris, *Social Forces in Urban Suicide* (Illinois, Dorsey Press, 1969) pp. 179–80.
54. Pope, *Durkheim's Suicide*, pp. 55–56.
55. Durkheim, *Suicide*, p. 382.
56. Ibid, p. 288.
57. B. D. Johnson, 'Durkheim's One Cause of Suicide', *American Sociological Review*, vol. 30 (1965) pp. 875–86. Also, to try to explain Durkheim's theory in terms of the one variable, integration, is to divorce it from the homo duplex concept in terms of which it was conceived. As Hynes has observed, 'One manifestation of Durkheim's homo duplex concept was his dichotomies, which he considered isomorphic, of social versus individual, moral rules versus sensual appetites, and concepts versus sensations. When Durkheim wrote on the differences between egoistic and anomic suicides he cast his argument in terms of "reflective intelligence" and "emotion".' E. Hynes, 'Suicide and Homo Duplex: an Interpretation of Durkheim's Typology of Suicide', *The Sociological Quarterly*, vol. 16 (1975) p. 95.
58. Durkheim, *Suicide*, p. 276.
59. Ibid, pp. 277–94.
60. Ibid, p. 315.
61. H. Hendin, 'Suicide: the Psychosocial Dimension', *Suicide and Life Threatening Behaviour*, vol. 8 (1978) p. 116.
62. R. J. Havighurst, 'Suicide and Education', in E. S. Shneidman (ed.), *On the Nature of Suicide* (San Francisco, Jossey-Bass, 1969) p. 55.
63. J. P. Gibbs, (ed.), *Suicide* (New York, Harper & Row, 1968) p. 7.
64. Pope, *Durkheim's Suicide*, p. 9.
65. For example in E. Durkheim, *Sociology and Philosophy* (Glencoe, Free Press, 1963) pp. 1–35.

66. As Giddens has observed, Durheim was not 'anti-individualist', rather he stressed that individualism had to be explained socially. Giddens, 'The Individual in the Writings of Emile Durkheim', *Studies in Social and Political Theory*, p. 273.
67. Durkheim, *Suicide*, p. 311.
68. Thus Durkheim wrote that: 'We see no objection to calling sociology a variety of psychology, if we carefully add that social psychology has its own laws which are not those of individual psychology.' Ibid, p. 312.
69. Ibid, p. 320. Wallwork has referred to this as 'relational social realism' whereby 'these facts exist neither apart from individuals nor in any single individual taken in isolation, for they only exist in and among associated individuals'. E. Wallwork, *Durkheim, Morality and Milieu* (Harvard University Press, 1972) p. 18.
70. Durkheim, *Suicide*, p.214.
71. E. Stengel, *Suicide and Attempted Suicide* (Harmondsworth, Penguin, 1973) p. 51.
72. P. Cresswell, 'Interpretations of Suicide', *British Journal of Sociology*, vol. 23 (1972) p. 143.
73. Pope, *Durkheim's Suicide*, p. 203.
74. Nye and Ashworth, 'Emile Durkheim', *British Journal of Sociology*, pp. 137–8.
75. Lukes, *Emile Durkheim*, p. 216.
76. Durkheim, *Suicide*, p. 299.
77. Ibid, p. 321.
78. R. Aron, *Main Currents of Sociological Thought*, vol. 2 (London, Weidenfeld & Nicolson, 1968) p. 34.

Chapter 2: The Sociologistic Perspective on Suicide

1. R. K. Merton, *On Theoretical Sociology* (New York, Free Press, 1967) p. 63.
2. H. C. Selvin, 'Durkheim's Suicide: Further Thoughts on a Methodological Classic', in Nisbet (ed.), *Emile Durkheim*, p. 136.
3. Although Pope has argued that in fact important aspects of *Suicide* are not reliably supported by the data, Pope, *Durkheim's Suicide*, pp. 63–154, this is not particularly relevant to the legacy bequeathed by the work because so many subsequent studies have *confirmed* 'Durkheim's' hypotheses.
4. Maris, *Social Forces in Urban Suicide*, p. 159.
5. R. L. Geisel, 'Suicide in Missouri: An Empirical Test of Durkheim's Social Integration Theory', unpublished paper.
6. S. Labovitz and M. B. Brinkerhoff, 'Structural Changes and Suicide in Canada', *International Journal of Comparative Sociology*, vol. 18 (1977) pp. 254–67.
7. P. Sainsbury, *Suicide in London*, (London, Chapman & Hall, 1955). In a basically similar type of ecological study of electoral wards of Edinburgh, McCulloch *et al.* found suicide correlated positively with the density of population, the divorce rate, juvenile delinquency and attempted suicide, but not with the number of migrants, old-age pensioners or rent arrears. J. W. McCulloch, A. E. Philip and G. M. Carstairs, 'The Ecology of Suicidal Behaviour', *British Journal of Psychiatry*, vol. 113 (1967) pp. 313–19. Chuaqui also found that suicide correlated positively with population density in an ecological study of the administrative divisions of Santiago, Chile: C. Chuaqui, 'Suicide in Santiago, Chile', *Public Health Report*, vol. 81 (1966) pp. 1109–17.

8. Stengel, *Suicide and Attempted Suicide*, p. 25; cf. G. E. Murphy and E. Robins, 'Social Factors in Suicide', *Journal of the American Medical Association*, vol. 199 (1967) pp. 303–8.

9. L. I. Dublin, *Suicide: A Sociological and Statistical Study*, (New York, Ronald, 1963).

10. Sainsbury, *Suicide in London*.

11. F. L. Nelson, 'Religiosity and Self-Destructive Crises in the Institutionalised Elderly', *Suicide and Life Threatening Behaviour*, vol. 7 (1977) p. 68.

12. Labovitz, in the introduction to his survey of suicide rates argued that general surveys are prior to theories because: 'First, they reveal the range and kinds of variation in the suicide rate that call for explanation. And second, they provide a basis for assessing the explanatory adequacy of any suggested cause of variation in suicide rates'. S. Labovitz, 'Variation in Suicide Rates', in Gibbs (ed.), *Suicide*, p. 58.

13. For example, E. H. Powell, 'Occupation, Status and Suicide: Toward a Redefinition of Anomie', *American Sociological Review*, vol. 23 (1958) pp. 131–9.

14. For a summary of these research findings see D. Lester, C. Reeve and K. Priebe, 'Completed Suicide and Month of Birth', *Psychological Reports*, vol. 27 (1970) p. 210. For a summary of the relationship between suicide and the moon, see P. K. Jones and S. L. Jones 'Lunar Association with Suicide', *Suicide and Life Threatening Behaviour*, vol. 7 (1977) pp. 31–39.

15. It is interesting that while critiques of empiricist techniques of explanation have a long history, many practitioners of research remain immune from them. For summaries of these critiques see A. J. Lally, 'Positivism and its Critics', in D. C. Thorne (ed.), *New Directions in Sociology* (Newton Abbott, David & Charles, 1976); Giddens, 'Positivism and its Critics', in Giddens, *Studies in Social and Political Theory*. For one of the most articulate critiques of empiricist research strategies see D. Willer and J. Willer, *Systematic Empiricism: a Critique of a Pseudo-Science* (Englewood Cliffs, Prentice-Hall, 1973).

16. For example, Giddens, 'The Suicide Problem in French Sociology', in *The Sociology of Suicide*, p. 46; J. D. Douglas, *The Social Meanings of Suicide*, pp. 79–83.

17. Douglas, for example, has suggested that 'Perhaps . . . *Suicide* has been too much of a challenge. Being so extensive and inclusive, it defied attempts at encompassment.' Douglas, *The Social Meanings of Suicide*, p. 79. Similarly, Alvarez, from a distance as it were, has observed that '[Durkheim's] influence on the lesser men who have followed him has been curiously deadening . . . As a result, the more that has been written, the narrower the field has become.' A. Alvarez, *The Savage God* (Harmondsworth, Penguin, 1974) p. 115.

18. For example, H. Hendin, *Black Suicide* (New York, Basic Books, 1969); R. Seiden, 'Why are the Suicides of Young Blacks Increasing?' *Public Health Reports*, vol. 87 (1972) pp. 3–8; J. Bush (ed.), *Suicide and Blacks*, (Los Angeles, Drew Post Graduate Medical School, 1976); R. Davis and J. F. Short, 'Dimensions of Black Suicide: A Theoretical Model', *Suicide and Life Threatening Behaviour*, vol. 8 (1978) pp. 161–73.

19. Newman *et al.* argue that the increasing suicide rates of women may be the product of the conflicting demands placed on the greater number of women who have to fulfil the roles of worker and homemaker. J. F. Newman, K. Whittemore and H. G. Newman, 'Women in the Labour Force and Suicide', *Social Problems*, vol. 21 (1973) pp. 220–30. Iga *et al.* explain the high rate of young Japanese females in terms of their unique vulnerability to role conflict. M. Iga, J. Yamamoto and T. Noguchi, 'The Vulnerability of Young Japanese Women to Suicide', *Suicide*, vol. 5 (1975) pp. 207–22.

20. Hendin, for example, argued that the relatively low suicide rate of Norwegians compared with Danes and Swedes stemmed from their different child-rearing practices. The former were allowed more freedom of emotional expression and this produced 'personality types' less prone to suicide. H. Hendin, *Suicide and Scandinavia* (New York, Grune & Stratton, 1964); cf. M. L. Farber, 'Suicide in France: Some Hypotheses', *Suicide and Life Threatening Behaviour*, vol. 9 (1979) pp. 154–62. Similarly Iga claimed that Japanese youth have a relatively high suicide rate on account of their 'weak egos'. M. Iga, 'Japanese Adolescent Suicide and the Social Structure', in E. S. Shneidman (ed.), *Essays in Self Destruction* (New York, International Science Press, 1967) pp. 224–50; while Hsu has argued that the relatively low suicide rate of Chinese Americans is to be explained in terms of their less individualistic, 'situation centred' life style making them less emotionally vulnerable to reversals. F. L. K. Hsu, *Americans and Chinese* (New York, Natural History Press, 1953).

21. More detailed accounts of the major sociological studies on suicide can be found, for example, in Douglas, *The Social Meanings of Suicide*, pp. 79–160; Gibbs (ed.), *Suicide*; A. F. Henry and J. F. Short, 'The Sociology of Suicide', in E. S. Shneidman and N. L. Farberow (eds), *Clues to Suicide* (New York, McGraw-Hill, 1957) pp. 58–69; Giddens (ed.), *The Sociology of Suicide*, pp. 3–151.

22. Halbwachs, *Les Causes du Suicide*.

23. In more recent studies Durkheim's notion of social integration which was essentially *moral* isolation, has been replaced by the idea of social isolation which is concerned mainly with *physical* isolation. For example, Dublin, *Suicide*, p 167; Sainsbury, *Suicide in London*, p. 76. In this context Stengel argued that the crucial factor is the experience of isolation. E. Stengel, 'Suicide and Social Isolation', *Twentieth Century*, vol. 173 (1964) p. 25.

24. B. D. Johnson, 'Durkheim's One Cause of Suicide'. Similarly, Martin has observed that: 'The task of explicating Durkheim's theory would be much simpler if it could be limited to *egoistic* suicide, since in this instance his theoretical position is clear and straightforward'. W. T. Martin, 'Theories of Variation in the Suicide Rate', in Gibbs (ed.), *Suicide*, pp. 74–96. Halbwachs, in adopting a broadly similar position, realised that altruistic suicide would have to be removed from the theory and he therefore argued that it was not really 'suicide' at all.

25. Thus Durkheim was able to 'identify characteristics of a population as indicative of a high degree of social integration *after* the establishment of the population's low suicide rate'. Gibbs and Martin, *Status Integration and Suicide*, p. 14.

26. For example, testing the theorem on individual states in the United States Gibbs and Martin correlated mean annual suicide rates, a (hypothetical) measure of total status integration, and a weighted status integration measure of thirty states. In most cases negative correlations were found between suicide rates and indices of status integration. Of 175 coefficients tested in the work 160 confirm the theory, although only a third of these are statistically significant to the 0.01 level. In total, 676 predictions were made of which 392 (58 per cent) were correct. On a chance basis only 172 correct predictions would have been expected. Gibbs and Martin, *Status Integration and Suicide*, p. 197. In a later paper, Gibbs and Martin have shown that a higher degree of predictability can be expected amongst groups where the suicide rate is consistent over a long period. In such groups there is less problem of a possible 'time lag' between the two measures. In other words, by implication, many of the theory's 'false' predictions could have been the result of the status integration of a group at a given time being matched (incorrectly) with its suicide rate at *another* time. Gibbs and

Martin, 'A Problem in Testing the Theory of Status Integration', *Social Forces*, vol. 52 (1974) pp. 332–9. However, Chambliss and Steel claim that many of Gibbs and Martin's correlations were due to the influence of a few extreme cases. W. J. Chambliss and M. F. Steel, 'Status Integration and Suicide', *American Sociological Review*, vol. 31 (1966) pp. 524–32.Bagley, although generally approving of the approach taken by Gibbs and Martin, has argued that 'authoritarianism' provides a better predictor of suicide rates, and that a greater degree of status integration can be expected in 'authoritarian communities' where individuals are more likely to be 'prevented from moving into atypical status sets'. C. Bagley, 'Authoritarianism, Status Integration and Suicide', *Sociology*, vol. 6 (1972) pp. 395–404.

27. W. J. Chambliss, 'Review of Status Integration and Suicide', *American Journal of Sociology*, vol. 71 (1966) pp. 731–2.

28. R. Hagedorn and S. Labovitz, 'A Note on Status Integration and Suicide', *Social Problems*, vol. 14 (1966) pp. 79–84.

29. For example, E. H. Powell, 'Occupation, Status and Suicide'; J. P. Gibbs and A. L. Porterfield, 'Occupational Prestige and Social Mobility of Suicides in New Zealand', *American Journal of Sociology*, vol. 66 (1960) pp. 147–52; W. Breed, 'Occupational Mobility and Suicide', *American Sociological Review*, vol. 28 (1963) pp. 179–88.

30. A. F. Henry and J. F. Short, *Suicide and Homicide* (Glencoe, Free Press, 1954).

31. The theory that suicide is aggression turned inwards against the self, and that such behaviour is to be explained in terms of various socialisation (especially childhood) experiences is employed in many works on suicide and owes most to Dollard's reformulations of Freud's insights. Briefly, Freud, in his original conception of suicide, argued that a (narcissistic) individual, enraged at having been denied a cherished goal, destroys the representation of that goal in himself and thereby destroys himself. S. Freud, 'Mourning and Melancholia', *Collected Papers of Sigmund Freud* vol. 4 (London, Hogarth Press, 1925). Dollard, applying his 'learning' approach to this idea, argued that it was those individuals, who at an early age are punished for the outward expression of aggression, who are more likely in later life to turn aggression inward when frustrated. J. Dollard, C. W. Dobb, H. E. Miller, O. H. Mowrer and R. R. Sears, *Frustration and Aggression* (Yale University Press, 1939). Menninger, in what remains the most famous attempt to explain suicide in terms of aggressive drives, argued that the true suicide act must contain three dimensions: the wish to kill (hate), the wish to be killed (guilt) and the wish to die (hopelessness). Suicide is thus displaced, or inverted, murder. K. Menninger, *Man Against Himself* (New York, Harcourt Brace, 1938).

32. Henry and Short hypothesise that males, whites, those aged 25–34 and army officers would have a greater preference for suicide as opposed to females, non-whites, those aged over 65 and enlisted men respectively, and claim that the data generally supports these hypotheses. Henry and Short, *Suicide and Homicide*, pp. 69–97. However, Buck and Weber, in a re-examination of the Henry and Short thesis, have argued that the crucial variable is not status, but the strength of the relational system. E. W. Buck and I. L. Webber, 'Social Status and Relational System of Elderly Suicides: A Re-examination of the Henry–Short Thesis', *Life Threatening Behaviour*, vol. 2 (1972) pp. 145–59.

33. M. Gold, 'Suicide, Homicide and the Socialisation of Aggression', *American Journal of Sociology*, vol. 63 (1958) p. 657.

34. Maris, *Social Forces in Urban Suicide*.

35. Ibid, pp. 167–72.

36. Ibid, p. 183

37. J. P. Gibbs, 'Suicide', in R. K. Merton and R. A. Nisbet (eds), *Contemporary Social Problems* (New York, Harcourt Brace, 1961), p. 228.

38. The urban ecologists were notable exceptions to this tendency. Cavan's work on suicide, for example, is rich in descriptive case study material although she did not, except by implication, link these examples of 'personal disorganisation' to the more general notion of social disorganisation. R. S. Cavan, *Suicide* (New York, Russell & Russell, 1965).

39. F. Achille-Delmas, *Psychologie Pathologique du Suicide* (Paris, Alcan, 1932). Discussed in Giddens, 'The Suicide Problem in French Sociology', in Giddens (ed.), *The Sociology of Suicide*, p. 41.

40. Stengel, *Suicide and Attempted Suicide*, p. 21.

41. It is interesting to note that, while Durkheim criticised Quetelet's theory of the 'average personality' on these grounds, he did not discuss the implications for his own theory. Durkheim, *Suicide*, p. 303.

42. Hendin, *Suicide and Scandinavia*.

43. W. S. Robinson, 'Ecological Correlations and the Behaviour of Individuals', *American Sociological Review*, vol. 15 (1950) pp. 351–7.

44. Selvin, 'Durkheim's Suicide', p. 126.

45. Some sociologists draw attention to the ecological fallacy, and yet still proceed to engage in a type of analysis which commits the error. See, for example, Bagley, Authoritarianism', p. 397.

46. Douglas, *The Social Meanings of Suicide*, p. 163.

47. J. D. Douglas, 'The Rhetoric of Science and the Origins of Statistical Thought: the Case of Durkheim's *Suicide*', in A. Tiryakian (ed.), *The Phenomenon of Sociology* (New York, Appleton-Century-Crofts, 1969) p. 53.

48. Ibid, p. 54. It may be noted that *Suicide* was the only one of Durkheim's works in which he used the hypothetical-deductive method and even here, he still used historical and biographical data. He did not argue, as some positivists have done, that this is *the* sociological method.

49. Durkheim, *Suicide*, pp. 36–7.

50. Ibid, p. 38.

51. Halbwachs, *Les Causes du Suicide*, p. 30; Alpert, *Emile Durkheim and his Sociology*, pp. 124–5; Gibbs and Martin, *Status Integration and Suicide*, p. 4; Douglas, *The Social Meanings of Suicide*, p. 75.

52. Durkheim, *Suicide*, pp. 167–8.

53. See Douglas, *The Social Meanings of Suicide*, pp. 13–76.

54. Even Gibbs and Martin who produced the most 'testable' sociological theory of suicide do not, for example, define their major concept, role conflict. It is merely assumed to be the product of incompatible statuses.

55. C. S. Kruijt, 'The Suicide Rate in the Western World since World War II, *Netherlands Journal of Sociology*, vol. 13 (1977) pp. 55–6.

56. A. L. Stinchcombe, *Constructing Social Theories*, (New York, Harcourt Brace, 1968) p. 13.

57. R. Pawson, 'Empiricist Explanatory Strategies: the Case of Casual Modelling', *Sociological Review*, vol. 26 (1978) p. 642.

58. E. Esquirol, *Des Maladies Mentales*, vol. 1 (1838) p. 639. Quoted in Giddens, 'The Suicide Problem in French Sociology', p. 37.

59. Ibid, pp. 38–47.

60. P. Courbon, 'Review of Halbwachs' *Les Causes du Suicide*', *Annales Medico-Psychologiques* (1 March 1931) p. 322. Quoted in Giddens, 'The Suicide Problem in French Sociology', p. 41.

61. There is considerable disagreement regarding the extent of the relationship between suicide and mental illnesses. Temoche *et al*. reviewed the different

estimates of the proportion of suicides exhibiting manifestations of mental illness and these ranged from 5 per cent to 94 per cent. A. Temoche, T. F. Pugh, and B. MacMahon, 'Suicide Rates among Current and Former Mental Institution Patients', *Journal of Nervous Mental Diseases*, vol. 138 (1964) pp. 124–30.

62. Stengel, for example, has written that: 'At the present state of knowledge, it is reasonable not to accept the suicidal act alone as a criterion of one of the typical mental disorders'. Stengel, *Suicide and Attempted Suicide*, p. 58. Many psychiatrists and other 'psychological' students of suicide have taken a keen interest in suicide rates and many 'social-factor' studies of suicide rates described above were undertaken by members of the medical profession.

63. For example, Henry and Short, *Suicide and Homicide*, p. 121; Giddens, 'A Typology of Suicide', *European Journal of Sociology*, vol. 7 (1966) pp. 276–95 (reprinted in Giddens (ed.), *The Sociology of Suicide*, pp. 97–120; Maris, *Social Forces in Urban Suicide*, p. 183; H. H. Krauss, 'Suicide – A Psychosocial Phenomenon', in Wolman (ed.) *Between Survival and Suicide*, pp. 25–54. The typical conception is that the 'psychologically orientated' approaches will explain why some individuals are more 'predisposed' to suicide than others, while the 'sociologically orientated' ones will reveal the conditions under which (vulnerable) individuals are more likely to kill themselves.

64. Stengel, *Suicide and Attempted Suicide*, p. 51.

65. Maris, *Social Forces in Urban Suicide*, p. 163.

66. R. A. Van Del, 'The Role of Death Romanticisation in the Dynamics of 'Suicide', *Suicide and Life Threatening Behaviour*, vol. 7 (1977) p. 47.

67. Durkheim, *The Elementary Forms of Religious Life*, translated by J. W. Swain, (New York, Free Press, 1965) p. 208.

68. Gibbs and Martin, *Status Integration and Suicide*, p. 209.

69. Durkheim, *Suicide*, pp. 277–96.

70. J. Wilkins, 'Suicidal Behaviour', *American Sociological Review*, vol. 32 (1967) pp. 286–98 (reprinted in Giddens (ed.), *The Sociology of Suicide*, pp. 398–418).

71. See, for example, Stengel, *Suicide and Attempted Suicide*, pp. 100–4; 'Attempted Suicides', in H. L. P. Resnik, *Suicidal Behaviours: Diagnosis and Management* (London, Churchill, 1968) pp. 171–89.

72. The Los Angeles Suicide Prevention Team, assisting the Los Angeles coroner in the investigation of 'equivocal' suicides, argued that a risk of death of one in six is likely to be recorded as suicide. Shneidman and Farberow, 'Sample Investigation of Equivocal Suicidal Deaths' in Shneidman and Farberow, *The Cry for Help* (New York, McGraw Hill, 1961) pp. 118–30.

73. S. Taylor, 'Suicide and the Renewal of Life', *Sociological Review*, vol. 26, (1978) p. 378.

74. J. I. Kitsuse, 'Societal Reaction to Deviant Behaviour: Problems of Theory and Method', in H. S. Becker (ed.), *The Other Side* (New York, Free Press, 1965) pp. 87–8.

75. See, for example, Gibbs, 'Conceptions of Deviant Behaviour: the Old and the New', *Pacific Sociological Review*, vol. 9 (1966) pp. 9–14; S. Box, *Deviance, Reality and Society* (London, Holt, Rinehart & Winston, 1971) pp. 11–15; I. Taylor, P. Walton and J. Young, *The New Criminology* (London, Routledge & Kegan Paul, 1973) pp. 139–171; A. V. Cicourel, *The Social Organisation of Juvenile Justice* (London, Heinemann, 1976) pp. 330–3; and for a recent defence see K. Plummer, 'Misunderstanding Labelling Perspectives', in D. Downes and P. Rock (eds), *Deviant Interpretations* (London, Martin Robertson, 1979) pp. 85–121.

76. Cohen has referred to this change in emphasis as a 'sceptical revolution' in the study of deviance: 'The new tradition is sceptical in the sense that when it sees

terms like "deviant" it asks "deviant to whom?" or "deviant from what?"; when told that something is a social problem, it asks "problematic to whom?" . . . In other words, these concepts and descriptions are not assumed to have a taken-for-granted status.' S. Cohen, *Folk Devils and Moral Panics* (London, Paladin, 1973) p. 12.

77. Gibbs and Martin, for example, have made it quite clear why they will continue to use suicide rates: 'The present research is based on the assumption that official suicide statistics are reliable to the point that their use in testing theories is justified. Douglas (*The Social Meanings of Suicide*), among others, has questioned that assumption; and three points should be made by way of a brief rejoinder. First, in testing a theory one need not assume that official suicide statistics are absolutely reliable or even approximately so; rather, one may assume that they are sufficiently reliable in a relative sense, that is, the proportionate difference between the 'true' number of suicides and the official number does not vary appreciably among populations. Second, it remains to be seen how one can demonstrate the absolute or relative reliability of even one suicide rate, let alone justify a generalisation from one or a few cases to all official suicide rates. Third, in so far as the goal is repeated tests of a theory, there is no practical alternative to the use of official suicide statistics.' Gibbs and Martin, 'A Problem in Testing the Theory of Status Integration', p. 336.

Chapter 3: Some Critiques of Official Suicide Rates

1. Stengel and Farberow, 'Certification of Suicide Around the World', in Farberow (ed.), *Proceedings of the Fourth International Conference for Suicide Prevention* (Los Angeles, Delmar, 1967) p. 8.
2. There are similarities between the problem of 'hidden suicides' and what criminologists refer to as the 'dark figure'. As Wiles has observed: 'The criminological literature still reports projects which espouse the axioms that individuals involved in criminal behaviour can be differentiated by variables other than their criminality and that this differentiation can be tested by comparing groups of convicted criminals with controls ostensibly without conviction. The contamination of control groups by the dark figure is all too frequently ignored.' P. N. P. Wiles, 'Criminal Statistics and Sociological Explanations of Crime', in W. G. Carson and P. Wiles (eds) *Crime and Delinquency in Britain* (London, Martin Robertson, 1971) p. 182. Generally, however, students of crime have been more aware of this problem than students of suicide. See, for example, F. H. McClintock, 'Criminological and Penological Aspects of the Dark Figure of Crime and Criminality', *Collected Studies in Criminological Research*, vol. 5, Council of Europe, (Strasbourg 1970); W. G. Skogan, 'The Validity of Official Crime Statistics: an empirical investigation', *Social Science Quarterly*, vol. 55 (1974) pp. 25–38; L. B. De Fleur, 'Biasing Influences on Drug Arrest Records: Implication for Deviance Research', *American Sociological Review*, vol. 40 (1975) pp. 88–103.
3. Dublin, for example, has estimated that in the United States the number of suicides probably exceeds the official rate by about 30 per cent. However, it is not at all clear on what criteria such an assessment is based. Dublin, *Suicide*, p. 2.
4. For example, P. Sainsbury and B. Barraclough, 'Differences Between Suicide Rates', *Nature*, vol. 220 (1968) p. 1252.
5. For example, Stengel and Farberow, 'Certification of Suicide', pp. 8–15.
6. Stengel and Cook, 'Contrasting Suicide Rates in Industrial Communities',

Journal of Mental Science, vol. 107 (1961) pp. 1009–14.

7. C. Hassall and W. H. Trethowan, 'Suicide in Birmingham', *British Medical Journal* (18 March 1972) pp. 717–18.

8. For example, Stengel has suggested that, 'the study of disparities and fluctuations of suicide rates in the same country is of greater scientific value than comparisons between different countries'. Stengel, *Suicide and Attempted Suicide*, p. 24.

9. J. Illman, 'Figures Hide True Rate of Suicides', *Pulse* (25 November 1972) p. 22.

10. Stengel and Farberow, 'Certification of Suicide', p. 8. Probably the most significant difference in the certification of suicide between different countries is that in most countries suicide is a judicial matter whereas in others it is not, (Sweden and Japan, for example). Of the thirty-seven countries who responded to Stengel and Farberow's questionnaire, eight used coroners, twenty used other legal officers (e.g. magistrates), one (Austria) a tribunal, and the remaining eight, medical officers. Stengel and Farberow observe that 'the suicide rates based on coroners' verdicts cannot be compared with those derived from medical judgements'. Other important (biasing) variables include whether or not suicide is an 'illegal' act, different autopsy rates and different procedures for issuing death certifications. Registration procedures also vary within countries; different states of America, provinces of Canada, and England and Scotland, for example, use different procedures for certifying suicide. Ibid, pp. 10–14. See J. H. Brown, 'Reporting of Suicide: Canadian Statistics', *Suicide*, vol. 5 (1975) pp. 21–8. Another important source of data, one rarely considered by students of suicide rates, is the reliability of the population census. Clearly, suicide rates are useless unless they can be related to correct population figures. Stengel and Farberow ask: 'Can it really be taken for granted that the population census is equally reliable everywhere, even in countries where millions have no homes of their own?' Ibid, p. 13. Apparently it can be – by sociologists. Gibbs and Martin, for example, make important tests on their theory of status integration with data from West Bengal. Gibbs and Martin, *Status Integration and Suicide*, pp. 154–8.

11. Stengel and Farberow, 'Certification of Suicide', p. 13.

12. McCarthy and Walsh estimated that the 'true suicide rate' of Dublin averaged 5.5 per 100,000 per year, approximately twice the official rate of between 2 and 2.7. They did not, however, discuss the criteria on which their rate was based; rather they were concerned to examine it for the 'familiar' social variables, such as marital status, social status, etc. P. D. McCarthy and D. Walsh, 'Suicide in Dublin', *British Medical Journal*, vol. 1 (1966) pp. 1393–6.

13. Zilboorg, for example, in a well-worn quotation, declared that: 'Statistical data on suicides, as they are compiled today, deserve little if any credence; it has been repeatedly pointed out by scientific students of the problem that suicide cannot be subjected to statistical evaluation, since all too many suicides are not reported as such . . . It is obvious that under these circumstances the statistical data available cover the smallest and probably least representative number of suicides: one is justified therefore, in discarding them as nearly useless in scientific evaluation of the problem.' G. Zilboorg, 'Suicide among Civilized and Primitive Races', *American Journal of Psychiatry*, vol. 92 (1936) p. 1349. Cf. G. Simpson, 'Editor's introduction to *Suicide*', p. 19. This scepticism appears to be quite common amongst the psychiatric profession, one of whom, on hearing my topic of research, remarked that 'any psychiatrist could have told you that suicide rates are no use'.

14. Zilboorg, it may be noted, qualified his critique with the phrase 'as they are

compiled today'. Another complaint made by researchers of a more psycho-analytic persuasion has been made against official suicide rates on the grounds many progressive and cumulative acts of self destruction – 'chronic suicides' in Menninger's terms – which are 'really' suicides, never get recorded as such. See O. Fenichel, *The Psychoanalytic Theory of Neurosis* (New York, Norton, 1945) p. 401–2. More recently Shneidman *et al.* have proposed a reclassification of suicidal acts in terms of the 'psychological dimension' of the death; giving 'unmeditated', 'premeditated' and 'submeditated' deaths. Shneidman, Farberow and Litman. **'A Taxonomy of Death–A Psychological Point of View', in Shneidman and Farberow (eds), *The Cry for Help*, pp. 129–35.**

15. Many researchers, although rejecting the available official statistics, still rely on the conventional methods of research. Belson, for example, gathered the data for his study of juvenile theft from self-report studies of 1400 boys, but he applied to this data 'traditional' hypothetico-deductive techniques. W. A. Belson, *Juvenile Theft: The Causal Factors*, (New York, Harper & Row, 1975). Further examples of attempts to construct alternative 'rates' of deviance are discussed in Taylor, Walton and Young, *The New Criminology*, pp. 11–19.

16. Ettlinger, 'Certification of Suicide in Sweden', in Farberow (ed.), *Proceedings of the Fourth Int. Conference*, p. 36. Cf. M. D. Warshauer and M. Moak, 'Problems in Suicide Statistics for Whites and Blacks', *American Journal of Public Health*, vol. 68 (1978) pp. 383–8.

17. Wilkins, 'Suicidal Behaviour'.

18. J. M. Atkinson, 'On the Sociology of Suicide', *Sociological Review*, vol. 16 (1968) pp. 83–92, also in Giddens (ed.), *The Sociology of Suicide*, pp. 87–96.

19. It is perhaps no coincidence that official statistics on deviant behaviour, chosen by those who wanted to build a positivist science of society to demonstrate their case, was also the battle ground chosen by those who wanted to undermine such an approach.

20. H. Garfinkel, *Studies in Ethnomethodology*, (Englewood Cliffs, Prentice-Hall, 1967).

21. A. Schutz, *The Phenomenology of the Social World* (Northwestern University Press, 1967) pp. 7–8. Quoted in Taylor, Walton and Young, *The New Criminology*, p. 194.

22. A. V. Cicourel, 'Basic and Normative Rules in the Negotiation of Status and Role', in D. Sudnow (ed.), *Studies in Social Interaction* (New York, Free Press, 1972).

23. Cicourel, *The Social Organisation of Juvenile Justice* (London, Heinemann, 1976).

24. Thus Cicourel's work on delinquency sought 'to discover those thoughts and taken-for-granted elements, participants of conversations and documents utilized for producing utterances and making decisions they routinely honour as "communication"'. Ibid, p. 333.

25. Kitsuse and Cicourel, 'A Note on the Uses of Official Statistics', *Social Problems*, vol. 12 (1963) pp. 131–9, also in W. J. Filstead (ed.), *An Introduction To Deviance: Readings in the Process of Making Deviants* (Chicago, Rand McNally, 1973) pp. 244–55, p. 248 (Filstead).

26. J. M. Atkinson, 'Societal Reactions to Suicide: the Role of Coroners' Definitions', in S. Cohen (ed.), *Images of Deviance* (Harmondsworth, Penguin, 1971) pp. 165–91; 'Critical Note: Suicide, Status Integration and Pseudo-Science', *Sociology*, vol. 7 (1973) pp. 437–45; *Discovering Suicide: Studies in the Social Organisation of Sudden Death* (London, Macmillan, 1978).

27. Douglas, *The Social Meanings of Suicide*, p. 170.

28. Ibid, p. 231. See also H. Sacks, 'Sociological Description', *Berkeley Journal of Sociology*, vol. 8 (1963) p. 8.
29. Ibid, p. 191
30. Thus Cicourel, for example, was 'concerned with the development of methods [which I view as basic to theory construction] for particular theoretical issues, while making both the researcher's and the actor's rules of procedure problematic elements in all research'. *The Social Organisation of Juvenile Justice*, p. vii. While Douglas stated that his work was 'directed at what seem to me to be fundamental problems in sociology . . . that this whole approach [i.e. hypothetical-deductive] involves certain misconceptions about the nature of social phenomena'. Douglas, *The Social Meanings of Suicide*, p. 338.
31. Douglas, *The Social Meanings of Suicide*, p. 183.
32. Garfinkel, 'Studies of the Routine Grounds of Everyday Actions', *Social Problems*, vol. II (1964) p. 229.
33. Cicourel, *The Social Organisation of Juvenile Justice*, p. 24.
34. B. Hindess, *The Use of Official Statistics in Sociology: A Critique of Positivism and Ethnomethodology* (London, Macmillan, 1973) p. 19.
35. Douglas, *The Social Meanings of Suicide*, p. 339.
36. Hindess, *The Use of Official Statistics in Sociology*, p. 24.
37. Douglas, *The Social Meanings of Suicide*, pp. 271–337.
38. Hindess, *The Use of Official Statistics in Sociology*, p. 26.
39. Cicourel, *The Social Organisation of Juvenile Justice*, pp. xviii–xix.
40. For example, in the cases of England, a predominantly Protestant country with a relatively low suicide rate, Durkheim observed that, 'the statistics of English suicides are not very exact. Because of the penalties attached to suicide, many cases are reported as accidental death'. Durkheim, *Suicide*, p. 160.
41. Durkheim, *Suicide*, pp. 148–9.
42. P. L. Berger and T. Luckmann, *The Social Construction of Reality* (Harmondsworth, Penguin, 1971) p. 119. An excellent discussion of the ideologies employed to try to transcend death is provided by R. J. Lifton, 'On Death and the Continuity of Life: A new Paradigm', in Wolman (ed.), *Between Survival and Suicide*, pp. 55–76.
43. Soon after the passing of the Suicide Act 1961 the Ministry of Health issued a memorandum advising doctors and authorities concerned that suicide was to be regarded as a social and a medical problem and all cases of attempted suicide should be seen by a psychiatrist.
44. J. Lofland, *Deviance and Identity* (Englewood Cliffs, Prentice-Hall, 1969) p. 150.
45. Douglas, *The Social Meanings of Suicide*, pp. 222–3.
46. Ibid, pp. 212–13.
47. Ibid, p. 216.
48. Ibid, p. 214.
49. For example, it could be argued that the more *suicide* is condemned, that is the more morally integrated a society is, then the more likely it is to find *concealment* an immoral act as well. Similarly, the less morally integrated a society, the more likely it is to be indifferent to concealment although the less likely it is to bother to conceal. The two may well, therefore, cancel each other out.
50. Another problem not considered by Douglas is how much *scope* officials actually have to allow their beliefs, preferences, etc., to influence their decisions.
51. Another source of systematic bias outlined by Douglas is that statistics-keeping organisations may vary in their efficiency, and that those of 'underdeveloped' countries, or rural areas, for example, would be relatively less efficient than

those of 'advanced countries or urban areas. Douglas, *The Social Meanings of Suicide*, pp. 225–6. Cf. Seiden, who has argued that the high suicide rate of San Francisco is probably in part due to its particular efficient registration procedures. R. H. Seiden, 'Suicide Capital? A Study of the San Francisco Suicide Rate', *Bulletin of Suicidology* (December 1967) pp. 1–7.

52. For example, M. E. Goss and J. I. Reed, 'Suicide and Religion: A Study of White Adults in New York City', *Life Threatening Behaviour*, vol. 1 (1971) pp. 163–77; E. W. Buck and I. L. Webber, 'Social Status and Relational System of Elderly Suicides'; J. F. Newman, K. R. Whittemore and H. G. Newman, 'Women in the Labour Force and Suicide'; Kruijt, 'The Suicide Rate in the Western World'.

53. Maris, *Social Forces in Urban Suicide*, p. 169. Cf. C. Bagley, 'Authoritarianism', p. 397.

54. Many students seem to assume that it is 'enough' to simply mention the 'inadequacy of the data' to resolve these problems. Thus De Vos, for example, having observed that, 'comparative cross cultural statistics are incomplete and can be misleading', then proceeds to use official suicide rates from three different continents in a comparative analysis! G. A. De Vos, 'Suicide in Cross-Cultural Perspective', in H. L. P. Resnik, *Suicidal Behaviours: Diagnosis and Management* (London, Churchill, 1968) pp. 105–34. Cf. S. J. Rojcewicz, 'War and Suicide', *Suicide and Life Threatening Behaviour*, vol. 1 (1971) p. 46.

55. Sainsbury and Barraclough, 'Differences Between Suicide Rates', p. 1252.

56. P. Cresswell, 'Suicide: the Stable Rates Argument', *Journal of Biosocial Science*, vol. 6 (1974) pp. 154.

57. Atkinson, *Discovering Suicide*.

58. Atkinson, 'Societal Reactions to Suicide', p. 186.

59. Atkinson, 'Suicide and the Student', *Universities Quarterly*, vol. 23 (1969) pp. 213–24.

Chapter 4: Proving Suicide

1. Atkinson, *Discovering Suicide*, p. 156.

2. J. Jervis, *The Office and Duties of Coroners*, W. B. Purchase and H. W. Wollaston (eds), (London, Sweet & Maxwell, 1957). For a fuller sociological discussion of coroners see Atkinson, *Discovering Suicide*, pp. 87–109.

3. A point certainly worth further investigation may be made here in relation to Douglas's hypothesis of varying rates of concealment. Coroners and their officials are bound by law and in my experience it seems unlikely that they would be influenced (certainly consciously) by the wishes of the deceased's significant others. In fact the potential for concealment, deliberate or accidental, is far greater *prior* to a case coming to official notice. Certainly there is a positive correlation between the 'referral rate' and the official suicide rate, but pursuing the implications of this potential source of bias would require expert medical knowledge and is, therefore, beyond the scope of this work. Indeed, there is little evidence of any kind on this point. However, in his research comparing coroners with medical examiners, Wayne noted that the former complained that, in their opinion, as many as 25 per cent of 'possibly unnatural sudden deaths' were not being referred to them. Wayne calculated that possibly as many as 16,000 sudden (and possibly unnatural) deaths were not being reported to the coroner. I. Wayne, *Suicide Statistics in the United States: An Exploration of some Factors Affecting the Quality of the Data*, (Washington, Bureau of

Social Science, 1969). See also H. R. M. Johnson, 'The Incidence of Unnatural Deaths which would have been Presumed to be Natural in Coroners' Autopsies', *Medical and Scientific Law*, vol. 9 (1969) pp. 102–6.

4. *Coroners' Rules* (HMSO, 1963).

5. Shneidman and Farberow (eds), *Clues to Suicide* pp. 197–215; see also, F. F. Wagner, 'Suicide Notes', *Danish Medical Journal*, vol. 116 (1960) pp. 62–4; C. J. Frederick, 'Suicide Notes: A Survey and Evaluation, *Bulletin of Suicidology* (March 1969) pp. 17–26.

6. All interview data are transcripts from tape recordings unless otherwise stated. Cf. observations of Atkinson, *Discovering Suicide*, p. 117.

7. T. J. Curphey, 'The Role of the Social Scientist in the Medicolegal Certification of Death from Suicide', in Shneidman and Farberow, *The Cry for Help* (New York, McGraw-Hill, 1961) pp. 110–17.

8. Ibid, p. 114.

9. An excellent comparison of history and psychology and the interpretation of the past is contained in F. Wyatt, 'The Reconstruction of the Individual and of the Collective Past', in R. W. White (ed.), *The Study of Lives* (New York, Atherton, 1963) pp. 305–20.

10. Under Section 4 of the Homicide Act 1957 the survivor of a suicide pact is guilty of manslaughter if in pursuance of the pact he kills the other, or is party to the killing of the other. Prior to this act, the survivor was technically guilty of murder.

11. Atkinson, 'Societal Reactions to Suicide', pp. 174–80.

12. In contrast, in deaths under trains, which are more commonly associated with suicide, coroners are interested to know whether or not the deceased was looking in the direction of the train and this is often considered as important evidence.

13. See, for example, J. M. McDonald, 'Suicide and Homicide by Automobile', *American Journal of Psychiatry*, vol. 121 (1964) pp. 366–70; C. L. Huffine, 'Equivocal Single-Auto Traffic Fatalities', *Life Threatening Behaviour*, vol. 1 (1971) pp. 83–95; A. D. Pokorny, J. P. Smith and J. R. Finch, 'Vehicular Suicides', *Life Threatening Behaviour*, vol. 2 (1972) pp. 105–19.

14. J. I. Coe, 'Sexual Asphyxias', *Life Threatening Behaviour*, vol. 4 (1974) pp. 171–5.

15. Atkinson, 'Societal Reactions to Suicide', p. 182.

16. *Guardian* (10 September 1977).p. 182.

17. Some of the problems in distinguishing the 'accidental' from the 'suicidal' drug death are discussed by Curphey, 'Drug Deaths: A Problem in Certification', in Farberow (ed.), *Proceedings of the Fourth International Conference* pp. 22–8.

18. In this context it is interesting to note that the statistics show that the suicide rate steadily increases with advancing age until the late sixties when it begins to decline. These researches suggest that a probable explanation for this is that it becomes increasingly difficult to *establish* and prove intent in an elderly and infirm person.

19. See, for example, Litman, Curphey, Shneidman, Farberow and Tabachnick, 'Investigation of Equivocal Suicides', *Journal of the American Medical Association*, vol. 184 (1963) pp. 924–9.

20. Stengel has referred to this as the 'appeal quality' of suicide and has argued that it is a characteristic of most suicidal acts. Stengel, *Suicide and Attempted Suicide*, pp. 113–17.

21. Atkinson, 'Societal Reactions to Suicide', p. 179.

22. Shneidman and Farberow, 'Sample Investigations of Equivocal Suicidal Deaths', in Shneidman and Farberow (eds), *The Cry for Help*, pp. 118–27;

Curphey, 'The Forensic Pathologist and the Multidisciplinary Approach to Death', in Shneidman (ed.), *Essays in Self Destruction* (New York, Science House, 1967) pp. 463–74.

23. Curphey, 'The Role of the Social Scientist in the Medicolegal Certification of Death from Suicide', p. 115.

24. Litman *et al.*, 'Investigations of Equivocal Suicides', p. 928.

25. *Daily Mirror*, (29 September 1977).

26. Atkinson, *Discovering Suicide*, pp. 149–157.

27. Of course, what officials demand for evidence of intent from the biography will vary depending on the evidence of intent that can be established from the circumstances of death. If death, for example, appears to be 'almost certainly suicide' from the circumstances of death, then they will require correspondingly less 'proof' from the biography and vice versa.

Chapter 5: Persons under Trains

1. I have excluded from these figures the forty-three people killed in the Moorgate disaster of that year.

2. The majority of these inquests I either attended myself or, occasionally, listened to tapes. When I was unable to attend an inquest, or when there were two at different courts on the same day, obliging friends helped. However, three of twenty-nine cases eventually excluded were left out because neither I nor one of my aides could attend the relevant inquest.

3. Stengel, *Suicide and Attempted Suicide* pp. 98–9. Cf. A. M. Pederson, M. Teft, H. M. Babigan, 'Risks of Mortality of Suicide Attempters Compared with Psychiatric and General Populations', *Suicide*, vol. 5 (1975) pp. 145–57.

4. I am grateful to the Lanchester Polytechnic for providing a grant for this part of the work.

5. For example, Breed, 'Occupational Mobility and Suicide'; Gibbs and Porterfield, 'Occupational Prestige'; Powell, 'Occupation, Status and Suicide'; H. H. Krauss and B. J. Krauss, 'A Cross-Cultural Study of the Thwarting Disorientation Theory of Suicide', *Journal of Abnormal Psychology*, vol. 73 (1968) pp. 353–7.

6. *Guardian* (5 June 1976).

7. *Daily Mirror* (24 June 1974).

8. Hindess, *The Use of Official Statistics in Sociology*, pp. 44–5.

Chapter 6: Individualistic Approaches to Suicide

1. Cf. Wilkins, 'Suicidal Behaviour'.

2. Suicidology has developed into a semi-autonomous discipline in the United States with its own professional organisation (American Association of Suicidology), its own journal (*Suicide and Life Threatening Behaviour*) and its own academic posts (for example, Professor of Thanatology).

3. S. Freud, 'Mourning and Melancholia', and 'Beyond the Pleasure Principle', in *Collected Works*, (London, Hogarth, 1925). For a review of psychoanalytic theory in suicide research see Litman and Tabachnik, 'Psychoanalytic Theories of Suicide', in Resnik (ed.), *Suicidal Behaviours*, pp. 73–81.

4. K. Menninger, *Man Against Himself* (New York, Harcourt Brace, 1938).
5. M. Von Andics, *Suicide and the Meaning of Life* (London, Hodge, 1947).
6. Although I am dealing here with works which employ the techniques of systematic empiricism which is the dominant mode of explanation in suicide research, there are, of course, a number of works which employ alternative perspectives. Some students, for example, have been more concerned with detailed reconstructions of suicidal acts, others with neo-existential studies of case histories and others with more ethical and philosophical issues. For a collection of papers based on an existential perspective see Shneidman (ed.), *On The Nature of Suicide*, pp. 103–42.
7. D. Lester, *Why People Kill Themselves* (Springfield, Thomas, 1972) p. 208.
8. For a good general discussion of these works see, E. Robins and P. O'Neal, 'Culture and Mental Disorder', *Human Organisation*, vol. 16 (1958) pp. 7–11; C. H. Fellner, 'Provocation of Suicide Attempts', *Journal of Nervous Mental Diseases*, vol. 133 (1961) pp. 55–8; Temoche *et al.*, 'Suicide Rates among Current and Former Mental Institution Patients'; I. W. Sletten, M. L. Brown, R. C. Evenson and H. Altman, 'Suicide in Mental Hospital Patients', *Diseases of the Nervous System*, vol. 33, (1972) pp. 328–35.
9. Lester, *Why People Kill Themselves*, p. 193.
10. N. L. Farberow and T. McEvoy, 'Suicide among Patients with Diagnoses of Anxiety Reaction or Depressive Reaction in General Medical and Surgical Hospitals', *Journal of Abnormal Psychology*, vol. 71 (1966) pp. 287–99; G. A. Foulds, 'Some Differences between Neurotics and Character Disorders', *British Journal of Social Clinical Psychology*, vol. 6 (1967) pp. 52–9; K. S. Vinoda, 'Personality Characteristics of Attempted Suicides', *British Journal of Psychiatry*, vol. 112 (1966) pp. 1143–50; G. E. Murphy *et al.*, 'Who Calls the Suicide Prevention Centre', *American Journal of Psychiatry*, vol. 126 (1969) pp. 314–24.
11. Temoche *et al.*, 'Suicide Rates'; A. D. Pokorny, 'Suicide Rates in Various Psychiatric Disorders', *Journal of Nervous Mental Diseases*, vol. 139 (1964) pp. 499–506; C. Perris and G. D'Elia, 'A Study of Bipolar (manic depressive) and Unipolar Recurrent Depressive Psychoses', *Acta Psychiatrica Scandinavica*, vol. 42 (1966) pp. 172–89; N. L. Farberow and D. McKinnon, 'Prediction of Suicide in Neuropsychiactric Hospital Patients', in C. Neuringer (ed.), *The Psychological Assessment of Suicidal Risk* (Springfield, Thomas, 1974).
12. L. Ljunberg, 'Hysteria', *Acta Psychiatrica Scandinavica*, vol. 32 (1957).
13. E. Johnson, 'A Study of Schizophrenia in the Male', *Acta Psychiatrica Scandinavica*, vol. 33, supplement 125 (1958).
14. N. L. Gittleson, 'The Relationship between Obsessions and Suicidal Attempts in Depressive Psychoses', *British Journal of Psychiatry*, vol. 112 (1966) pp. 889–90.
15. Many of this last type of studies have been interested in 'social factors' as well as 'clinical' ones. Broadly, it is hypothesised that in a group of say, depressives there will be a relatively high incidence of suicidal behaviour as this type of illness makes individuals more prone to suicide. Therefore, if one compares 'suicidal' and 'non-suicidal' depressives one may be in a better position to begin to 'isolate' those ('external') factors, social isolation for example, which, when combined with depression (and/or other 'internal' factors) make suicide more likely. H. J. Walton, 'Suicidal Behaviour in Depressive Illness', *Journal of Mental Science*, vol. 104 (1958) pp. 884–91; S. Farnham-Diggory, 'Self Evaluation and Subjective Life Expectancy among Suicidal and Non-Suicidal Psychotic Males', *Journal of Abnormal Social Psychology*, vol. 69 (1964) pp. 628–34; E. B. Ritson, 'Suicide among Alcoholics', *British Journal of Medical*

Psychology, vol. 41 (1968) pp. 235–42; G. E. Murphy and E. Robins, 'Social Factors in Suicide', *Journal of the American Medical Association*, vol. 199 (1967) pp. 303–8; H. Warnes, 'Suicide in Schizophrenics', *Diseases of the Nervous System*, vol. 29 (1968) pp. 35–40; A. M. Penderson, B. M. Tefft and H. M. Babigan, 'Risk of Mortality of Suicide Attempters Compared with Psychiatric and General Populations', *Suicide*, vol. 5 (1975) pp. 145–57.

16. J. Tuckman, W. F. Youngman and G. Kriezman, 'Suicide and Physical Illness', *Journal of General Psychology*, vol. 75 (1966) pp. 291–6; T. L. Dorpat, W. F. Anderson and H. S. Ripley, 'The Relationship of Physical Illness to Suicide', in Resnik (ed.), *Suicidal Behaviours*, pp. 209–19.

17. Farberow *et al.*, 'Suicide among General Medical and Surgical Hospital Patients with Malignant Neoplasms', *New Physician*, vol. 13 (1964) pp. 6–12.

18. T. Morris, *Deviance and Control*, pp. 78–97.

19. P. I. Robinson, 'Suicide', *Postgraduate Medicine*, vol. 32 (1962) pp. 154–9. R. S. Paffenbarger and D. P. Asnes, 'Chronic Diseases in Former College Students', *American Journal of Public Health*, vol. 56 (1966) pp. 1026–36.

20. A. Piney, 'A Peculiar Bodily Disproportion', *Lancet*, vol. 2 (1935) pp. 972–3; W. H. Sheldon, *The Varieties of Temperament* (New York, Harper, 1942); M. A. Gjukic, 'A Contribution to the Problem of Lymphatic Constitution', *Z Menschl Vererb-U Konstitutionslehre*, vol. 34 (1957) pp. 303–22.

21. W. F. Bunney and J. A. Fawcett, 'Possibility of a Biochemical Test for Suicide Potential', *Archives of General Psychiatry*, vol. 13 (1965); Bunney and Fawcett, 'Biochemical Research in Depression and Suicide', in Resnik (ed.) *Suicidal Behaviours*, pp. 144–59; D. M. Shaw, F. E. Camps and N. G. Eccleston, '5-Hydroxytryptamine in the Hindbrain of Depressive Suicide', *British Journal of Psychiatry*, **vol. 113(1967) pp. 1407-11; D. M. Shaw *et al.*, 'Brain Electrolytes** in Depressive and Alcoholic Suicides', *British Journal of Psychiatry*, vol. 115 (1969) pp. 69–79; G. Krieger, 'The Plasma Level of Cortisol as a Predictor of Suicide', *Diseases of the Nervous System*, vol. 35 (1974) pp. 237–40; G. Krieger, 'Is there a Biochemical Predictor of Suicide?', *Suicide*, vol. 5 (1975) pp. 228–31.

22. Not only have the results of such work been as yet inconclusive or invalid (see, for example, B. Levy and E. Hansen, 'Failure of the Urinary Test for Suicide Potential', *Archives of General Psychiatry*, vol. 20 (1969) pp. 415–18), but these students are not investigating causes of suicide as such. Rather Bunney and his associates are hypothesising that suicidal actions take place when an individual is in great mental anguish and that this stress might be *reflected* in certain biochemical changes, namely high levels of 17–OHCS (a hormone secreted by the adrenal cortex) in the urine of (potentially) suicidal patients. They are then looking for a measure of stress rather than an explanation of it. Cf. S. H. Snyder 'Biology', in S. Perlin (ed.), *A Handbook for the Study of Suicide* (Oxford University Press, 1975) p. 128. The problem of genetic explanations is, of course, trying to isolate the genetic variable. The few studies in this area have been extremely tentative in their findings. See, for example, L. B. Shapiro, 'Suicide', *Journal of Nervous Mental Diseases*, vol. 81 (1935) pp. 547–53; F. J. Kallman, F. J. De Porte, J. De Porte and L. Feingold, 'Suicide in Twins and Only Children', *American Journal of Human Genetics*, vol. 1 (1949) pp. 113–26. For an overview see D. Lester, 'Note on the Inheritance of Suicide', *Psychological Report*, vol. 22 (1968) pp. 89–94.

23. J. Bowlby, *Child Care and the Growth of Love*, (Harmondsworth, Penguin, 1965).

24. See, for example, Hendin, 'Growing Up Dead: Student Suicide', in Shneidman (ed.), *Suicidology: Contemporary Developments*, pp. 317–34.

25. For example, J. Tuckman and W. F. Youngman, 'Attempted Suicide and

Family Disorganisation', *Journal of Genetic Psychology*, vol. 105 (1964) pp. 187–93.

26. For an overview see, D. Lester, 'Sibling Position and Suicidal Behaviour', *Journal of Individual Psychology*, vol. 22 (1966) pp. 204–7.

27. For example, D. Lester, 'The Relation between Discipline Experiences and the Expression of Aggression', *American Anthropologist*, vol. 69 (1967) pp. 734–7; M. L. Farber, 'Factors Determining the Incidence of Suicide within Families', *Suicide and Life Threatening Behaviour*, vol. 7 (1977) pp. 3–6. (Also many of the cultural and subcultural studies of suicide rates, Hendin's, *Suicide and Scandinavia*, for example, are based upon an implicit acceptance of the child-rearing and expression of aggression theory.)

28. Walton, 'Suicidal Behaviour in Depressive Illness'; J. G. Bruhn, 'Broken Homes among Attempted Suicides and Psychiatric Outpatients', *Journal of Mental Science*, vol. 108 (1962) pp. 772–9; S. Greer, 'The Relationship between Parental Loss and Attempted Suicide: A Controlled Study', *British Journal of Psychiatry*, vol. 100 (1964) pp. 698–705; T. L. Dorpat, J. K. Jackson and H. S. Ripley, 'Broken Homes and Attempted Suicide', *Archives of General Psychiatry*, vol. 12 (1965) pp. 213–16; N. McConaghy, J. Linane and R. C. Buckle, 'Parental Deprivation and Attempted Suicide', *Medical Journal of Australia*, vol. 1 (1966) pp. 886–92; K. M. Koller and J. N. Castanos, 'Parental Deprivation and Attempted Suicide in a Prison Population', *Medical Journal of Australia*, vol. 1 (1969) pp. 858–61.

29. For an overview of research findings see Koller and Castanos, 'The Influence of Childhood Parental Deprivation in Attempted Suicide', *Medical Journal of Australia*, vol. 1 (1968) pp. 396–9. One of the problems that makes comparisons difficult is the inability of researchers to agree on a definition of parental deprivation. See Stengel, *Suicide and Attempted Suicide*, pp. 54–5.

30. As an illustration of this in a general context see Eysenck's views on Freud. H. J. Eysenck, *Fact and Fiction in Psychology* (Harmondsworth, Penguin, 1965) pp. 95–131.

31 N. L. Farberow and A. G. Devries, 'An Item Differentiation of MMPI's of Suicidal Neuropsychiatric Hospital Patients', *Psychological Reports*, vol. 20 (1967) pp. 607–17; W. G. Dahlstrom, G. S. Welsh, L. E. Dahlstrom, *An MMPI Handbook* (University of Minnesota Press, 1972).

32. L. Srole, 'Social Integration and Certain Corollaries', *American Sociological Review*, vol. 21 (1956) pp. 709–16; D. Lester, 'Anomie and Suicidal Behaviour', *Psychological Reports*, vol. 26 (1970) p. 532; F. V. Wenz, 'Anomie and Level of Suicidality in Individuals', *Psychological Reports*, vol. 36 (1975) pp. 817–18.

33. A. R. Jensen, 'The Maudsley Personality Inventory', *Acta Psychology*, vol. 14 (1958) pp. 314–25.

34. I. H. Scheier and R. B. Cattell, *Handbook for the Neuroticism Scale Questionaire* (Champaign, Institute for Personality and Ability Testing, 1961). With reference to suicide see, for example, A. E. Philip and J. W. McCulloch, 'Some Psychological Features of Persons who have Attempted Suicide', *British Journal of Psychiatry*, vol. 114 (1968) pp. 1299–1300.

35. M. Iga, 'Relation of Suicide Attempts and Social Structure in Kamakura', *International Journal of Social Psychiatry*, vol. 12 (1966) pp. 221–32; D. Lester, 'Resentment and Dependency in the Suicidal Individual', *Journal of General Psychiatry*, vol. 81 (1969) pp. 137–45.

36. E. Pomeroy, A. R. Mahrer and D. J. Mason, 'An Aggressive Syndrome in Hospital Patients', *Proceedings of the American Psychological Association* (1965) pp. 239–40; S. Eisenthal, 'Suicide and Aggression', *Psychological*

Reports, vol. 21 (1967) pp. 745–51; F. A. Whitlock and A. D. Broadhurst, 'Attempted Suicide and the Experience of Violence', *Journal of Biosocial Science*, vol. 1 (1969) pp. 353–68.

37. D. Lester, 'Suicide as an Aggressive Act', *Journal of General Psychology*, vol. 79 (1968) pp. 83–6.

38. R. B. Cattell, H. W. Eher, H. M. Tatsvoka, *Handbook for the Sixteen Personal-Factor Questionnaire Campaign* (Illinois, Campaign, 1970).

39. H. B. Kaplan, *Self Attitudes and Deviant Behaviour* (California, Goodyear, 1975); H. B. Kaplan, A. D. Pokorny, 'Self Attitudes and Suicidal Behaviour', *Suicide and Life Threatening Behaviour*, vol. 6 (1976) pp. 23–35.

40. M. Kovacs, A. T. Beck, M. A. Weissman, 'Hopelessness: An Indicator of Suicidal Risk', *Suicide*, vol. 5 (1975) pp. 98–103; A. T. Beck, M. Kovacs, M. A. Weissman, 'Hopelessness and Suicidal Behaviour: An Overview', *Journal of the American Medical Association*, vol. 234 (1975) pp. 1146–9; R. C. Bedrosian, A. T. Beck, 'Cognitive Aspects of Suicidal Behaviour', *Suicide and Life Threatening Behaviour*, vol. 9 (1979) pp. 87–96.

41. S. Ganzler, 'Some Interpersonal and Social Dimensions of Suicidal Behaviour', *Dissertation Abstracts*, vol. 28 (1967) pp. 1192–3; D. W. Pierce, 'Suicidal Intent and Self Injury', *British Journal of Psychiatry*, vol. 130 (1977) pp. 377–85.

42. E. Ringel, *Der Selbstmord: Abschluss Einer Krankhaften Psychischen Entwicklung* (Vienna, Maudrich, 1953); *Selstmordverhutung* (Bern, Huber, 1969). Ringel has recently summarised his main ideas in English translation: E. Ringel, 'The Pre-suicidal Syndrome', *Suicide and Life Threatening Behaviour*, vol. 6 (1976) pp. 131–49.

43. For a discussion of the methodology see Shneidman, 'Logical Content Analysis: An Explication of Styles of "Concludifying"', in G. Gerbner *et al.* (eds), *The Analysis of Communication Content* (New York, Wiley, 1969).

44. They refer to this as 'catalogic': 'The suicide says in effect, "I [i.e. as experienced by others] will get attention, that is, certain other people will cry, go to a funeral, sing hymns, relive memories, and the like". But he also implies or states that even after death, I [i.e. myself] will go through these experiences, that is, "I will be cried over: I will be attended to" – as though the individual would be able to experience these occurrences. This is the heart of the semantic fallacy or ambiguity.' Shneidman and Farberow, 'The Logic of Suicide', in Shneidman and Farberow (eds), *Clues to Suicide*, p. 33; Shneidman, 'Suicide Notes Reconsidered', *Psychiatry*, vol. 36 (1973) pp. 379–94.

45. P. Tripodes, 'Reasoning Patterns in Suicide Notes', in Shneidman (ed.), *Suicidology: Contemporary Developments*, pp. 207–25. See also, Shneidman and Farberow 'Some Comparisons between Genuine and Simulated Suicide Notes in terms of Mowrer's Concepts of Discomfort and Relief', *Journal of General Psychology*, vol. 56 (1957) pp. 251–6; Ogilvie, Stone and Shneidman, 'Some Characteristics of Genuine versus Simulated Suicide Notes', *Bulletin of Suicidology* (March 1969) pp. 27–32; V. J. Henken, 'Banality Reinvestigated: A Computer-Based Content Analysis of Suicide and Forced Death Documents', *Suicide and Life Threatening Behaviour*, vol. 6 (1976) pp. 26–43.

46. C. Neuringer, 'Dichotomous Evaluations in Suicidal Individuals', *Journal of Consultative Clinical Psychology*, vol. 25 (1961) pp. 445–9; 'Rigid Thinking in Suicidal Individuals', *Journal of Consultative Clinical Psychology*, vol. 28 (1964) pp. 54–8; 'The Cognitive Organisation of Meaning in Suicidal Individuals', *Journal of General Psychology*, vol. 76 (1967) pp. 91–100; 'Divergences between Attitudes Towards Life and Death among Suicidal, Psychosomatic, and Normal Hospitalised Patients', *Journal of Consultative Clinical Psychology*, vol. 32 (1968) pp. 59–63.

47. C. Neuringer, 'Current Developments in the Study of Suicidal Thinking', in Shneidman (ed.), *Suicidology*, pp. 234–52.
48. Ringel, 'The Pre-suicidal Syndrome', p. 131.
49. C. E. Osgood, G. J. Suci and P. H. Tannenbaum, *The Measurement of Meaning* (University of Illinois Press, 1957).
50. Neuringer, 'Dichotomous Evaluations in Suicidal Individuals'; 'Current Developments in the Study of Suicidal Thinking', pp. 238–9.
51. See, for example, Giddens, *New Rules of Sociological Method* (London, Hutchinson, 1976) p. 20.
52. In the study of social class, for example, some students have illustrated that individuals' perceptions of their 'class position could only be understood in terms of their *overall perception of society*'. See, for example, E. Bott, *Family and Social Network* (London, Routledge & Kegan Paul, 1957); H. Popitz *et al.*, 'The Worker's Image of Society', translated by C. Ryan in T. Burns (ed.), *Industrial Man* (Harmondsworth, Penguin, 1969) pp. 281–324; J. H. Goldthorpe *et al.*, *The Affluent Worker in the Class Structure* (Cambridge University Press, 1969). Similar comments would seem to be applicable to attitudes towards life and death. Neuringer, however, assumes that these attitudes can be conveniently divorced from the social contexts that make them 'meaningful'; C. Neuringer, 'Divergences between Attitudes Towards Life and Death among Suicidal, Psychosomatic and Normal Hospitalised Patients'. This may be directly contrasted with the view of 'meaning' taken, for example, by Douglas, *The Social Meanings of Suicide*, pp. 253–4.
53. Although, of course, the nature of the phenomenon is such that it makes such an approach extremely difficult. In practice the researcher is dependent on someone who was 'involved', whether the subject or another, giving an account of 'what happened' which is subject to the kind of difficulties outlined in the previous Part of this work. Furthermore, suicide is often seen as a medical problem, i.e. with the 'causes' firmly located in the suicidal individual and, therefore, analysis often takes the laboratory/in-depth case-study form, which tends to divorce actor from social context. On the other hand, as far as most sociologists are concerned, explanation is a statistical exercise involving comparative group rates.
54. D. Willer and J. Willer, *Systematic Empiricism: a Critique of a Pseudo-science* (Englewood Cliffs, Prentice-Hall, 1973) pp. 68–9.
55. The same appears to be true of 'medical studies' generally. See R. Harris, 'Why I am Browned Off with Quantitative Methodology', *Medical Sociology News*, vol. 5 (1977) pp. 4–9.
56. For example, Dorpat and Ripley, 'The Relationship between Attempted and Committed Suicide', *Comprehensive Psychiatry*, vol. 8 (1967) pp. 74–89.
57. For example, Dorpat and J. W. Boswell, 'An Evaluation of Suicidal Intent in Suicidal Attempts', *Comprehensive Psychiatry*, vol. 4 (1963) pp. 117–25.
58. For example, P. Canter, 'Frequency of Suicidal Thought and Self-Destructive Behaviour among Females', *Suicide and Life Threatening Behaviour*, vol. 6 (1976) pp. 92–100.
59. Douglas, *The Social Meanings of Suicide*, pp. 235–340.
60. For an aggressive statement of this view of 'naturalism' see D. Matza, *Delinquency and Drift* (New York, Wiley, 1964); *Becoming Deviant* (Englewood Cliffs, Prentice-Hall, 1969). For an excellent summary of the 'newer' existential approaches see P. K. Manning, 'Existential Sociology', *Sociological Quarterly*, vol. 14 (1973) pp. 200–25.
61. Thus many students take as their starting point Weber's definition of sociological understanding as the interpretation of human action in terms of the actor's

subjective meaning. M. Weber, *The Theory of Social and Economic Organisation*, (New York, Free Press, 1964) p. 88. (For the contradictions inherent in Weber's own approach see, for example, H. H. Gerth and C. W. Mills, *From Max Weber* (London, Routledge & Kegan Paul, 1948) pp. 56–8.

62. See Z. Bauman, *Hermeneutics and Social Science* (London, Hutchinson, 1978).

63. Cavan, *Suicide*; Sainsbury, *Suicide in London*; J. W. Wallace, A. E. McCulloch, *Suicidal Behaviour* (Oxford, Pergamon, 1972).

64. N. E. Connor and R. W. Maris, 'Exchange, Balance and Formal Organisation in Psychotherapeutic Interactions', *Suicide and Life Threatening Behaviour*, vol. 6 (1976) pp. 150–68.

65. R. L. Akers, 'A Social Learning Analysis of the Suicidal Process', in R. L. Akers, *Deviant Behaviour* (California, Wadsworth, 1977) pp. 297–304.

66. Ibid, p. 304.

67. Of course, in spite of one or two rather shallow attempts at synthesis – for example E. M. Schur, *Labelling Deviant Behaviour* (New York, Harper & Row, 1971) – the important differences between interactionism and phenomenology should not be overlooked. In modern works the primary influence of the former is Mead's psychology (mediated by Blumer) while for the latter it is Schutz's philosophy (mediated by Garfinkel).

68. W. A. Rushing, 'Deviance, Interpersonal Relations and Suicide', *Human Relations*, vol. 22 (1969) pp. 61–75; 'Situational Contexts and the Relationship of Alcoholism and Mental Illness to Suicide', in Rushing (ed.), *Deviant Behaviour and Social Process* (Chicago, Rand McNally, 1975) pp. 474–80.

69. E. M. Lemert, *Human Deviance, Social Problems and Social Control* (Englewood Cliffs, Prentice-Hall, 1967) p. 40.

70. W. Breed, 'Five Components of a Basic Suicide Syndrome', *Life Threatening Behaviour*, vol. 2 (1972) pp. 3–17; see also, 'Suicide and Loss in Social Interaction', in Shneidman (ed.), *Essays in Self Destruction*, pp. 188–201; 'Suicide and Particular Social Statuses or Conditions', in Gibbs (ed.), *Suicide*, pp. 209–27. Cf. D. H. Miller, *Suicidal Careers: Toward a Symbolic Interactionist Theory of Suicide* (School of Social Welfare, University of California, 1967); D. H. Miller, W. Dawson and R. Barnhouse, *Reconstruction of Self: Toward a Symbolic Interactionist Theory of Rehabilitation* (San Francisco Department of Mental Hygiene, 1968).

71. Breed, 'Occupational Mobility and Suicide among White Males', *American Sociological Review*, vol. 28 (1963) pp. 179–88.

72. Breed, 'Five Components of a Basic Suicide Syndrome' p. 4.

73. Ibid, p. 7.

74. This is not, of course, to imply that there were no contradictions in Durkheim's own position. In fact, as Nye and Ashworth have argued, in his attempts to avoid both nominalism and realism, Durkheim 'was driven towards a dialectical synthesis he was never able to formulate'. Nye and Ashworth, 'Emile Durkheim', pp. 133–4. The point being made here is simply that Breed has not gone 'beyond' Durkheim.

75. A. L. Kobler and E. Stotland, *The End of Hope* (New Yorks, Free Press, 1964).

76. Ibid, p. 1.

77. J. Jacobs, 'A Phenomenological Study of Suicide Notes', *Social Problems*, vol. 15 (1967) pp. 60–72 (reprinted in Giddens (ed.), *The Sociology of Suicide*, pp. 332–48). See also, J. Jacobs, 'The Use of Religion in Constructing the Moral Justification of Suicide', in Douglas (ed.), *Deviance and Respectability: the Social Construction of Moral Meanings* (New York, Basic Books, 1970) pp. 229–50. For a similar approach to delinquency see D. Matza and G. Sykes, 'Juvenile Delinquency and Subterranean Values', *American Sociological*

Review, vol. 26 (1961) pp. 712–19.

78.   J. Jacobs, 'A Phenomenological Study of Suicide Notes', p. 347 (Giddens).

79.   Idem. See also J. Jacobs, *Adolescent Suicide*, (New York, Wiley, 1971).

80.   Another problem specifically related to studies such as Jacobs's that employ suicide notes, is that note writers are not a random sample of suicides, but possibly more common to certain types of suicide. See, for example, S. L. Cohen and J. E. Fiedler, 'Content Analysis of Multiple Messages in Suicide Notes', *Life Threatening Behaviour*, vol. 4 (1974) pp. 75–95.

81.   Douglas, 'The Sociological Analysis of the Social Meanings of Suicide', *European Journal of Sociology*, vol. 7 (1966) pp. 249–75. Reprinted in Giddens (ed.), *The Sociology of Suicide*, pp. 121–51; Douglas, *The Social Meanings of Suicide*.

82.   Douglas, *The Social Meanings of Suicide*, pp. 235–54.

83.   A notion developed by some into a critique of the very conception of a social 'science'. See P. Winch, *The Idea of a Social Science* (London, Routledge & Kegan Paul, 1967).

84.   Although, of course, the validity of much of this data is subject to the same kinds of criticisms that Douglas himself raised against official suicide rates.

85.   Douglas, 'The Sociological Analysis of the Social Meanings of Suicide', p. 137 (Giddens).

86.   Ibid, pp. 137–44.

87.   Douglas, *The Social Meanings of Suicide*, pp. 328–9.

88.   Ibid, p. 254.

89.   Ibid, p. 253.

90.   Bauman, *Hermeneutics and Social Science*, pp. 194–224.

91.   Giddens, *New Rules of Sociological Method*, pp. 55–6.

92.   A. Giddens, 'A Theory of Suicide', in Giddens (ed.), *Studies in Social and Political Theory*, p. 303.

93.   See, for example, L. H. Farber, 'The Phenomenology of Suicide', in E. S. Shneidman (ed.), *On the Nature of Suicide*, pp. 103–10.

94.   See R. Bhasker, 'On the Possibility of Social Scientific Knowledge and the Limits of Naturalism', *Journal of the Theory of Social Behaviour*, vol. 8 (1978) pp. 1–28.

95.   Taylor, 'Suicide and the Renewal of Life'.

Chapter 7: Suicide and the Gamble with Death

1.   Douglas, 'The Sociological Analysis of the Social Meanings of Suicide', p. 133 (Giddens).

2.   Taylor, 'Suicide and the Renewal of Life', pp. 375–8.

3.   Matza, *Becoming Deviant*, p. 17.

4.   Wilkins, 'Suicidal Behaviour', pp. 398–9 (Giddens).

5.   R. W. Ettlinger and P. Flordah, 'Attempted Suicide', *Acta Psychiatrica Neurologica Scandinavica*, vol. 103 (1955).

6.   A. Arieff, R. McCulloch and D. B. Rotman, 'Unsuccessful Suicide Attempts', *Diseases of the Nervous System*, vol. 9 (1948) p. 179.

7.   G. Rains and S. Thompson, 'Suicide: Some Basic Considerations', *Digest of Neurology and Psychiatry*, vol. 18 (1950) pp. 101–2.

8.   Stengel, 'To Die or not to Die', *New Society* (15 March 1973) p. 581.

9.   Stengel, 'Attempted Suicides', in Resnik (ed.), *Suicidal Behaviours*, p. 174. See also, Stengel, 'Some Unexplored Aspects of Suicide and Attempted Suicide', *Comprehensive Psychiatry*, vol. 1 (1960) pp. 71–8; *Suicide and Attempted Suicide*, pp. 121–36.

10. Stengel and Cook, *Attempted Suicide* (Oxford University Press, 1958) ch. 4; N. Krietman, P. Smith and E. Tan, 'Attempted Suicide in Social Networks', *British Journal of Preventive Social Medicine*, vol. 23 (1969) pp. 116–23; M. Rosenbaum and J. Richman, 'Family Dynamics and Drug Overdoses', *Life Threatening Behaviour*, vol. 2 (1972) pp. 19–21. (This last study for example found that in 89 per cent of the sample the overdose was taken in the home or in the presence of family members.)

11. Stengel and Cook, *Attempted Suicide*, pp. 38–44; Stengel, *Suicide and Attempted Suicide*, pp. 92–3; J. Hirsh, 'Methods and Fashions of Suicide', *Mental Hygiene*, vol. 44 (1960) pp. 3–11; A. Capstick, 'The Methods of Suicide', *Medicolegal Journal*, vol. 29 (1961) pp. 33–8; K. A. Achte and L. Ginman, 'Suicide Attempts with Narcotics and Poisons', *Acta Psychiatrica Scandinavica*, vol. 42 (1966) pp. 214–32; R. C. B. Aitken, D. Buglass and N. Krietman, 'The Changing Patterns of Attempted Suicide in Edinburgh', *British Journal of Preventive Social Medicine*, vol. 23 (1969) pp. 111–15.

12. E. Robins, S. Gassner, S. Kayes, R. H. Wilkinson and G. E. Murphy, 'The Communication of Suicidal Intent: A Study of 134 Consecutive Cases of Successful (Completed) Suicide', *American Journal of Psychiatry*, vol. 115 (1959) pp. 724–33; W. B. Delong and E. Robins, 'The Communication of Suicidal Intent Prior to Psychiatric Hospitalisation', *American Journal of Psychiatry*, vol. 117 (1961) pp. 695–705; F. R. Kumler, 'Communication between Suicide Attempters and Significant Others', *Nursing Research*, vol. 13 (1964) pp. 191–200; G. E. Murphy and E. Robins, 'The Communication of Suicidal Ideas', in Resnik (ed.), *Suicidal Behaviours*, pp. 163–70.

13. **Robins *et al.*, 'The Communication of Suicidal Intent', pp. 724–6; Stengal, *Suicide and Attempted Suicide*, p. 100.**

14. Stengel, 'Attempted Suicides', p. 174.

15. Stengel, *Suicide and Attempted Suicide*, pp. 121–9.

16. J. M. S. Weiss, 'The Gamble with Death in Attempted Suicide', *Psychiatry*, vol. 20 (1957) pp. 17–25. Reprinted in Giddens (ed.), *The Sociology of Suicide*, pp. 384–97.

17. Litman and Farberow, 'Emergency Evaluation of Self-Destructive Potentiality', in Farberow and Shneidman (eds), *The Cry For Help*.

18. S. Futterman, 'Suicide: the Psychoanalytic Point of View', in Farberow and Shneidman (eds), *The Cry For Help*, pp. 167–77.

19. D. Lester and G. Lester, *Suicide: the Gamble with Death*, (Englewood Cliffs, Prentice-Hall, 1971).

20. Litman *et al.*, 'Investigations of Equivocal Suicides', p. 927.

21. R. Firth, 'Suicide and Risk-Taking in Tikopia Society', *Psychiatry*, vol. 24 (1961) pp. 1–17. Reprinted in Giddens (ed.), *The Sociology of Suicide*, pp. 197–222.

22. Ibid, pp. 218–19 (Giddens).

23. V. Jensen and T. Petty, 'The Fantasy of being Rescued in Suicide', *Psychoanalytic Quarterly*, vol. 27 (1959) p. 337.

24. J. E. Lennard-Jones and R. Asher, 'Why Do They Do It?', *Lancet* vol. 1 (1959) p. 1138.

25. N. Kreitman and N. Chowdury, 'Distress Behaviour: A Study of Selected Samaritan Clients and Parasuicides ('Attempted Suicide') Patients', *British Journal of Psychiatry*, vol. 123 (1973) pp. 1–8; N. Kreitman (ed.), *Parasuicide* (New York, Wiley, 1977).

26. Stengel, 'A Matter of Communication', in Shneidman (ed.), *On the Nature of Suicide* (San Francisco, Jossey-Bass, 1969) p. 78.

27. Litman and Farberow, 'Emergency Evaluation', p. 51. See also, L. S. Kubie, '**Multiple Determinants of Suicidal Efforts', *Journal of Nervous and Mental***

Disease, vol. 138 (1964) pp. 3–8.
28. M. Kovacs, A. T. Beck, 'The Wish to Live and the Wish to Die in Attempted Suicides', *Journal of Clinical Psychology*, vol. 33 (1977) pp. 361–65.
29. Stengel, *Suicide and Attempted Suicide*, pp. 121–2.
30. J. Wilkins, 'Suicidal Behaviour', pp. 398–9 (Giddens).
31. Durkheim, *Suicide*, p. 44. Of course, in this definition the actor's motives and intentions have been excluded. Halbwachs was the first to complain at this and argue that a definition of suicide must include the idea that the act be performed by the victim himself with the *intention* of producing his death. See V. Verkko, *Homicides and Suicides in Finland and Their Dependence on National Character* (Copenhagen, Forlag, 1951).
32. Durkheim, *Suicide*, p. 46.
33. As noted earlier the Suicide Prevention Centre Team suggested that to take a needless chance of one in six for death was suicidal. Litman *et al.*, 'Investigations of Equivocal Suicides', p. 928.
34. Taylor, 'Suicide and the Renewal of Life', p. 378. The definition which comes closest to this was advanced by Stengel, 'To Die or Not to Die', p. 582.
35. Weiss, 'The Gamble with Death'.
36. E. H. Schmidt, P. O'Neal and E. Robins, 'Evaluation of Suicide Attempts as a Guide to Therapy', *Journal of the American Medical Association*, vol. 155 (1954) pp. 549–57.
37. Dorpat and Boswell, 'An Evaluation of Suicidal Intent in Suicide Attempts', *Comprehensive Psychiatry*, vol. 4 (1963) pp. 117–125.
38. D. Lester, 'Suicidal Behaviour: A Summary of Research Findings', *Buffalo Suicide Prevention and Crisis Service* (1970).
39. J. W. Worden, 'Lethality Factors and the Suicide Attempt', in Shneidman (ed.), *Suicidology: Contemporary Developments*, pp. 131–62. See also A. D. Weisman and J. W. Worden, 'Risk–Rescue Rating in Suicide Assessment', *Archives of General Psychiatry*, vol. 26 (1972) pp. 553–560.
40. The difference between 'measurement' and 'scaling' is well explained by the Willers. Broadly, measurement transcends, or is independent of, the particular things it is measuring while scales are dependent upon the things from which they are derived. 'Measurement' and 'scaling', although often confused, are in fact 'completely unrelated pursuits'. Willer and Willer, *Systematic Empiricism*, pp. 106–24.
41. Schmidt *et al.*, 'Evaluation of Suicide Attempts', pp. 555–6.
42. Dorpat and Boswell, 'An Evaluation of Suicidal Intent', pp. 122–3.
43. Farberow and Shneidman, 'Attempted, Threatened and Completed Suicide', *Journal of Abnormal Social Psychology*, vol. 50 (1955) p. 230; F. B. Davis, 'Sex Differences in Suicide and Attempted Suicide', *Diseases of the Nervous System*, vol. 29 (1968) pp. 193–4; I. W. Sletten, R. C. Evenson and M. L. Brown, 'Some Results from an Automated Statewide Comparison among Attempted, Committed and Non-Suicidal Patients', *Life Threatening Behaviour*, vol. 3 (1973) pp. 191–9. (The last study, for example, found that the sample of completed suicides (compared with attempters and non-attempters) contained more males, fewer blacks, fewer separated and divorced, a higher level of education, more people with a professional occupation, more neurotically depressed and schizophrenic patients, more relatives who committed suicide and considerably more relatives who were mentally ill, pp. 194–5).
44. One hypothesis, which has as yet received little empirical support, is that some individuals have a greater propensity to take risks than others and therefore, these individuals are more likely to engage in suicidal gambles with death. See P. F. Kennedy, A. L. Phanjoo and W. O. Shekim, 'Risk-taking in the Lives of

Parasuicides (Attempted Suicides)', *British Journal of Psychiatry*, vol. 119 (1971) pp. 281–6; R. L. Adams, M. B. Giffen and F. Garfield, 'Risk-taking among Suicide Attempters', *Journal of Abnormal Psychology*, vol. 82 (1972) pp. 262–7.

45. R. D. Laing, *The Politics of Experience* (Harmondsworth, Penguin, 1967) p. 79.
46. Stengel, *Suicide and Attempted Suicide*, pp. 116–17.
47. Stengel, 'Attempted Suicides', p. 172.
48. Stengel and Cook, *Attempted Suicide*, p. 86.
49. Stengel and Cook, *Attempted Suicide*: Pokorny, 'A Follow-up Study of 618 Suicidal Patients, *American Journal of Psychiatry*, vol. 122 (1966) pp. 1109–16; D. H. Rosen, 'The Serious Suicide Attempt: Epidemological and Follow-up Study of 886 Patients', *American Journal of Psychiatry*, vol. 127 (1970) pp. 764–70; N. Retterstol and B. Strype, 'Suicide Attempters in Norway: A Personal Follow-up Examination', *Life Threatening Behaviour*, vol. 3 (1973) pp. 283–97; K. G. Dahlgren, 'Attempted Suicides – 35 Years Afterward', *Suicide and Life Threatening Behaviour*, vol. 7 (1977) pp. 75–9.
50. First opportunity re-attempts do, of course, occur. In the London Transport study, for example, a girl who had survived a train jump virtually unharmed tried to throw off her rescuers and touch the positive rail shouting, 'Help me, I want to die': such cases, however, are very much the exception.
51. Stengel, *Suicide and Attempted Suicide*, p. 116.
52. J. Lonnqvist, P. Niskanen, K. A. Achte and L. Ginman, 'Self Poisoning with Follow-up Considerations', *Suicide*, vol. 5 (1975) pp. 39–46.
53. P. Udsen, Prognosis and Follow-up of Attempted Suicide', *International Anæsthesiology Clinics*, vol. 4 (1966) pp. 379–88; R. Ettlinger, 'Somantic Sequelae', in J. Waldenstrom, T. Larsonn and N. Ljungstedt (eds), *Suicide and Attempted Suicide* (Stockholm, Nordiska Bokhandelns Forlag, 1972).
54. Dorpat and Ripley, 'The Relationship between Attempted and Committed Suicide', *Comprehensive Psychiatry*, vol. 8 (1967) pp. 74–89.
55. The term is Stengel's. Stengel, *Suicide and Attempted Suicide* pp. 113–16.
56. Stengel and Cook, *Attempted Suicide*; P. E. Sifneos, 'Manipulative Suicide', *Psychiatric Quarterly*, vol. 40 (1966) pp. 525–37; J. W. Bonnar and R. K. McGee, 'Suicidal Behaviour as a Form of Communication in Married Couples', *Suicide and Life Threatening Behaviour*, vol. 7 (1977) pp. 7–16.
57. For example, Kobler and Stotland, *The End of Hope*, p. 1. Stengel has argued that all suicidal acts, fatal or not, convey this appeal effect: 'Therefore to divide suicidal acts into those aiming at self destruction and those meant to be cries for help is, in my opinion, mistaken. They are not either one or other but both at the same time'. Stengel, 'A Matter of Communication', p. 78.
58. See A. L. Bearman, 'The Epidemology of Life Threatening Events', *Suicide*, vol. 5 (1975) pp. 67–77.
59. D. H. Rosen, 'Suicide Survivors: Psychotherapeutic Implications of Egocide', *Suicide and Life Threatening Behaviour*, vol. 6 (1976) pp. 209–15.
60. Ibid, p. 211.
61. Idem.
62. Alvarez, *The Savage God: A Study of Suicide*, p. 291.
63. Ibid, pp. 302–6.
64. Taylor, 'Suicide and the Renewal of Life', p. 380.
65. J. Cohen, *Chance, Skill and Luck* (Harmondsworth, Penguin, 1960).
66. Stengel, 'A Matter of Communication', p. 78.
67. Taylor, 'Suicide and the Renewal of Life'.
68. G. Green, *A Sort of Life* (London, Bodley Head, 1971).

69. Alvarez, *The Savage God*, p. 33.
70. S. Plath, 'Lady Lazarus', from *Ariel* (New York, Harper & Row, 1961). Quoted in Alvarez, *The Savage God*, pp. 33–34.
71. Ibid, p. 34.
72. Green, *A Sort of Life*. A state of mind captured well (and subsequently corrected) by Rhinehart's Diceman. 'Life is islands of ecstasy in an ocean of ennui, and after the age of thirty land is seldom seen. At best we wander from one much-worn sandbar to the next, soon familiar with each grain of sand we see,' L. Rhinehart, *The Diceman* (London, Panther, 1972) p. 10. See also G. Simmel, 'The Adventurer', in G. Simmel, *The Sociology of George Simmel*, translated and edited by K. Wolff (New York, Free Press, 1950) pp. 187–98.
73. N. Tabacknick, 'The Psychology of the Fatal Accidents', in Shneidman (ed.), *Essays in Self Destruction*, pp. 399–420.
74. Cohen and Taylor take a rather similar approach in their study of long-term imprisonment. They use the experiences of those who have written about 'survival in extreme situations' to gain some insights into the experiences of long-term prisoners. 'Gradually we realised that we were not just trying to understand another group of prisoners. Instead we were looking at the ways in which men in general might react to an extreme situation . . . Once we realised this we were able to turn to a range of other studies which looked at the more general question of how men deal with the stress produced by a massive disruption in their normal lives.' S. Cohen and L. Taylor, *Psychological Survival: The Experience of Long-term Imprisonment* (Harmondsworth, Penguin, 1972) p. 41.
75. H. McIlvanney, 'Why the Grand Prix Gladiators Can't Kick the Habit', *Observer Magazine* (14 September 1975) p. 27.
76. Ibid.
77. Camus has captured this state of being well; 'the danger lies in the subtle instant that precedes the leap. Being able to remain on that dizzy crest – that is integrity and the rest is subterfuge.' A. Camus, *The Myth of Sisyphus* (Harmondsworth, Penguin, 1975).
78. K. Menninger, *Man Against Himself*.
79. Shneidman, 'Orientations to Death: A Vital Aspect of the Study of Lives', in R. White (ed.), *The Study of Lives* (New York, Atherton, 1963) pp. 200–27.
80. Neuringer, 'Methodological Problems in Suicide Research', *Journal of Consulting Psychology*, vol. 26 (1962) pp. 273–8.
81. E. Goffman, *Where the Action is* (London, Allen Lane, 1969) p. 111.
82. This is why the phrase 'has to await the outcome' was explicitly included in the definition of a suicidal act.
83. Goffman, *Where the Action is*, pp. 111–13.
84. Taylor, 'Suicide and the Renewal of Life', pp. 382–3.
85. C. Brasher, 'The Man who was an Island', *Observer*, (23 January 1978).
86. Ashworth, 'Sport as Symbolic Dialogue', in E. Dunning (ed.), *The Sociology of Sport* (London, Cass, 1971) pp. 40–46.
87. Ibid, p. 44.
88. Ibid, p. 45.
89. Idem.
90. Goffman, *Where the Action is*, p. 143.
91. T. Hardy, *Jude the Obscure* (London, Macmillan, 1971) p. 77.
92. *Sun*, (12 April 1975).
93. For example, Stengel, 'Attempted Suicides', pp. 176–9; Farberow and Shneidman, 'Attempted, Threatened and Completed Suicide', pp. 230–3; Sletten, Evenson and Brown, 'Some Results from an Automated Statewide Comparison, pp. 191–3.

94. Lester, *Why People Kill Themselves*; Dorpat and Boswell, 'An Evaluation of Suicidal Intent'; Weisman and Worden, 'Risk–Rescue Rating'; J. Tuckman and W. Youngman, 'A Scale for Assessing Risk of Attempted Suicides', *Journal of Clinical Psychology*, vol. 24 (1968) pp. 17–19.
95. Worden, 'Lethality Factors and the Suicide Attempt', p. 140.
96. Taylor, 'The Confrontation with Death', *Suicide and Life Threatening Behaviour*, vol. 8 (1978) pp. 89–98.

Chapter 8: The Ordeal and the Sacrifice

1. See, for example, R. Harre, *The Principles of Scientific Thinking* (London, Macmillan, 1970); R. Keat and J. Urry, *Social Theory as Science* (London, Routledge & Kegan Paul, 1975); R. Bhasker, *A Realist Theory of Science* (Brighton, Harvester, 1978).
2. For example, Durkheim's claim that 'now we know the factors in terms of which the suicide rate varies, we may define the reality to which this rate corresponds and which express it numerically'. Durkheim, *Suicide*, p. 297.
3. A view well articulated by Douglas, *The Social Meanings of Suicide*, pp. 22–33.
4. See Hirst, *Durkheim, Barnard and Epistemology*. Although, in his 'dismissal' of the Durkheimian enterprise, Hirst bases his argument almost exclusively on *The Rules of Sociological Method*, while, as I have tried to show here, there is some distance between this treatise and Durkheim's more substantive works. I shall argue in relation to *Suicide* that the claims of an empiricist epistemology advanced by Durkheim have relatively little importance. Issue may also be taken with Hirst's claim that sociology must necessarily degenerate into theoretical ideology. In short, exposing contradictions in an epistemological position does not *necessarily* destroy the substantive position.
5. We may note in this context that there is no need for modern positivists to 'treat social facts as things' because, for them, they *are* things. Thus in Kruijt's work, for example, 'anomie' was a (useful) descriptive term for something more 'real', i.e. urbanisation and secularisation. Kruijt, 'The Suicide Rate in the Western World', p. 55. Durkheim, in contrast, was concerned with the objective study of *moral* phenomena and, had his concern been merely with the relationship between physical phenomena, the 'thing-like' nature of these 'social facts' would have been self evident.
6. See R. Bhasker, *A Realist Theory of Science*, Chapter 2 and, in particular, his demonstration that philosophies of science presuppose a 'closed system' of enquiry and experimentation unavailable to the social sciences. The consequence of this is that positivist notions, causation and 'Popperian' notions of falsification must be abandoned along with social science's claims of predictability
7. Douglas, *The Social Meanings of Suicide*, p. 22.
8. See Giddens, 'Positivism and its Critics' (p. 29), where he observes that 'positivism . . . has become a term of abuse than a technical term of philosophy'.
9. It is perhaps interesting that of the English-speaking sociologists who have undertaken research in suicide, only Douglas and Giddens have made serious and perceptive studies of Durkheim's *Suicide*.
10. C. Lévi-Strauss, 'French Sociology', in G. Gurvitch and W. E. Moore (eds), *Twentieth Century Sociology* (New York, Philosophical Library, 1945) pp. 524–5; see also S. Clarke, 'The Origins of Lévi-Strauss's Structuralism', *Sociology*, vol. 12 (1978) p. 416.
11. Thus for Radcliffe-Brown, for example, 'natural science is the systematic

investigation of the universe as it is revealed to us through the senses. Social phenomena constitute a distinct class of natural phenomena ... direct observation reveals to us that human beings are connected by a complex network of social relations. I use the term social structure to denote this framework of actually existing relations.' A. R. Radcliffe Brown, *Structure and Function in Primitive Society* (London, Cohen & West, 1952) p. 190. Cf. B. Malinowski, *A Scientific Theory of Culture and Other Essays*, (Oxford University Press, 1944); E. E. Evans-Pritchard, *Social Anthropology*, (London, Routledge & Kegan Paul, 1951); E. Leach *Political Systems of Highland Burma; a study of Kachin social structure* (London, Bell, 1954). S. F. Nadel, *The Theory of Social Structure* (London, Cohen & West, 1957).

12. Most influentially Parsons, who argued that 'theory is confined to the formulation and logical relations of propositions containing empirical facts in direct relation to the observations of the facts and thus empirical verification of the propositions'. T. Parsons, *The Structure of Social Action* (New York, Free Press, 1968) p. 49.

13. See for example, J. Piaget, *Structuralism*, translated by C. Maschler (London, Routledge & Kegan Paul, 1971) pp. 3–16; R. Boudon, *The Uses of Structuralism* (London, Heinemann, 1971) pp. 1–15; M. Glucksman, 'The Structuralism of Lévi-Strauss and Althusser', in J. Rex (ed.), *Approaches to Sociology* (London, Routledge & Kegan Paul, 1974) pp. 230–45.

15. J. Piaget, *Structuralism*, p. 98.

16. According to Lévi-Strauss, 'We shall have hope of overcoming the opposition between the collective nature of culture and its manifestations in the individual, since the so-called "collective consciousness" would, in the final analysis, be no more than the expression on the level of individual thought and behaviour, of certain time and space modalities of the universal laws which make up the unconscious activity of the mind.' C. Lévi-Strauss, *Structural Anthropology*, trans. C. Jacobson and B. Schoepf (London, Allen Lane, 1968) p. 65.

17. N. Chomsky, *Syntactic Structures* (The Hague, Mouton, 1957); 'Verbal Behaviour by B. F. Skinner', *Language*, vol. 35 (1959) pp. 26–58; *Aspects of the Theory of Syntax* (Cambridge, M.I.T. Press, 1965). Neither, of course, are 'rationalist' theories 'irrefutable'. In this context in relation to Chomsky's work see, for example, J. R. Searle, 'Chomsky's Revolution in Linguistics', *New York Review* (29 June 1972) pp. 16–24.

18. For a summary see Giddens, *Central Problems in Social Theory* (London, Macmillan, 1979) pp. 9–48; Keat and Urry, *Social Theory as Science*, pp. 137–40.

19. A view not incompatible with realism. See Keat and Urry, *Social Theory as Science*, pp. 167–75.

20. Bauman, *Hermeneutics and Social Science*, pp. 194–224. For an alternative view, building up from specific to more general 'patterns of meaning' see Douglas, *The Social Meanings of Suicide*, Part IV.

21. Many structuralist approaches make broadly similar distinctions, an original formulation of which is located in Saussure's distinction between langue and parole. F. de Saussure, *Course in General Linguistics* (London, Owen, 1960). For more general application see R. Barthes, *Elements of Semiology* (London, Cape, 1967).

22. Shneidman, 'Classification of Suicidal Phenomena', *Bulletin of Suicidology* (July 1968).

23. B. Klopfer, 'Suicide: the Jungian Point of View', in Shneidman and Farberow, (eds), *The Cry for Help*.

24. For example, Kessel, Kreitman and Philip, amongst others, have suggested that the concept of 'attempted suicide' is misleading because it is so often applied to cases which are not fact suicides. They propose, instead, 'self-poisoning'. N. Kessel 'Self Poisoning – Part I', *British Medical Journal*, vol. 2 (1965) pp. 1265–70; N. Kreitman and A. E. Philip, 'Letter to the Editor', *British Journal of Psychiatry*, vol. 115 (1969) pp. 746–7.

25. Shneidman, 'Orientations to Death: A Vital Aspect in the Study of Lives', in White (ed.), *The Study of Lives* (New York, Atherton, 1963) pp. 200–28.

26. Cf. Willer and Willer, *Systematic Empiricism*.

27. For an original formulation in sociological research see M. Seeman, 'On the Meaning of Alienation', *American Sociological Review*, vol. 24 (1959) pp. 783–91; Cf. R. Blauner, *Alienation and Freedom: the Factory Worker and his Industry* (New York, Wiley, 1964). For the empiricist operationalisation of 'anomie' in relation to suicidal behaviour see F. V. Wenz, 'Self Injury Behaviour, Economic Status and Family Anomie Syndrome amongst Adolescents', *Adolescence*, vol. 14 (1979) pp. 387–98. In such approaches 'anomie' or 'alienation' are seen at one end of a continuum with normality at the other. Thus Seeman, for example, identified 'powerlessness', 'meaninglessness', 'normlessness', 'isolation' and 'self-estrangement' as the major dimensions of alienation. Therefore, presumably the *least* alienated are those in situations of unrestrained power with no normative constraints on them, to whom all is totally meaningful, who have complete certainty regarding what the future holds for them, are totally integrated and know all about themselves. It seems reasonable to suppose, however, that not only would such individuals be extremely 'alienated', but totally insane. See L. Feuer, 'What is Alienation? The Career of a Concept', in M. Stein and A. Vidich (eds), *Sociology on Trial* (Englewood Cliffs, Prentice-Hall, 1963).

28. From the vast amount of case literature that I have collected over the years of research I have tended to select ones which are fairly 'well known' in the field of suicide research. However, they are presented here not as 'tests' of the theory, but rather as illustrations of it.

29. Taylor, 'Suicide and the Renewal of Life', p. 386.

30. McClelland, in a study of women with fatal illnesses, has suggested that many relate to death as a 'Harlequin figure' to whom they submit as they would to a lover who comes to take them away to their death. D. C. McClelland, 'The Harlequin Complex', in White (ed.), *The Study of Lives*.

31. Robins *et al.*, 'The Communication of Suicidal Intent', p. 726.

32. Cavan, *Suicide*, p. 279.

33. *Guardian* (26 January 1977).

34. Quoted in Shneidman, 'Suicide Notes Reconsidered', in Shneidman (ed.), *Suicidology: Contemporary Developments*, p. 265.

35. See for example, Jacobs, 'A Phenomenological Study of Suicide Notes'.

36. Cavan, *Suicide*, p. 281.

37. Ibid, pp. 282–3.

38. A. E. Moll, 'Suicide: Psychopathology', *Canadian Medical Journal*, vol. 74 (1956) p. 106.

39. *Daily Mirror* (8 October 1977).

40. In some cases the submission may be 'extended' to include another, as for example, in a case quoted by West involving an elderly couple with rapidly deteriorating health, where the husband killed the wife before taking his own life as part of an agreement. D. J. West, *Murder Followed by Suicide* (London, Heinemann, 1965) p. 49.

41. From personal communication.

42. L. Binswanger, 'The Case of Ellen West', in R. May (ed.), *Existence* (New York, Basic Books, 1958) p. 292.
43. N. N. Holland, 'Literary Suicide: A Question of Style', *Psychocultural Review*, vol. i (1977) pp. 285–303.
44. S. Plath, *The Bell Jar* (London, Faber, 1966).
45. M. Savage, *Addicted to Suicide*, (Santa Barbara, Capra, 1975); B. R. Soloman, 'O My Hunger! My Hunger: Death in the Poetry of Anne Sexton', *Life Threatening Behaviour*, vol. 2 (1972) pp. 268–84.
46. Hendin, 'Growing up Dead: Student Suicide', in Shneidman (ed.), *Suicidology: Current Developments*, pp. 322–34.
47. Ibid, p. 327.
48. F. Simone, F. Felici, P. Valerio and P. Montella, 'Suicide in the Literary Work of Cesare Pavese', *Suicide and Life Threatening Behaviour*, vol. 7 (1977) pp. 184–5. See also Alvarez *The Savage God*, pp. 149–50.
49. Simone *et al.*, 'Suicide in the Literary Work of Cesare Pavese', p. 188.
50. Cavan, *Suicide*, pp. 235–6.
51. Ibid, p. 244.
52. Ibid, pp. 240–1.
53. I have not used the seemingly more obvious term 'symbiosis' in this context because it implies a mutual interdependence, which is not necessarily the case; for the attachment of the suicidal individual is in all probability not returned. Relatively few studies have been undertaken of *both* partners to a suicidal 'communication'. See J. V. Hattem, 'Precipitating Role of Discardant Interpersonal Relationships in Suicidal Behaviour', *Dissertation Abstracts*, vol. 25 (1964) pp. 1335–6; R. A. Harris, 'Factors Related to Continued Suicidal Behaviour in Dyadic Relationships', *Nursing Research*, vol. 15 (1966) pp. 72–5; Bonnar and McGee, 'Suicidal Behaviour as a Form of Communication in Married Couples'.
54. Stengel, *Suicide and Attempted Suicide*, pp. 113–16; Shneidman and Farberow (eds), *The Cry for Help*, Introduction.
55. Shneidman, Prologue to *On the Nature of Suicide*, p. 15.
56. Stengel, 'A Matter of Communication', in Shneidman (ed.), *On the Nature of Suicide*, p. 78.
57. Kobler and Stotland, *The End of Hope*, p. 1.
58. Robins *et al.*, 'The Communication of Suicidal Intent'.
59. As Stengel has observed, 'The effects of suicidal attempts . . . are complex. Those close to the attempter, and sometimes society as a whole, tend to behave as they feel they ought to behave had the outcome been fatal.' Stengel, 'A Matter of Communication', pp. 77–8.
60. Taylor, 'Dying to Live: study of adolescent suicide attempts'.
61. Shneidman and Farberow, 'Sample Investigations of Equivocal Suicidal Deaths', in Shneidman and Farberow (eds), *The Cry for Help*, pp. 122–23.
62. Taylor, 'Dying to Live'.
63. Bonnar and McGee, 'Suicidal Behaviour', p. 15.
64. Stengel and Cook, *Attempted Suicide*.
65. Ibid, p. 79.
66. Weiss, 'The Gamble with Death in Attempted Suicide', p. 392 (Giddens).
67. Bonnar and McGee, 'Suicidal Behaviour', pp. 7–8.
68. S. M. Jourard, 'The Invitation to Die', in Shneidman (ed.), *On the Nature of Suicide*, p. 132.
69. R. E. Litman, 'Immobilisation Response to Suicidal Behaviour', Archives of General Psychiatry vol. 2 (1964) pp. 282–5.
70. S. Perlin and C. W. Schmidt, 'Psychiatry', in S. Perlin (ed.), *A Handbook for the Study of Suicide* (Oxford University Press, 1975) p. 157.

71. Kobler and Stotland, *The End of Hope*. Cf. R. L. Coser, 'Suicide and the Relational System: A Case Study in a Mental Hospital', *Journal of Health and Social Behaviour*, vol. 17 (1976) pp. 318–27.
72. Quoted in Douglas, *The Social Meanings of Suicide*, pp. 311–12.
73. According to West, about one third of all murders are followed by the suicide of the perpetrator. D. J. West, *Murder Followed by Suicide*.
74. Cavan, *Suicide*, pp. 163–4.
75. West, *Murder Followed by Suicide*, pp. 50, 86–7 respectively.
76. Perlin and Schmidt, 'Psychiatry', p. 157.
77. This case was taken from my participant-observation study at the coroner's office.
78. *Guardian* (9 October 1978).
79. For example, Stengel, 'A Matter of Communication', p. 78.
80. For example, Jacobs, 'A Phenomenological Study of Suicide Notes', p. 347 (Giddens).
81. Jourard, 'The Invitation to Die', p. 132.
82. Kobler and Stotland, *The End of Hope*.
83. See Durkheim, *Suicide*, pp. 217–28.

General Conclusions

1. R. Bhasker, 'Scientific Knowledge and the Limits of Naturalism', p. 4.

Bibliography

Adams, R. L., Giffen, M. B. and Garfield, F. (1972) 'Risk-taking among Suicide Attempters', *Journal of Abnormal Psychology*, vol. 82, pp. 262–7.

Aitken, R. C. B., Buglass, D. and Kreitman, N. (1969) 'The Changing Patterns of Attempted Suicide in Edinburgh', *British Journal of Preventive Social Medicine*, vol. 23, pp. 111–15.

Akers, R. L. (1977) *Deviant Behaviour: a Social Learning Approach*, California, Wadsworth.

Alpert, H. (1961) *Emile Durkheim and his Sociology*, New York, Russell & Russell.

Alvarez, A. (1971) *The Savage God: a Study of Suicide*, Harmondsworth, Penguin.

Arieff, A., McCulloch, R. and Rotman, D. B. (1948) 'Unsuccessful Suicide Attempts', *Diseases of the Nervous System*, vol. 9.

Aron, R. (1968) *Main Currents of Sociological Thought*, vol. 2, London, Weidenfeld & Nicolson.

Ashworth, C. E. (1971) 'Sport as Symbolic Dialogue', in Dunning, E. (ed.), *The Sociology of Sport*, London, Cass, pp. 40–6.

Atkinson, J. M. (1968) 'On the Sociology of Suicide', *Sociological Review*, vol. 16, pp. 83–92.

Atkinson, J. M. (1971) 'Societal Reactions to Suicide: the Role of Coroners' Definitions', in Cohen, S. (ed.), *Images of Deviance*, Harmondsworth, Penguin, pp. 165–91.

Atkinson, J. M. (1973) 'Critical Note: Suicide, Status Integration and Pseudo-Science', *Sociology*, vol. 7, pp. 437–45.

Atkinson, J. M. (1978) *Discovering Suicide*, London, Macmillan.

Bagley, C. (1973) 'Authoritarianism, Status Integration and Suicide', *Sociology*, vol. 6, pp. 395–404.

Barthes, R. (1967) *Elements of Semiology*, London, Cape.

Bauman, Z. (1978) *Hermeneutics and Social Science*, London, Hutchinson.

Benoit-Smullyan, E. (1948) 'The Sociologism of Emile Durkheim and his School', in Barnes, H. E. (ed.), *An Introduction to the History of Sociology*, Chicago, Pheonix, pp. 500–21.

Berger, P. L. and Luckmann, T. (1967) *The Social Construction of Reality*, Harmondsworth, Penguin.

Berman, A. L. (1975) 'The Epidemology of Life Threatening Events', *Suicide*, vol. 5, pp. 67–77.

Bhasker, R. (1978) *A Realist Theory of Science*, Sussex, Harvester.

Bhasker, R. (1978) 'On the Possibility of Social Scientific Knowledge and the Limits of Naturalism', *Journal of the Theory of Social Behaviour*, vol. 8, pp. 1–28.

Bierstedt, R. (1966) *Emile Durkheim*, London, Weidenfeld & Nicolson.

Biller, O. A. (1977) 'Suicide Related to the Assassination of President John F. Kennedy', *Suicide and Life Threatening Behaviour*, vol. 7, pp. 40–4.

Binswanger, L. (1958) 'The Case of Ellen West', in May, R. (ed.), *Existence*, New York, Basic Books.

Bonnar, J. W. and McGee, R. K. (1977) 'Suicidal Behaviour as a Form of Communication in Married Couples', *Suicide and Life Threatening Behaviour*, vol. 7, pp. 7–16.

Breed, W. (1963) 'Occupational Mobility and Suicide among White Males', *American Sociological Review*, vol. 28, pp. 179–88.

Breed, W. (1972) 'Five Components of a Basic Suicide Syndrome', *Life Threatening Behaviour*, vol. 2, pp. 3–17.

Brown, J. H. (1975) 'Reporting of Suicide: Canadian Statistics', *Suicide*, vol. 5, pp. 21–8.

Brown, T. R. and Sheran, T. J. (1972) 'Suicide Prediction: A Review', *Life Threatening Behaviour*, vol. 2, pp. 67–98.

Buck, E. W. and Webber, I. L. (1972) 'Social Status and Relational System of Elderly Suicides: A Re-examination of the Henry–Short Thesis', *Life Threatening Behaviour*, vol. 2, pp. 145–59.

Buckle, H. T. (1871) *History of Civilization in England*, vol. 1, London, Longman.

Bunney, W. F. and Fawcett, J. A. (1965) 'Possibility of a Biochemical Test for Suicide Potential', *Archives of General Psychiatry*, vol. 13, pp. 323–9.

Cain, A. C. (ed.) (1972) *Survivors of Suicide*, Springfield, Thomas.

Canter, P. (1976) 'Frequency of Suicidal Thought and Self-Destructive Behaviour Among Females', *Suicide and Life Threatening Behaviour*, vol. 6, pp. 92–100.

Capstick, A. (1960) 'The Recognition of Emotional Disturbance and the Prevention of Suicide', *British Medical Journal*, vol. 1, pp. 1179–82.

Capstick, A. (1961) 'The Methods of Suicide', *Medicolegal Journal*, vol. 29, pp. 33–8.

Cavan, R. S. (1965) *Suicide*, New York, Russell & Russell.

Chambliss, W. J. and Steel, M. F. (1966) 'Status Integration and Suicide', *American Sociological Review*, vol. 31, pp. 524–32.

Chomsky, N. (1959) 'Verbal Behaviour by B. F. Skinner', *Language*, vol. 35, pp. 26–58.

Cicourel, A. V. (1976) *The Social Organisation of Juvenile Justice*, London, Heinemann.

Coe, J. I. (1974) 'Sexual Asphyxias', *Life Threatening Behaviour*, vol. 4, pp. 171–5.

Cohen, J. (1964) *Behaviour in Uncertainty and its Social Implications* New York, Basic Books.

Cohen, S. and Taylor, L. (1972) *Psychological Survival*, Harmondsworth, Penguin.

Connor, N. E. and Maris, R. W. (1976) 'Exchange, Balance and Formal Organisation in Psychotherapeutic Interactions', *Suicide and Life Threatening Behaviour*, vol. 6, pp. 150–68.

Cresswell, P. (1972) 'Interpretations of Suicide', *British Journal of Sociology*, vol. 23, pp. 133–45.

Cresswell, P. (1974) 'Suicide: the Stable Rates Argument', *Journal of Biosocial Science*, vol. 6, pp. 148–56.

Dahlgren, K. G. (1945) *On Suicide and Attempted Suicide*, Lund, Lindstadts.

Dahlgren, K. G. (1977) 'Attempted Suicides – 35 years Afterward', *Suicide and Life Threatening Behaviour*, vol. 7.

Davis, R. and Short, J. F. (1978) 'Dimensions of Black Suicide: A Theoretical Model', *Suicide and Life Threatening Behaviour*, vol. 8, pp. 161–73.

De Fleur, L. B. (1975) 'Biasing Influences on Drug Arrest Records: Implications for Deviance Research', *American Sociological Review*, vol. 40, pp. 88–103.

Delong, W. B. and Robins, E. (1961) 'The Communication of Suicidal Intent Prior to Psychiatric Hospitalisation', *American Journal of Psychiatry*, vol. 117, pp. 695–705.

Dorpat, T. L. and Boswell, J. W. (1963) 'An Evaluation of Suicidal Intent in Suicidal Attempts', *Comprehensive Psychiatry*, vol. 4, pp. 117–25.

Dorpat, T. L. and Ripley, H. S. (1967) 'The Relation Between Attempted and Committed Suicide', *Comprehensive Psychiatry*, vol. 8, pp. 74–89.

Douglas, J. D. (1966) 'The Sociological Analysis of the Social Meanings of Suicide', *European Journal of Sociology*, vol. 7, pp. 249–75.

Douglas, J. D. (1967) *The Social Meanings of Suicide*, Princeton University Press.

Douglas, J. D. (1969) 'The Rhetoric of Science and the Origins of Statistical Thought: the Case of Durkheim's *Suicide*', in Tiryakian, A. (ed.), *The Phenomenon of Sociology* New York, Appleton-Century-Crofts.

Douglas, J. D. (ed.), (1970) *Deviance and Respectability*, New York, Basic Books.

Dublin, L. I. (1963) *Suicide: A Sociological and Statistical Study*, New York, Ronald.

Durkheim, E. (1950) *The Rules of Sociological Method*, translated by Solvay, S. A. and Mueller, J. H., New York, Free Press.

Durkheim, E. (1952) *Suicide: A Study in Sociology*, translated by Spaulding, J. A. and Simpson, G., London, Routledge & Kegan Paul.

Durkheim, E. (1965) *The Elementary Forms of Religious Life*, translated by Swain, J. W., New York, Free Press.

Edwards, J. E. and Whitlock, F. A. (1968) 'Suicide and Attempted Suicide in Brisbane', *Medical Journal of Australia*, vol. 1, pp. 932–8.

Ettlinger, R. W. and Flordah, P. (1955) 'Attempted Suicide', *Acta Psychiatrica Scandinavica*, vol. 103.

Farber, M. L. (1965) 'Suicide and the Welfare State', *Mental Hygiene*, vol. 49, pp. 371–3.

Farber, M. L. (1977) 'Factors Determining the Incidence of Suicide within Families', *Suicide and Life Threatening Behaviour*, vol. 7, pp. 3–6.

Farberow, N. L. (ed.) (1967) *Proceedings of the Fourth International Conference for Suicide Prevention*, Los Angeles, Delmar.

Farberow, N. L. (ed.) (1975) *Suicide in Different Cultures*, Baltimore, University Park Press.

Filstead, W. J. (ed.) (1973) *An Introduction to Deviance: Readings in the Process of Making Deviants*, Chicago, Rand McNally.

Firth, R. (1961) 'Suicide and Risk-taking in Tikopia Society', *Psychiatry*, vol. 24, pp. 1–17.

Freud, S. (1925) 'Mourning and Melancholia', *Collected Papers*, vol. 4, London, Hogarth.

Garfinkel, H. (1967) *Studies in Ethnomethodology*, Englewood Cliffs, Prentice-Hall.

Gibbs, J. P. (1961) 'Suicide', in Merton, R. K. and Nisbet, R. A. (eds), *Contemporary Social Problems*, New York, Harcourt Brace.

Gibbs, J. P. (1966) 'Conceptions of Deviant Behaviour: the Old and the New', *Pacific Sociological Review*, vol. 9, pp. 9–14.

Gibbs, J. P. (ed.) (1968) *Suicide*, New York, Harper & Row.

Gibbs, J. P. and Porterfield, A. L. (1960) 'Occupational Prestige and Social Mobility of Suicides in New Zealand', *American Journal of Sociology*, vol. 66, pp. 147–52.

Gibbs, J. P. and Martin, W. T. (1964) *Status Integration and Suicide: A Sociological Study*, University of Oregon Press.

Gibbs, J. P. and Martin, W. T. (1974) 'A Problem in Testing the Theory of Status Integration', *Social Forces*, vol. 52, pp. 332–9.

Giddens, A. (1965) 'The Suicide Problem in French Sociology', *British Journal of Sociology*, vol. 16, pp. 3–15.

Giddens, A. (1966) 'A Typology of Suicide', *European Journal of Sociology*, vol. 7, pp. 276–95.

Giddens, A. (ed.) (1971) *The Sociology of Suicide*, London, Cass.

Giddens, A. (1976) *The New Rules of Sociological Method*, London, Hutchinson.

Giddens, A. (1977) *Durkheim*, London, Fontana.

Giddens, A. (1977) *Studies in Social and Political Theory*, London, Hutchinson.

Giddens, A. (1979) *Central Problems in Social Theory*, London, Macmillan.

Glucksman, M. (1974) 'The Structuralism of Lévi-Strauss and Althusser', in Rex, J. (ed.), *Approaches to Sociology*, London, Routledge & Kegan Paul.

Goffman, E. (1969) *Where the Action is*, London, Allen Lane.

Gold, M. (1958) 'Suicide, Homicide and the Socialisation of Aggression', *American Journal of Sociology*, vol. 63, pp. 651–61.

Goss, M. E. W. and Reed, J. T. (1971) 'Suicide and Religion: A Study of White Adults in New York City', *Suicide and Life Threatening Behaviour*, vol. 1, pp. 163–77.

Greene, G. (1971) *A Sort of Life*, London, Bodley Head.

Halbwachs, M. (1930) *Les Causes du Suicide*, Paris, Alcan.

Harre, R. (1970) *The Principles of Scientific Thinking*, London, Macmillan.

Hartelius, H. (1957) 'Suicide in Sweden', *Acta Psychiatric Scandinavica*, vol. 32.

Hassall, C. and Trethowan, W. H. (1972) 'Suicide in Birmingham', *British Medical Journal*, vol. 2, pp. 717–18.

Hendin, H. (1964) *Suicide and Scandinavia*, New York, Grune & Stratton.

Henken, V. J. (1976) 'Banality Reinvestigated: A Computer-Based Content Analysis of Suicide and Forced Death Documents', *Suicide and Life Threatening Behaviour*, vol. 6, pp. 26–43.

Henry, A. F. and Short, J. F. (1954) *Suicide and Homicide*, Glencoe, Free Press.

Hindess, B. (1973) *The Use of Official Statistics in Sociology*, London, Macmillan.

Hirsh, J. (1959) 'Suicide', *Mental Hygiene*, vol. 43, pp. 516–26.

Hirsh, J. (1960) 'Methods and Fashions of Suicide', *Mental Hygiene*, vol. 44, pp. 3–11.

Hirst, P. Q. (1975) *Durkheim, Barnard and Epistemology*, London, Routledge & Kegan Paul.

Holland, N. N. (1977) 'Literary Suicide: A Question of Style', *Psychocultural Review*, vol. 3, pp. 285–303.

Horton, J. (1964) 'The Dehumanisation of Anomie and Alienation a Problem in the Ideology of Knowledge', *British Journal of Sociology*, vol. 15, pp. 283–300.

Iga, M. (1966) 'Relation of Suicide Attempts and Social Structure in Kamakura', *International Journal of Social Psychiatry*, vol. 12, pp. 221–32.

Iga, M. (1971) 'A Concept of Anomie and Suicide in Japanese College Students', *Life Threatening Behaviour*, vol. 1, pp. 232–44.

Iga, M., Yamamoto, J. and Noguchi, T. (1975) 'The Vulnerability of Young Japanese Women to Suicide', *Suicide*, vol. 5, pp. 207–222.

Illman, J. (25 Nov 1972) 'Figures Hide True Rate of Suicides', *Pulse*.

Jacobs, J. (1967) 'A Phenomenological Study of Suicide Notes', *Social Problems*, vol. 15, pp. 60–72.

Jacobs, J. (1971) *Adolescent Suicide*, New York, Wiley.

Jensen, V. and Petty, T. (1959) 'The Fantasy of Being Rescued in Suicide', *Psychoanalytic Quarterly*, vol. 27, pp. 332–9.

Johnson, B. D. (1965) 'Durkheim's One Cause of Suicide', *American Sociological*

Review, vol. 30, pp. 875–86.

Kalish, R. A. (Dec 1968) 'Suicide', *Bulletin of Suicidology*, pp. 37–43.

Kaplan, H. B. and Pokorny, A. D. (1976) 'Self Attitudes and Suicidal Behaviour', *Suicide and Life Threatening Behaviour*, vol. 6, no. 1, pp. 23–35.

Keat, R. and Urry, J. (1975) *Social Theory as Science*, London, Routledge & Kegan Paul.

Kennedy, P. F., Phanjoo, A. L. and Shekim, W. O. (1971) 'Risk-taking in the Lives of Parasuicides (Attempted Suicides)', *British Journal of Psychiatry*, vol. 119, pp. 281–6.

Kessel, N. (1965) 'Self Poisoning', *British Medical Journal*, vol. 2, pp. 1265–70.

Kitsuse, J. I. (1965) 'Societal Reaction to Deviant Behaviour: Problems of Theory and Method', in Becker, H. S. (ed.), *The Other Side*, New York, Free Press, pp. 81–102.

Kitsuse, J. I. and Cicourel, A. V. (1963) 'A Note on the Use of Official Statistics', *Social Problems*, vol. 12, pp. 131–9.

Kobler, A. L. and Stotland, E. (1964) *The End of Hope*, Glencoe, Free Press.

Koller, K. M. and Castanos, J. N. (1968) 'The Influence of Childhood Parental Deprivation in Attempted Suicide', *Medical Journal of Australia*, vol. 1, pp. 396–9.

Kovacs, M. and Beck, A. T. (1977) 'The Wish to Live and the Wish to Die in Attempted Suicides', *Journal of Clinical Psychology*, vol. 33, pp. 361–5.

Kreitman, N. (ed.) (1977) *Parasuicide*, New York, Wiley.

Kreitman, N., Smith, P. and Tan, E. (1969) 'Attempted Suicide in Social Networks', *British Journal of Preventive Social Medicine*, vol. 23, pp. 116–23.

Kreitman, N. and Chowdury, N. (1973) 'Distress Behaviour: A Study of Selected Samaritan Clients and Parasuicides (Attempted Suicide) Patients', *British Journal of Psychiatry*, vol. 123, pp. 1–8.

Krieger, G. (1975) 'Is there a Biochemical Predictor of Suicide?', *Suicide*, vol. 5, pp. 228–31.

Kruijt, C. S. (1960) *Suicide: Sociological and Statistical Investigations*, Door, Van Gorium.

Kruijt, C. S. (1977) 'The Suicide Rate in the Western World since World War II', *The Netherlands Journal of Sociology*, vol. 13, pp. 55–65.

Kubie, L. S. (1964) 'Multiple Determinants of Suicidal Efforts', *The Journal of Nervous Mental Diseases*, vol. 138, pp. 3–8.

Labovitz, S. and Brinkerhoff, M. B. (1977) 'Structural Changes and Suicide in Canada', *International Journal of Comparative Sociology*, vol. 18, pp. 254–67.

La Capra, D. (1972) *Emile Durkheim: Sociologist and Philosopher*, Cornell University Press.

Laing, R. D. (1967) *The Politics of Experience*, Harmondsworth, Penguin.

Lemert, E. M. (1967) *Human Deviance, Social Problems and Social Control*, Englewood Cliffs, Prentice-Hall.

Leogrande, E. (1975) *A Second Chance to Live: The Suicide Syndrome*, New York, Da Capo.

Lester, D. (1968) 'Suicide as an Aggressive Act', *Journal of General Psychology*, vol. 79, pp. 83–6.

Lester, D. (1970) 'Suicidal Behaviour: A Summary of Research Findings', *Buffalo Suicide Prevention and Crisis Service*.

Lester, D. (1972) *Why People Kill Themselves*, Springfield, Thomas.

Lester, D. and Lester, G. (1971) *Suicide: The Gamble with Death*, Englewood Cliffs, Prentice-Hall.

Lévi-Strauss, C. (1945) 'French Sociology', in Gurvitch, G. and Moore, W. E. (eds), *Twentieth Century Sociology*, New York, Philosophical Library.

Lévi-Strauss, C. (1968) *Structural Anthropology*, London, Allen Lane.
Lewis, A. (1956) 'Statistical Aspects of Suicide', *The Canadian Medical Association Journal*, vol. 74, pp. 99–104.
Litman, R. E., Curphey, T., Shneidman, E. S., Farberow, N. L. and Tabacknick, N. (1963) 'Investigations of Equivocal Suicides', *Journal of the American Medical Association*, vol. 184, pp. 924–9.
Lofland, J. (1969) *Deviance and Identity*, Englewood Cliffs, Prentice-Hall.
Lonnqvist, J., Niskanen, P., Achte, K. A. and Ginman, L. (1975) 'Self Poisoning with Follow-up Considerations', *Suicide*, vol. 5, pp. 39–45.
Lukes, S. (1975) *Emile Durkheim: His Life and Work: A Historical and Critical Study*, London, Peregrine.
MacMahon, B., Johnson, S. and Pugh, T. (1963) 'The Relation of Suicide Rates to Social Conditions', *Public Health Report*, no. 78.
Manning, P. K. (1973) 'Existential Sociology', *Sociological Quarterly*, vol. 14, pp. 200–25.
Maris, R. W. (1969) *Social Forces in Urban Suicide*, Illinois, Dorsey Press.
Masaryk, T. G. (1970) *Suicide and the Meaning of Civilization*, translated by Weist, W. B. and Batson, R. G., University of Chicago Press.
Matza, D. (1969) *Becoming Deviant*, Englewood Cliffs, Prentice-Hall.
McCarthy, P. D. and Walsh, D. (1966) 'Suicide in Dublin', *British Medical Journal*, vol. 1, pp. 1393–6.
McCulloch, J. W., Philip, A. E., and Carstairs, G. M. (1967) 'The Ecology of Suicidal Behaviour', *British Journal of Psychiatry*, vol. 113, pp. 313–19.
Menninger, K. (1938) *Man Against Himself*, New York, Harcourt Brace.
Mintz, R. S. (1970) 'Prevalence of Persons in the City of Los Angeles who have Attempted Suicide', *Bulletin of Suicidology*, vol. 7.
Morris, T. (1976) *Deviance and Control: the Secular Heresy*, London, Hutchinson.
Morselli, H. (1903) *Suicide: An Essay in Comparative Moral Statistics*, New York, Appleton.
Neuringer, C. (1967) 'The Cognitive Organisation of Meaning in Suicidal Individuals', *Journal of General Psychology*, vol. 76, pp. 91–100.
Neuringer, C. (1962) 'Methodological Problems in Suicide Research', *Journal of Consulting Psychology*, vol. 26, pp. 273–8.
Neuringer, C. (ed.) (1974) *The Psychological Assessment of Suicidal Risk*, Springfield, Thomas.
Newman, J. F., Whittemore, K. R. and Newman, H. G. (1973) 'Women in the Labour Force and Suicide', *Social Problems*, vol. 21, pp. 220–9.
Nisbet, R. A. (1963) 'Sociology as an Art Form', in Stein, M. and Vidich, A. (eds), *Sociology on Trial*, Englewood Cliffs, Prentice-Hall, pp. 148–62.
Nisbet, R. A. (ed.) (1965) *Emile Durkheim*, Englewood Cliffs, Prentice-Hall.
Nisbet, R. A. (1967) *The Sociological Tradition*, London, Heinemann.
Ogilvy, M., Stone, P. J. and Shneidman, E. S. (March 1969) 'Some Characteristics of Genuine versus Simulated Suicide Notes', *Bulletin of Suicidology*, pp. 27–32.
Paerregaard, G. (1975) 'Suicide among Attempted Suicides', *Suicide*, vol. 5, pp. 140–4.
Parsons, T. (1968) *The Structure of Social Action*, New York, Free Press.
Pawson, R. (1978) 'Empiricist Explanatory Strategies: The Case of Causal Modelling', *Sociological Review*, vol. 26, no. 3, pp. 613–45.
Perlin, S. (ed.), (1975) *A Handbook for the Study of Suicide*, Oxford University Press.
Pearson, G. (1975) *The Deviant Imagination*, London, Macmillan.
Piaget, J. (1971) *Structuralism*, translated by Maschler, C., London, Routledge & Kegan Paul.

Plath, S. (1966) *The Bell Jar*, London, Faber & Faber.
Pokorny, A. D. (1966) 'A Follow-up Study of 618 Suicidal Patients', *American Journal of Psychiatry*, vol. 122, pp. 1109–16.
Pokorny, A. D., Smith, J. P. and Finch, J. R. (1972) 'Vehicular Suicides', *Life Threatening Behaviour*, vol. 2, pp. 105–19.
Pope, W. (1976) *Durkheim's Suicide: A Classic Analyzed*, University of Chicago Press.
Porterfield, A. L. (1952) 'Suicide and Crime in Folk and Secular Society', *American Journal of Sociology*, vol. 57, pp. 331–8.
Powell, E. H. (1958) 'Occupation, Status and Suicide: Toward a Redefinition of Anomie', *American Sociological Review*, vol. 23, pp. 131–40.
Quetelet, M. A. (1842) *A Treatise on Man*, Edinburgh, Chambers.
Renolds, D. K. and Farberow, N. L. (1976) *Suicide: Inside and Out*, University of California Press.
Resnik, H. L. P. (ed.) (1968) *Suicidal Behaviours: Diagnosis and Management*, London, Churchill.
Retterstol, N. and Strype, B. (1973) 'Suicide Attempters in Norway: A Personal Follow-up Examination', *Life Threatening Behaviour*, vol. 3. pp. 283–97.
Ringel, E. (1976) 'The Pre-suicidal Syndrome', *Suicide and Life Threatening Behaviour*, vol. 6, pp. 131–49.
Robins, E. and O'Neal, P. (1958) 'Culture and Mental Disorder: A Study of Attempted Suicide', *Human Organisation*, vol. 16, pp. 7–11.
Robins, E., Gassner, S., Kayes, S., Wilkinson, R. H. and Murphy, G. E. (1959) 'The Communication of Suicidal Intent: A Study of 134 Consecutive Cases of Successful (Completed) Suicide', *American Journal of Psychiatry*, vol. 115, pp. 724–33.
Rock, P. and McIntosh, M. (eds) (1974) *Deviance and Control*, London, Tavistock.
Rojcewicz, S. J. (1971) 'War and Suicide', *Suicide and Life Threatening Behaviour*, vol. 1, pp. 46–54.
Rook, A. (1959) 'Student Suicides', *British Medical Journal*, vol. 1, pp. 595–602.
Rootman, I. (1973) 'A Cross Cultural Note on Durkheim's Theory of Suicide', *Life Threatening Behaviour*, vol. 3, pp. 83–95.
Rosen, D. H. (1970) 'The Serious Suicide Attempt: Epidemological and Follow-up Study of 886 Patients', *American Journal of Psychiatry*, vol. 127, pp. 764–70.
Rosen, D. H. (1976) 'Suicide Survivors: Psychotherapeutic Implications of Ego-cide', *Suicide and Life Threatening Behaviour*, vol. 6, pp. 209–15.
Rosenbaum, M. and Richman, J. (1972) 'Family Dynamics and Drug Overdoses', *Life Threatening Behaviour*, vol. 2, pp. 19–21.
Rushing, W. A. (1969) 'Deviance, Interpersonal Relations and Suicide', *Human Relations*, vol. 22, pp. 61–75.
Rushing, W. A. (1975) 'Deviance, Disrupted Social Relations, Interpersonal Contexts and Suicide', in Rushing, W. A. (ed.), *Deviant Behaviour and Social Process*, Chicago, Rand McNally.
Sainsbury, P. (1955) *Suicide in London*, London, Chapman & Hall.
Sainsbury, P. (1968) 'Suicide in Depression', in Coppen, A. and Walk, A. (eds), *Recent Developments in Affective Disorders*, British Journal of Psychiatry special publication, pp. 1–13.
Sainsbury, P. and Baraclough, B. (1968) 'Differences Between Suicide Rates', *Nature*, vol. 220, p. 1252.
Savage, M. (1975) *Addicted to Suicide*, Santa Barbara, Capra.
Schmidt, E. H., O'Neal, P. and Robins, E. (1954) 'Evaluation of Suicide Attempts as a Guide to Therapy', *Journal of the American Medical Association*, vol. 155, pp. 549–57.
Shneidman, E. S. (1963) 'Orientations Towards Death: A Vital Aspect of the Study

of Lives', in White, R. W. (ed.), *The Study of Lives*, New York, Atherton, pp. 200–28.

Shneidman, E. S. (ed.) (1967) *Essays in Self Destruction*, New York, International Science Press.

Shneidman, E. S. (July 1968) 'Classification of Suicidal Phenomena', *Bulletin of Suicidology*.

Shneidman, E. S. (ed.) (1969) *On the Nature of Suicide*, San Francisco, Jossey-Bass.

Shneidman, E. S. (1973) *Deaths of Man*, New York, Quadrangle Books.

Shneidman, E. S. (ed.) (1976) *Suicidology: Contemporary Developments*, New York, Grune & Stratton.

Shneidman. E. S. and Farberow, N. L. (1961) *The Cry For Help*, New York, McGraw-Hill.

Shneidman, E. S. and Farberow, N. L. (eds) (1957) *Clues to Suicide*, New York, McGraw-Hill.

Sifneos, P. E. (1966) 'Manipulative Suicide', *Psychiatric Quarterly*, vol. 40, pp. 525–37.

Simone, F., Felici, F., Valerio, P. and Montella, P. (1977) 'Suicide in the Literary Work of Cesare Pavese', *Suicide and Life Threatening Behaviour*, vol. 7, pp. 183–8.

Skogan, W. G. (1974) 'The Validity of Official Crime Statistics: An Empirical Investigation', *Social Science Quarterly*, vol. 55, pp. 25–38.

Sletten, I. W., Evensen, R. C. and Brown, M. L. (1973) 'Some Results from an Automated Statewide Comparison among Attempted, Committed and Non-suicidal Patients', *Life Threatening Behaviour*, vol. 3, pp. 191–9.

Solomon, B. R. (1972) '"O My Hunger! My Hunger!": Death in the Poetry of Anne Sexton', *Life Threatening Behaviour*, vol. 2, pp. 268–84.

Stengel, E. (1960) 'Some Unexplored Aspects of Suicide and Attempted Suicide', *Comprehensive Psychiatry*, vol. 1, pp. 71–80.

Stengel, E. (1960) 'The Complexity of Motivations to Suicide Attempts', *Journal of Mental Science*, vol. 106, pp. 1388–93.

Stengel, E. (1973) *Suicide and Attempted Suicide* (revised edition), Harmondsworth, Penguin.

Stengel, E. (15 Mar. 1973) 'To Die or not to Die', *New Society*.

Stengel, E. and Cook, N. G. (1958) *Attempted Suicide*, Oxford University Press.

Stengel, E. and Cook, N. G. (1961) 'Contrasting Suicide Rates in Industrial Communities', *Journal of Mental Science*, vol. 107, pp. 1009–14.

Straus, J. H. and Straus, M. A. (1953) 'Suicide, Homicide and Social Structure in Ceylon', *American Journal of Sociology*, vol. 58, pp. 461–9.

Sudnow, D. (ed.) (1972) *Studies in Social Interaction*, New York, Free Press.

Swinscow, D. (1951) 'Some Suicide Statistics', *British Medical Journal*, vol. 1, p. 1417.

Tabachnick, N. D. and Klugman, D. J. (1965) 'No Name: A Study of Anonymous Suicidal Telephone Calls', *Psychiatry*, vol. 28, pp. 79–85.

Tabachnick, N. D., Litman, R. E., Osman, M., Jones, W. L., Cohn, J., Kasper, A. and Moffat, J. (1966) 'Comparative Psychiatric Study of Accidental and Suicidal Death', *Archives of General Psychiatry*, vol. 14, pp. 60–9.

Taylor, I., Walton, P. and Young, J. (1973) *The New Criminology*, London, Routledge & Kegan Paul.

Taylor, S. (1973) 'Interpreting Suicide' (paper given at British Sociological Association Conference, Manchester).

Taylor, S. (25 Oct 1977) 'Suicide: Public Purpose and Private Grief', *Community Care*, pp. 23–5.

Taylor, S. (1978) 'Suicide and the Renewal of Life', *Sociological Review*, vol. 26.

Taylor, S. (1978) 'The Confrontation with Death', *Suicide and Life Threatening Behaviour*, vol. 8.

Tuckman, J., Kleiner, R. J. and Lavell, M. (1959) 'Emotional Content of Suicide Notes', *American Journal of Psychiatry*, vol. 116, pp. 59–63.

Tuckman, J. and Youngman, W. F. (1962) 'Suicide Risk among Persons Attempting Suicide', *Public Health Reports*, vol. 77, pp. 585–90.

Turner, R. (ed.) (1974) *Ethnomethodology*, Harmondsworth, Penguin.

Van Del, R. A. (1977) 'The Role of Death Romanticisation in the Dynamics of Suicide', *Suicide and Life Threatening Behaviour*, vol. 7.

Walderstrom, J., Larsonn, T. and Ljungstedt, N. (eds) (1972) *Suicide and Attempted Suicide*, Stockholm, Nordiska Bokhandelns Forlag.

Wallwork, E. (1972) *Durkheim, Morality and Milieu*, Harvard University Press.

Walton, H. J. (1958) 'Suicidal Behaviour in Depressive Illness', *Journal of Mental Science*, vol. 104, pp. 884–91.

Weisman, A. D. (1971) 'Is Suicide a Disease?', *Life Threatening Behaviour*, vol. 1, pp. 219–31.

Weiss, J. M. S. (1957) 'The Gamble with Death in Attempted Suicide', *Psychiatry*, vol. 20, pp. 17–25.

Wenz, F. V. (1975) 'Anomie and Level of Suicidology in Individuals', *Psychological Reports*, vol. 36, pp. 817–18.

West, D. J. (1965) *Murder Followed by Suicide*, London, Heinemann.

Wiles, P. N. P. (1971) 'Criminal Statistics and Sociological Explanations of Crime', in Carson, W. G. and Wiles, P. (eds), *Crime and Delinquency in Britain*, London, Martin Robertson, pp. 174–91.

Wilkins, J. (1967) 'Suicidal Behaviour', *American Sociological Review*, vol. 32, pp. 286–98.

Willer, D. and Willer, J. (1973) *Systematic Empiricism: a Critique of a Pseudo-Science*, Englewood Cliffs, Prentice-Hall.

Winch, P. (1958) *The Idea of a Social Science and its Relation to Philosophy*, London, Routledge & Kegan Paul.

Wolman, B. B. (ed.) (1976) *Between Survival and Suicide*, New York, Gardner.

Worden, J. W. (1972) 'Risk-Rescue Rating in Suicide Assessment', *Archives of General Psychiatry*, vol. 26, pp. 553–60.

Yap, P. M. (1958) 'Suicide in Hong Kong', *Journal of Mental Science*, vol. 104, pp. 266–301.

Index